For my

friend, Donna.

Love

Bret

Threads of Gold

BRENDA JOSEE
Editor in Chief

PAULA KIRK
Managing Editor

HARVEST HOUSE PUBLISHERS
Eugene, Oregon 97402

WALK THRU THE BIBLE
Atlanta, Georgia 30341

Design by Paz Design Group, Salem, Oregon

THREADS OF GOLD
Copyright © 1998 by Walk Thru the Bible Ministries
Published by Harvest House Publishers
Eugene, Oregon 97402

Library of Congress Cataloging-in-Publication Data

Threads of gold / Walk Thru the Bible Ministries.
    p. cm.
  ISBN 1-56507-910-8
   1. Women—Prayer-books and devotionals—English.   2. Devotional
calendars. I. Walk Thru the Bible (Educational ministry)
BV4527.T49 1998
242'.643—dc21   98-16021
                                                      CIP

Printed in the United States of America.

98 99 00 01 02 03 / DH / 10 9 8 7 6 5 4 3 2 1

His Touch

The aroma in the air was definitely not that of scented pot-pourri. The stinging odors of sweaty people and dirty animals were almost visible in the swirling dust raised by the crowd following Jesus. The adults were exhilarated, and the children were exhausted. Most of those folks were curiously skeptical and maybe even confused. But everyone listened carefully to see and hear what Jesus might do next. By His words and actions, Jesus was proving Himself to be the Messiah, the Son of God. But the authorities called Him a liar.

One persistent lady believed He was who He said He was. Though she couldn't get His undivided attention, she pushed close enough to reach the hem of His robe.

She hoped that merely touching His robe would be sufficient to heal her. How wonderful she must have felt when her hopes were realized and she was immediately—instantaneously—freed from her suffering. This is the only incident recorded in the New Testament where a person reached out to touch Jesus and healing power flowed from Him. But the story doesn't end there. Jesus knew someone had touched Him. He turned and sought her out. Fearful and trembling, she came forward to tell Him the truth. Then came the wonderful words of benediction and blessing that would set her free and ignite the rest of her life: "Daughter, your faith has healed you. Go in peace and be freed from your suffering" (Mark 5:34).

We should applaud that woman's determination. We need to find a similar inner determination to touch the heart of God with our prayers and our praises and experience His touch in our lives.

Frequently it's only out of the painful experiences in our lives that we seek the Lord and become aggressive in our study of His Word. Why do we wait for a crisis—a spouse who wants a divorce, a sick child, an ailing parent, a wayward teenager—before seeking the Lord fervently? Because our spiritual devotion is not at the level it should be, and nothing makes that more obvious than a crisis.

Recognizing the power of God at work in your life is an exciting way to live. The pace of life for most of us seems to propel us at breakneck speed from morning till night. Do you ever catch a glimpse of yourself in a mirror and wonder, "Who is that woman?"

The stories in this book are based on real-life experiences of women from many different walks of life.

Please take little snatches of time you can squeeze from your schedule and allow the Lord to speak to your heart about the tapestry He is weaving of your life.

We have so many choices available to us. The colors and textures of our tapestries are not only divinely prescribed by God, but they are also shaped and influenced by our choices. Just as the woman with the issue of blood was determined to touch Jesus for healing, make two of your choices the pursuit of a better understanding of God's design for your life and developing a closer relationship with Jesus.

Threads of Gold was developed from the women's devotional magazine *Tapestry*, which is also published under the title *Journey* and distributed by LifeWay Press.

A very special thanks goes to Selma Wilson who had vision and determination to encourage women in their walk with the Lord.

A Note of Thanks . . .

We offer sincere appreciation to the dedicated writers who have faithfully contributed to *Tapestry* magazine during the last four years. They've willingly shared their stories and those of their sisters and friends to give us deeper insights into how God works in women's lives. Thank you all.

Kim Allen	Shelba Nivens
Jane Bateman	Pam Nixon
LeAnne Benefield	Yolanda Olsen
Martha Comeaux	Lisa Orvis
Bonnie Harvey	Barb Peil
Judith Hayes	Helen Ryser
Janice Hopkins	Nanette Thorsen Snipes
Brenda Josee	Carla Summers
Paula Kirk	Sandi Tompkins
Millicent Manning	Pauline Triplett
Charlotte Mathis	Patty Wills
Liz McFadzean	Selma Wilson
Sue Nelson	Lezlie Winberry

THREADS OF WINTER

Rejoicing

Rejoicing

We are entering a season of adventure: celebrations, New Year's resolutions, hearts and flowers. The journey ahead holds several unknowns, and it is easy to find ourselves a bit anxious about the future. For most of us the holidays are filled with visiting family and friends, but we frequently find ourselves overcommitted and under-energized. Then on the heels of a highly active season come the long days of winter. The letdown can be hard to deal with. But there is an answer!

Nothing can energize us more than choosing to rejoice! It's a great way to keep perspective during this special season. Write down your thoughts of praise in a journal. Begin by reading Scripture and then, in your own words, write your interpretation of the passage. Conclude with personal praises to the Lord.

As you pray for specific family members, include in your journal praise reports about them. My, what that does to clarify perspective! Many of your prayers are petitions to the Lord, but you'll find a beautiful release by concentrating on rejoicing in Him, too.

The truest form of rejoicing is praising Him for everything in our lives. Remember the angels who proclaimed the arrival of Jesus? They were rejoicing and singing praises.

Rejoice in His birth.
Rejoice in the New Year.
Rejoice in His love for you.

Divine Perspective

*I have brought you glory on earth by completing
the work you gave me to do.*

JOHN 17:4

*W*hat is your mission in life? Have you ever written out a personal mission statement for your life? Your marriage? Your family?"

A mission statement? For myself? Wow! My heart pounded as I listened to my favorite speaker at a recent Bible conference. After she read her own mission statement, along with other examples, she gave us 15 minutes to prayerfully pen our own. She added this inspiring thought: "Be who God made you to be. Live His dream for you."

God has a dream for me? What could it be? I'm sure I've already messed it up many times. These thoughts pummeled my mind as I stared at the blank sheet of paper. Then I shook them off and focused on God. *Father, please guide me. What is Your dream for me?* For help I turned to Jeremiah 29:11 and then Ephesians 2:10, verses the speaker had suggested. She had also said, "Whatever your heart desires for your life, that's most likely what God desires as well. List those things and then formulate your statement."

My exciting life—this will be the shortest mission statement in history. I thought about my family, my home, my church, my first-graders, my seedlings growing in the garage, my sewing, and my dormant rosebushes waiting for spring. I thought of my love for the Lord, His Word, and prayer. Then I began to see it. I was a nurturer. I loved creating and tending things. Suddenly I could see how God had been using me.

Is this God's dream for me? Have I really been glorifying Him all along?

I quickly wrote out my mission statement. Something about seeing God's dream for me written out on paper made my heart pound again. I realized how exciting my life really is—when I see it through God's eyes.

There are many advantages to writing out a personal mission statement, but a key one is its time-saving value. When you are asked to take on a new responsibility or task, check your statement. If the request doesn't square with it, then you will have peace when you say no.

Steps of Faith

*Heavenly Father, what a joy it is to know You have dreams for me.
What are they? Let me live Your dreams for me.*

A Caring Heart

The sacrifices of God are a broken spirit; a broken and contrite heart, O God, you will not despise.

PSALM 51:17

Jack and I were going to spend Thanksgiving with his sister, Lindy, and her husband, Andrew. I wasn't too happy about it because, to me, Lindy wasn't much of a housekeeper. Jack said I was a perfectionist with impossible standards. But they weren't impossible—just very high. I took great pride in my clean, well-ordered house. After all, wasn't the Proverbs 31 woman a good housekeeper?

When we arrived at their house, we exchanged hugs and kisses. Andrew poured us all some coffee, and I followed Jack and Lindy into the den.

As the two of them talked excitedly, I did a quick survey of the room: a huge pile of magazines about to fall over; CDs stuffed into the CD holder any old way instead of alphabetically; an enlarged and lopsided photo of Lindy and Andrew on a recent mission trip hanging over the sofa.

"So," Jack said, "tell us about your mission trip."

"It was incredible!" Lindy said. "The people were so grateful for our help in building the new church. Several people who'd never been there before came to our Bible study." Was that a cobweb over her head in the corner?

"Jack, you'd have been so proud of your little sister. Those women just gravitated toward her," Andrew said.

Jack smiled. "I'm not surprised. God has given her a gift with people."

As I sat there listening, a light began to dawn on me. It wasn't that Lindy wasn't a good housekeeper. It's just that I was more interested in a clean house than a caring heart. All along, I'd wanted Lindy to be like me when I should have been striving to be more like her— more like Christ. God, forgive me for my pride.

Are you a perfectionist at home or at work? Perfectionism is often a sign of pride and self-sufficiency, and it needlessly uses up time and energy. Instead of trying to achieve perfection, should you be focusing your energy on the Lord?

Steps of Faith

Dear Father, forgive me for being a perfectionist. Forgive me for the pride that leads me to it. Help me to keep from projecting my perfectionism on others.

Forgiven

All have sinned and fall short of the glory of God.

ROMANS 3:23

$\mathcal{I}$ don't need forgiveness from God. I don't even believe in God." With that, Andi walked out of the kitchen, leaving her neighbor Sherry clutching a bag of Christmas cookies.

Lord, Sherry prayed, *I told You I'm not any good at this! Now she's never going to be receptive to You.* Sherry had been sharing her faith with Andi over the last few months, and Andi had never reacted this way. What had happened?

In a few minutes, Andi came back in and began to fill a tray with cookies. "I'm sorry. I guess I got defensive. It's just that I consider myself a pretty good person, you know? But I shouldn't have jumped on you like that, especially since you're helping me get ready for my open house!"

"It's okay," Sherry said, arranging raw vegetables on a tray. "I know how you feel. Except for an occasional bad mood, I used to think I was okay. But something was missing from my life, and no matter what I did, I was never happy. Then one day I went to church, and the pastor said that Jesus, who lived a perfect life, died so sinners could be forgiven. I realized that no matter how good I thought I was, I was still a sinner. I still needed to be forgiven by God. That's when I asked Jesus to come into my heart and cleanse me of my sins."

"How do you know He did it?" Andi asked.

"Because I've never been the same since," Sherry said, tears in her eyes. "He set me free, and I know He lives in me."

Andi didn't say anything else, but Sherry knew she was thinking about what she had said. She knew they'd talk again.

Everyone needs God's forgiveness. We're all sinners, and without Jesus Christ in our lives, we're destined to spend eternity separated forever from the God we so long to be near. Have you asked Him to forgive you? Does Jesus live in your heart?

Steps of Faith

Father, thank You that my salvation doesn't depend on me. I could never be worthy of it. Thank You for forgiving my sins, just as You promised.

A Quiet Ministry

Let the little children come to me, and do not hinder them,
for the kingdom of God belongs to such as these.

LUKE 18:16

On Christmas Eve eight years ago, Jerry and I walked into the church we had passed many times since we moved here. Neither of us had been to church in years, but for weeks we had planned to come to this candlelight service. We wanted to put more meaning into our holiday celebration, because now we had a child, Lucas, our four-month-old son. I was nervous about leaving him with strangers in the nursery. Nervous, that is, until I met Bethany.

The candlelight service was beautiful, but what I remember most about that night was the care and concern Bethany Newton, the children's ministry director, showed to Lucas, Jerry, and me. She smiled warmly and held Lucas gently. She described the church's children's program and made us feel as if we were the most important people in the world. We went back the next Sunday and the next and the next. In April, I accepted Jesus as my Savior, Jerry recommitted his life to Christ, and we joined the church. In May, we dedicated Lucas in front of our new church family.

Over the years, Bethany has helped bring many couples like us to Christ. Her ministry is reaching children and their parents for Christ, yet she goes about it in a quiet way. She doesn't get as much recognition as someone in the spotlight does, but she's loved and respected by all who know her. Her quiet, gentle spirit models Jesus to everyone.

I wonder how many children have come to know and love the Lord over the years because of Bethany and her ministry? I know of one very special little boy who has. Praise God!

Have you ever felt that, since you're not a church leader, you can't have a ministry? Regardless of whether you're a missionary or nursing-home volunteer, a music director or youth worker, a Christian counselor or custodian, your work is a ministry if it's done for the Lord.

Steps of Faith

Dear Lord, what a pleasure it is to serve You! Thank You for the opportunities You've given me to minister in Your holy name. Help me to remember that I can serve You regardless of the work I'm doing.

Mission in Life

*I have brought you glory on earth by completing
the work you gave me to do.*

JOHN 17:4

$\mathcal{R}$oy and I rode home in silence from the church. Our pastor's wife, Elaine, had just been buried. During the funeral service we had listened in wonder to all she had accomplished in her short 46 years on earth. How could she have done it? As a pastor's wife, Elaine's time, energy, and resources were certainly limited.

We learned later that when Elaine was in college, she had formulated a personal mission statement, with John 17:4 as her life verse. Every major decision Elaine made had been set against her stated purpose. If it squared, it was right; if it didn't, it wasn't.

Roy and I decided to do the same. With guidance from the Bible and other books, we determined what was unique about us: 1) our gifts and abilities; 2) our personal passions; 3) our personalities; 4) our responsibilities; 5) our experiences and education; 6) our network; 7) our resources; and 8) our allegiances, the top one being Jesus Christ.

On separate sheets of paper we wrote out our thoughts about each category. A picture of who we are individually and what we want to accomplish together came into focus as we listed all the words, phrases, and thoughts that best described each of us.

Finally, we consolidated it into one general statement: "Our life purpose is to glorify God by enriching the lives of our family, friends, and those within our circle of influence by modeling an approach to living that is centered around Jesus Christ and a study of God's Word."

Since then Roy and I no longer feel pressured to serve on every committee or volunteer for every activity. We know our purpose, and we stick to it.

One reason many women find themselves wasting time, energy, and resources is that they haven't really determined their purpose in life. Have you formulated a personal mission statement? When you do, you will discover the joy and peace that comes with having a focused approach to life.

Steps of Faith

Dear Father, I know You have a purpose for my life. Help me discover it. And after I have done so, please give me the strength, wisdom, and courage to live by it, for Your glory.

F
R
I
D
A
Y

13

Schedule or Agenda?

Be very careful, then, how you live—
not as unwise but as wise.

EPHESIANS 5:15

W
E
E
K
E
N
D

Living by a schedule was never a problem for me. My goals and schedule kept my life moving at a healthy, productive clip. Nothing got in my way.

And that was the problem. Projects, not people, had top priority in my life. When my three-year-old, Matthew, asked if he could schedule a time to read a story, I knew something had to change.

I began to examine the truly valuable things in my life. Were they all those meetings and deadlines? Or were they the people—people who hurt, ask questions, and have eternal souls? I prayed for strength and wisdom to make the best choices.

God answered that prayer two days later. My schedule was packed, and I had already missed my deadline. As I was eating lunch at my desk, the phone rang. I usually let voice mail answer, but something made me pick it up. It was my 14-year-old daughter, Maggie, and she was crying. Her first boyfriend had just broken up with her at lunch. My heart quietly broke for her.

Maggie wanted to go home. Bargaining with her, I told her I'd pick her up at school at 3 P.M. if she'd stay. Then the two of us could go off alone and talk. Before we hung up, I prayed with her and told her I loved her. When I hung up, I wept for my baby girl.

Although my schedule was still packed, my agenda cleared the afternoon for Maggie. Sure, the project was late, but the world didn't end. And what a sweet time Maggie and I had discussing dealing with the opposite sex, being a godly young woman, and falling in love.

That's the kind of agenda my family, my Lord, and I can live with.

"Life happens on the way to something else." A great deal of life is made up of interruptions. Even Jesus faced constant interruptions. He turned each one into an opportunity to advance His mission. Ask God to help you strike the right balance between your projects and people who interrupt.

Steps of Faith

My Lord and Savior, I confess that sometimes I put projects and other things ahead of the needs of the people closest to me. I want Your agenda to be my agenda. Help me to be sensitive to Your Spirit's guidance the next time I feel pulled on both sides.

What Would He Do?

Do to others as you would have them do to you.
LUKE 6:31

*M*organ, age nine, and Lydia, age seven, had been playing quietly with their dolls in front of the television when Lydia let out a bloodcurdling scream. "Mommy, Mommy! Look what Morgan did to my baby!" She sobbed as she ran into the kitchen. Morgan had cut off the doll's hair.

Morgan was old enough to know better, so I told her she should trade dolls with Lydia. Morgan began to cry and refused. Trying to remain calm, I began to reason with her. Nothing worked. Finally I said, "Now, Morgan. What would Jesus do?"

"I don't know what He would do, and I don't care!" she cried. "You always ask that, and I don't know."

Didn't know? How could my daughter not know? Was Morgan just being stubborn, or did she really not know? Both options were troubling. I asked God to show me what to do.

That night, as the girls and I settled down to read from their children's Bible, I prayed that the Holy Spirit would speak to Morgan's heart through the Scripture. We turned to Luke 6 and began reading the section that contained the Golden Rule. I knew Morgan's Sunday school class had learned that verse several months ago and hoped that the lesson had not been lost on her.

I tried not to watch her as I read, but I couldn't help it.

After we finished reading, we bowed our heads to pray. Then, as soon as we said our amens, Morgan slid off the bed, picked up her doll, and handed it to Lydia. "Jesus says I should do this. I would want you to do it for me. I'm sorry, Lydia."

Have you ever wondered how much the world would change if you, your family, or your church lived out the Golden Rule? Charles Sheldon did when he wrote *In His Steps* almost 100 years ago, and so have 15 million of his readers. Consider reading this classic to your family or giving it to someone you love.

Steps of Faith

Almighty Father, thank You for the life of Your Son, Jesus Christ. His example to me answers so many questions and directs my family and me on the path of love. I realize that the closer I am to Jesus, the easier it is to follow in His steps. May His goodness shine through my life.

One at a Time

How lovely is your dwelling place, O Lord Almighty!
PSALM 84:1

*B*ecause we were having Thanksgiving dinner at my brother's and I had done most of my Christmas shopping during the summer, I found myself in an unusual but wonderful situation: a whole week off at Thanksgiving and nothing to do! Except some long-needed household reorganization.

But where would I begin? After 17 years and three children, the thought of tackling such a chore was overwhelming. As I sat on the end of my bed, I fixed my eyes upon the top drawer of the dresser— my underwear drawer. As I stared at it, I realized that if I organized it, I might be able to put my socks and stockings in there as well. Then I would have another drawer.

Hmmm. I slowly walked to the drawer, pulled it open, and went to work. In 15 minutes one drawer was reorganized, another was empty. And I felt great! Then it occurred to me that if I did one drawer at a time, one room at a time, the task wouldn't be so over-whelming.

As I planned my Thanksgiving week, I set aside a few hours each morning to concentrate on one room. What a feeling of satisfaction I had as I slowly, methodically restored order to my house that week. And to my surprise, it became a special time with the Lord. I played praise music, sang, and prayed for my family and friends. It was therapeutic as well. I was focusing on something other than myself and seeing immediate results.

Since then I've been able to maintain a moderate amount of order using this system. Whether it's the kitchen pantry, the family room, or the guest bathroom, I just take it one room at a time.

Consider reorganizing one drawer at a time, one shelf at a time, one room at a time. After the first one, you'll not only feel better about your surroundings, you'll be inspired to do more!

Steps of Faith

Lord Almighty, I can only imagine how lovely Your dwelling place is! May I honor and glorify You by making the dwelling place You have given me one of grace and order. Thank You, Lord, that because I am made in Your image, I can appreciate the beauty of order.

Jehovah-Jireh

*So Abraham called that place
The LORD Will Provide.*

GENESIS 22:14

*T*he story of Abraham and Sarah has been a great comfort for my husband, Jim, and me. When we married in our thirties, we felt as though God had promised us children. But by the time I was 36, we had spent thousands of dollars on infertility treatments, endured several miscarriages, and could no longer handle the emotional strain of the process. To add to the challenge, Jim is paralyzed from the waist down. Children seemed out of the question.

Romans 4:18-21 strengthened our faith. We finally decided to let God provide children for us if that was His will. How? That wasn't our problem. God could do it.

About one month after relinquishing our hopes to God's control, we learned about a sister and brother, ages seven and four, in an orphanage outside of Moscow. We filed all the paperwork and received their pictures on my birthday. Jim's uncle, who travels extensively, offered us his frequent-flyer miles, enough to cover all the airfare (a $4,000 value). My family donated two bedroom sets. Neighbors and friends gave us new and used toys, books, and clothes.

Every time we thought God was out of surprises, He'd surprise us again. We were concerned about Jim's nine-hour flight to Moscow without access to a bathroom. Jim mentioned this when the airline called to check on his needs for the flight. He was told that we would be one of the first people to fly their new jet that had wheelchair-accessible bathrooms! What a God!

Every foreseen and unforeseen issue was covered. It was clear the right Person was in control this time—the One who will provide.

Jehovah-Jireh, the name by which Abraham addressed God on Mount Moriah, means "God will provide." Often our focus becomes so limited that we forget that God not only has the power to provide, but He wants to provide as well. Do you know God as your *Jehovah-Jireh?*

Steps of Faith

Jehovah-Jireh, thank You for the countless blessings in my life. I see all of them as Your provision, gifts from Your hand. You know all my needs, even the ones I don't know about yet, and I trust You to provide for them all.

Only One Way?

*No one can lay any foundation other than the one
already laid, which is Jesus Christ.*

1 CORINTHIANS 3:11

*S*usan could see Ted across the ballroom engrossed in conversation with his supervisor, George, and some other men. *Hmm. He must be talking about sports or politics. I'd better rescue him—and his audience!* But as Susan approached the men she heard these words and said a quick prayer:

"But Jesus Himself said in John 14:6, 'No one comes to the Father except through me.' Are you saying Jesus was lying?"

"I thought you were intelligent, Ted," George shot back, ignoring Ted's question. "How can you be so intolerant? Jesus was a good man, but so were Mohammed, Buddha, and Confucius. If you'd get your head out of the Bible and show a little love you'd see that all religions lead to God."

"I didn't say that they won't," Ted replied, instantly getting everyone's attention. "But Jesus did. Either He is a lunatic, a liar, or He spoke the truth. Of all the world's religious teachers, Jesus Christ is the only one who claimed to be God [John 10:30; 12:45; 14:10], loved His followers so much that He willingly gave His sinless life [John 8:46] to pay for their sins [John 3:16], and then gave sinners the hope of eternal life [Romans 5:8] by conquering death when He rose from the grave [Romans 14:9; Colossians 1:18]. Mohammed, Buddha, and Confucius are still dead—but Jesus Christ lives! We know He was not a lunatic, and not many people believe He was a liar. That leaves only one option open. He spoke the truth. Because He claims to be the only way to God, I have to believe it."

On the way home Susan squeezed Ted's hand. Studying apologetics was the beginning of a new adventure. As they prayed for George and the others, she thanked God for giving her Ted as a partner.

Have you ever been challenged or even ridiculed for believing that Jesus Christ is the only way to God? Spend some time in the Bible and books that compare other religions to Christianity. They will help you reason with nonbelievers as you defend your faith.

Steps of Faith

My Lord and Savior, how my heart praises You for Your love and sacrifice for me. How unworthy I am apart from You. Let Your presence in my life strengthen me and shine through me as I lead others to the eternal hope that is found only in You.

Let It Shine

*Let your light shine before men, that they may see your good
deeds and praise your Father in heaven.*

MATTHEW 5:16

In the church where I grew up, services always seemed gloomy to me. Very little light filtered in through the stained-glass windows. The pastors terrified me, because they always looked so stern. *That's what God's like,* I thought, *always mad at me. He doesn't like me.*

The best part of church was going to Sunday school. I can still feel the warm, blinding sunlight streaming over me as the teachers led us out of the dark church to our classes. When I was eight, Mr. Beasley was my Sunday school teacher. He was different from the others. He smiled a lot, and all he seemed to talk about was how much Jesus loved us. I loved Mr. Beasley because he made me feel good when I thought about God. On promotion Sunday, he gave each of us a little Bible. (It was my first Bible.)

On the way home from church that day, I asked my parents why Mr. Beasley was different. My mother told me he was "born again." I had never heard of that and asked her what it meant. She didn't know.

By the time I was 11, my family had stopped going to church, and at 25, I had really messed up my life. My heart longed for God's forgiveness, but I thought it was too late. *God can't love me. He knows how bad I've been.*

I often thought about Mr. Beasley, wondering how he could have been so happy and excited about a God who was so stern. Then I met Chuck. His joy and love for the Lord reminded me of Mr. Beasley's, so I trusted him. He explained what it means to be "born again" and soon led me to Christ.

Mr. Beasley died in 1992. He was a gifted teacher who had been willing to let his light shine in a class of eight-year-olds. Because he did, I got my first glimpse of Jesus. Now my light is shining.

Is your light shining for the world to see and praise God for? Or are you hiding it? The goodness of Christ in the life of a believer shines bright in a world darkened by sin. Ask God to show you where your light can shine the brightest.

Steps of Faith

*Lord, Your goodness fills my heart with joy and peace. Lead me in
Your way so that the light of Your holiness will shine through me.
Reveal any hidden sins that shadow my joy and love for You.*

Living with Less

Whoever loves discipline loves knowledge, but he who hates correction is stupid.

PROVERBS 12:1

Pat looked at the mess in front of her and shook her head. Why had she let this go for so long? The closets, the garage, the utility closet, the pantry—each one was a disaster! She was disgusted and silently began to berate herself for her lack of discipline.

A knock at the door interrupted her thoughts. She was glad to see her old friend Lisa. As they settled down to a cup of coffee, Pat expressed her frustration to Lisa and was surprised to see her friend smiling.

"Oh, Pat, I can help you! It took me awhile, but I learned how to live with less years ago! My life is much simpler now!" Lisa said.

"Learn to live with less stuff?" Pat repeated.

In a few minutes, Lisa explained her rules for clutter control:

- Start at one end of the house and do one area at a time. Make piles to throw away, give away, or store elsewhere.

- Make a six-month rule. If you haven't used it in six months, get rid of it.

- Keep your inside closets filled with items you use regularly. Store the rest in marked boxes in the garage. This is the best place for seasonal items.

- Get boxes of a similar size and label them: A1, A2, etc. Write the contents of each box on a three-by-five card. Keep the cards in the house. When you need something, flip through the cards to locate it instead of rummaging through all the boxes.

"There are lots of books on organizing," Lisa said. "Get a book, get a friend, and get busy!"

Managing the "things" in our lives takes time, organization, and maintenance. Many books and systems are out there. Find one that works for you, start small, and begin! Our God is a God of order—in all ways.

Steps of Faith

Dear God, You created an orderly world and I do not want to live in chaos. Help me to stay on top of my possessions and to learn the joy of living more simply.

A Fight for Right

Who is going to harm you if you are eager to do good?
But even if you should suffer for what is right, you are blessed.

1 PETER 3:13,14

*A*s a high-school English teacher I'm not allowed to share my faith or quote the Bible during class time; however, I'm a faculty sponsor for a student-initiated and student-led Christian club that meets on campus after school for a short Bible study and prayer time.

One day Mr. Jones, the principal, received a call from Mrs. Murrow, who was incensed that our group was allowed to meet on campus. She said our club was unconstitutional and demanded that it be denied classroom space. Although Mr. Jones explained to her that the club was indeed legitimate, Mrs. Murrow began to circulate a petition among students and parents.

The issue polarized the school and community. Emotions and tempers raged on both sides. As faculty sponsor, I had to defend my beliefs to students, teachers, and parents. It really tested my faith and the faith of each club member. (Our club prayer time was no longer brief!)

Finally Mr. Jones and the PTA called a special meeting. The room was packed. As Mrs. Murrow spoke, she restated her claims but also insisted that we study other religious writings along with the Bible. In addition she accused me of brainwashing and manipulating club members.

When it was my turn, I spoke briefly about James Madison, the Constitution, and the Bible. Then several club members gave one-minute testimonies about how the club had enriched their faith and their lives.

Those students and I were never same. We had been forced to defend our values to the world, and we had done it without flinching. And after the smoke cleared, we still had a Christian club—with six new members!

Do you know how to mount a defense when your values are attacked? Consider what Jesus did when He cleared the temple (Matthew 21:12,13). He was disruptive, but He never lost His integrity. He forced the people out, but He never abused them. He disturbed their merchandise, but He didn't destroy it. He didn't hate them—He hated their behavior.

Steps of Faith

Oh Father, I don't like confrontation, so I'm often tempted to remain silent when my beliefs are attacked. Let me learn from Jesus. He knew how to fight for right.

Tale of Two Desks

*I will listen to what God the LORD will say; he promises peace
to his people, his saints—but let them not return to folly.*

PSALM 85:8

$\mathcal{T}$ he desks still rest against the same wall in the spare room. A small filing cabinet still stands in between—the old battle line. It's peaceful here, now. Vestiges of the virtual battlefield are hardly noticeable.

The desk on the left belongs to my husband, Andy, a CPA. As expected, it is organized—neat little piles allowing ample work space. He works here on the weekends. The other is mine. I'm a free-lance writer. "Creatively cluttered" best describes my desk, but it has seen messier days.

Shortly after Andy and I married, Andy began to complain about my desk. The mess overflowed from the desk to the floor—dictionaries, telephone books, reference books, pads of paper strewn all over the floor. He'd get mad and push all of it onto my side of the filing cabinet. Then I'd get mad because he'd ruined my "system"!

But I'd really unnerve him when I'd water the plants I had hiding the ugly surge protector that sat at the back corner of my desk. I kept an old plastic cup filled with water right next to it. Both computers, the printer, his calculator, and the telephone/answering machine were plugged into it. More than once he warned me not to water the plants there.

Then one day my cat, after napping on top of my monitor, jumped down onto the desk. He landed on a marker hidden under a sheet of paper, lost his footing, and knocked the cup of water all over the surge protector.

Words cannot adequately describe the horror that followed. The worst part was calling Andy. Most of our equipment was damaged, and at one point, I thought our marriage might be as well. Only much prayer, humility, and forgiveness, along with a lot of dollars, have brought us back up to speed. Needless to say, the plants have been moved to another room.

Are you and your husband opposites when it comes to clutter control? If you are the messy spouse, remember there is a point at which too much clutter, coupled with a lack of wisdom, can be dangerous and expensive. Check the safety of all your clutter pockets soon.

Steps of Faith

*Father, make me wise to see where I need to change any foolish
habits—especially those that disturb the people I love.*

Captive Thoughts

Finally, brothers, whatever is true, whatever is noble,
whatever is right, whatever is pure, whatever is lovely,
whatever is admirable—if anything is excellent or
praiseworthy—think about such things.

PHILIPPIANS 4:8

*S*he said *what?*" Sandy asked incredulously. "How dare Kim draw that conclusion because she feels there is some tension in my marriage. She, of all people, knows what Michael and I have been through—and how far we've come. How low can you get?" For the next fifteen minutes Sandy and Patsy said a lot of nasty things about Kim.

After they hung up, Sandy's heart and head were pounding. Kim had betrayed her, and all she wanted to do was talk about it. Within days, Sandy had gotten to the point that her first thoughts in the morning and final thoughts in the evening centered on Kim.

To get even, Sandy called all the women in her Sunday school class, except Kim, with "a special prayer request." That afternoon Sandy rehearsed every detail to eight pairs of eager ears. But when she reached Donna, the wife of the Sunday school teacher, she got a different response. Donna asked Sandy to meet her for coffee that night.

At the diner Donna gently talked with Sandy about her obsession with this issue. Sandy tearfully admitted it and asked for help. Donna suggested she memorize 2 Corinthians 10:5 and Philippians 4:8, and recite these verses every time she was tempted to think or talk negatively about Kim. In a couple of weeks she and Kim could talk about reconciliation. (Sandy doubted that would ever happen.)

Sandy followed Donna's advice and to her amazement, within several days her anger and hurt had practically vanished. She even found herself praying that God would restore her friendship with Kim.

Goodness begins in your mind, and for that matter so does evil. You have the power to "take captive every thought to make it obedient to Christ" (2 Corinthians 10:5), especially when you use the greatest of all spiritual weapons: "the sword of the Spirit, which is the word of God" (Ephesians 6:17).

Steps of Faith

Lord, the Bible says, "Your righteousness is like the mighty mountains" (Psalm 36:6). One of the few things more awesome than that is that You have imparted that same righteousness to me. May I live it to Your glory.

Path to Peace

*You will keep in perfect peace [her] whose mind is
steadfast, because [she] trusts in you.*

ISAIAH 26:3

It had been four months since my husband had been laid off. With still no job in sight, I could see him spiraling into depression. Six Sunday papers, brimming with employment opportunities, sat on his desk—untouched. The man who normally needed only five hours of sleep now needed twelve. The man who never watched television was now hooked on talk shows and sitcom reruns. He'd gained 20 pounds.

On the other hand I'd found a temporary full-time job, was snatching about five hours of sleep per night, had no time for television, and had *lost* 20 pounds. In my attempt to tend to a depressed husband, restless children, numerous household chores, and a new job, I became a nervous wreck. All I did was worry.

I was working as a proofreader for a printing company. Ironically, as much time as the job consumed, all that reading was a wonderful escape from the fears and pressures I constantly exerted on myself. Then one day I was proofing a brochure for a religious conference. Isaiah 26:3 was printed in bold, italic type across the three panels of the brochure. I quickly wrote it out on a yellow sticky note and placed it on my computer screen. Every time I read Isaiah 26:3, I could feel peace, fresh and alive, welling up inside me. Pretty soon I had that verse plastered everywhere: my bathroom mirror, the refrigerator, the dashboard of my car, and my checkbook. And anytime I felt anxiety creeping up, I recited it out loud.

Looking back, it's a good thing I didn't know that five more months of unemployment stretched before us. But that's not even an issue now. God faithfully provided for all of my family's needs—even my need for peace.

Have you allowed a situation or a person to rob you of the peace God wants you to enjoy? The Bible tells us that peace is a fruit of the Holy Spirit (Galatians 5:22,23). Cultivate the fruit of peace by keeping your heart and mind steadfastly on the Lord, trusting Him to take care of everything.

Steps of Faith

*Oh Lord my God, You have safely led me through so many trials.
When I look back on them, I know it was Your remarkable peace
that sustained me. Keep my heart in "perfect peace" any time my
faith is tested.*

Christmas Teardrop

*Do not cast me away when I am old; do not forsake me
when my strength is gone.*

PSALM 71:9

*O*ne little tear stood ready to fall, and try as she might, Grandma Amy could not stop its escape. Five-year-old Julia saw the tear and, without knowing the possible consequences, announced, "Grandma's crying!"

Around the table, all laughter and friendly bantering stopped abruptly and every eye turned toward Amy DeLaney Anderson, the matriarch of this clan who had gathered for Christmas dinner together.

"Mother, what's wrong?" asked her gentle daughter, Beth, with genuine concern.

"Has something upset you?" asked her son, Edward.

Julia slipped out of her chair and into Grandma Amy's arms. "She misses Grandpa! He's in heaven, you know," she said with great authority.

Grandma Amy hugged her close. "Yes, I do miss him, sweetheart. It's not the same without Grandpa here, is it?"

Around the table, heads nodded sadly, relief in their expressions. Grandma Amy was all right, just missing her husband of 55 years. That was understandable.

In a few hours, the house will be quiet again, she thought. *All of you will say goodbye and go back to your busy lives, leaving me alone again.*

Grandma Amy felt a familiar ache go through her insides. She felt like her heart was breaking. So close to the surface was her pain that the words were out of her mouth before she could call them back, "I am so lonely. Help me, please!"

Immediately, love flowed around the table and all over Grandma Amy as she was hugged and reassured. Plans were made for weekend outings, promises given of daily phone calls and mini-visits, even invitations to spend holidays at the beach.

Holidays can be lonely times for the older generation, despite the whirlwind of activities surrounding them. Do you have any "Grandma Amys" in your midst? Be sensitive and ask how they are really doing—before, during, and after holidays. Plan to include them in some of your family's activities.

Steps of Faith

*Dear Father, grant me the privilege of helping ease the loneliness of
an elderly person this holiday season and throughout the year.*

25

A Joyful Noise

*It is good to praise the LORD and make music to
your name, O Most High.*

PSALM 92:1

I can't sing. I mean, I do sing, but I can't carry a tune or harmonize. And I never remember all the words. Still, I like to make a joyful noise unto the Lord!

Sometimes, the words to a worship chorus will trigger a response in my heart that opens my tear ducts, a physical phenomenon that I can't explain. Other times, the melody is so sweet, my heart soars and my voice follows suit.

I sing the loudest in the shower. There's something about the acoustics in the bathroom that make me sound much better than I am. I sing the best in the car, with the windows down and the stereo cranked up. I sing the worst in church with everybody listening to me.

I used to worry about it, but I don't anymore.

Sometimes when I'm singing and making a joyful noise, I feel God's pleasure. I have a theory that my not-so-good voice is transformed into angelic music when my heart is bursting with praise.

It seldom happens when I'm in church and distracted by what people around me are wearing.

It seldom happens when I'm aware that others are listening to me, like at my women's Bible study.

It seldom happens when I'm thinking about shopping or the book I'm reading or the movie I saw last night.

But when I'm totally thinking about Jesus, when my heart is filled with gratitude, and when praise saturates my entire being, that's when I connect with heaven. That's when my voice sounds beautiful. That's when I know my "noise" is truly made beautiful by joy.

Music gives you the chance to express your love for God. Whether singing with others or alone, let your heart be turned toward God. If you've never sung to the Lord when you're alone, why not give it a try? During your quiet time, softly sing a favorite praise chorus—just for Him.

Steps of Faith

Dear Father, You are worthy of praise and my voice is the instrument You have given me to worship You. Let me be a sweet, sweet sound in Your ear.

A Family Divided

Be completely humble and gentle; be patient,
bearing with one another in love.

EPHESIANS 4:2

Carolyn and Carl argued as small children, and now, in their retirement years, they continued to disagree. Their father had recently passed away, and the siblings couldn't agree on how to disburse the family furniture and keepsakes.

"Dad promised me the grand piano!" exclaimed Carolyn.

"But you have the dining room set," Carl protested loudly.

This had been going on for months. It was as though I was watching children argue over the largest cookie in the jar. My family was falling apart over possessions. It saddened me as I watched my own mother and her brother in this verbal battle that seemed unending.

"Mother, please don't do this! We have all that we need—we don't want further friction. We have lost Papa and now his belongings are dividing the family."

My mother had had a difficult childhood and rarely shared those memories with me. I knew she was dealing with painful hurts and needed someone to listen to her recollections of the years gone by.

"I'm sorry for your anguish, Mom," I said as I tried to comfort her. "Perhaps it is time to reconcile the differences between you and Carl and begin to forgive. We can't go on in this battle. The conflict in your generation is now affecting your children and your grandchildren."

That evening I heard her on the phone. "Carl, we need to get this settled. Papa wouldn't want us. . . . "

My heart lightened.

Is there someone in your family who needs your forgiveness? You can choose to act in love and not out of past painful memories. You can choose to release your hurt and move into forgiveness. Allow God to comfort you and begin to restore your family!

Steps of Faith

Father in heaven, thank You for my loving parents and my dear grandparents. Thank You for the beautiful inheritance You have given me. Thank You for healing fractured families.

The Gift of Peace

Grace and peace to you from God our Father and
the Lord Jesus Christ, who gave himself for our sins to rescue
us from the present evil age, according to the will
of our God and Father.

GALATIANS 1:3,4

*M*y life is a testimony to Proverbs 22:6: "Train a child in the way he should go, and when he is old he will not turn from it." The problem was what I did between when I was a child and when I was "old."

I don't know exactly when I began to stray, but I do remember a moment in college when I said to myself, "It's time to start having fun. Being a nice girl just isn't worth it." It was downhill from there: a few too many drinks, foul language, marijuana, broken promises, waking up next to someone I didn't know, an abortion, cheating on finals, gossip, betrayals, and, finally, publicly denying my Lord.

However, even while I wallowed in sinful rebellion, some Sunday nights I'd sneak into the balcony of my old church, sing the familiar hymns, and listen to every word of the sermon. God would not let me go.

By the time I repented and rededicated my life to Christ, my sins had so scarred and maimed me that I couldn't believe the cross was enough to cover me. My reputation inside and outside the church was destroyed. I was tormented with guilt and fear of God's judgment. Then, after weeks of prayer and immersing myself in God's Word, I came upon Romans 8:31: "If God is for us, who can be against us?" At this point I began to accept the possibility that God, at least, was *for* me, so I clung to that verse, reciting it to myself 100 times a day.

Twelve years later, as a 37-year-"old" woman, I know the gift of God's steadfast peace. I trust that I will never turn from it again.

Do you remember the moment in your life when you recognized your sinfulness as compared to God's infinite holiness? At that moment you realized your need for a Savior, and God the Father was right there with you, offering you peace with Him through His perfect Son, Jesus.

Steps of Faith

Lord God, no one can compare with You. You are my Deliverer from the ravages of my sin, no matter how awful, and the Provider of peace and blessings. There is no other Lord in my life. Thank You for rescuing me from evil.

The Missed Christmas

Turn to me and be gracious to me, for I am lonely and afflicted.

PSALM 25:16

*H*annah put on a happy face, but her heart was breaking as her ex-husband walked down the sidewalk with two-year-old Jacob in his arms and four-year-old Jeremy toddling along beside him. *Oh, Lord, how will I possibly get through this Christmas?* she wondered.

Hannah tried to reassure herself that she would be okay, that she was glad Greg wanted to spend Christmas with the boys. After all, some fathers didn't want their children at all. And besides, she'd had them last year. It was his turn.

Greg had even suggested that he take Jeremy and she keep Jacob at home with her. But the boys were so close, she reasoned, and in the end, keeping them together seemed best.

Under the Christmas tree were presents for each of the boys from her, but the toys from Santa would arrive at Greg's house this year. They had discussed what to purchase and agreed ahead of time. Jeremy and Jacob would return after dinner at Nana and Papa's house.

Yes, it will be a grand day for them, she thought, knowing Greg's parents' devotion to the boys. *They won't even miss me.*

The ringing telephone brought Hannah out of her doldrums and she put on her best Christmas voice when she answered, "Merry Christmas!"

"Goodnight, Mommy!" she heard Jacob's and Jeremy's sweet voices at the other end of the phone. "We miss you, Mommy!"

Thanks, Lord, I needed that!

Will your children be away this Christmas, spending time with their father in another house, maybe even another state? If so, make sure that you have friends to spend the time with, or perhaps volunteer to work at a hospital or a homeless shelter. As you release your children into the Lord's care during this separation, you will find that He cares for you—even in those lonely moments.

Steps of Faith

Dear God, help me not to just "get through" this Christmas, but to focus on You and the marvelous miracle You accomplished. Help my kids to have a special holiday with their dad. Help me to encourage this relationship for their sakes.

Soothing My Spirit

Because you are my help,
I sing in the shadow of your wings.

PSALM 63:7

*A*n unexpected phone call had brought the darkest news a mother would ever have to hear: "Your son passed away last night."

"No, this can't be true! Someone has made a terrible mistake!" I cried out.

It was true, my precious son had died in his sleep that night. My son, who loved the Lord, was now with Him—and I was left behind! My heart was broken. I felt empty and alone. How could I trust God with anything again? How could I go to church or pray? Would I ever sing again?

Many months passed before my desire returned to attend church, but there I was, in church singing praise songs. "Lord, I want to know You more. . . ." The words were flowing from my mouth as the tears rolled down my cheeks. Music was soothing and restoring my spirit, as it had many times in the past. How could I have forgotten the other times when I had been so down and the Lord had come through? Powerful words encased in beautiful music nourished me once again. The words I had sung so many times in the past sounded fresh and new to me that day.

"Yes, Lord, I do want to know You more!" My heart was healing!

It has been a year now since my son died and I miss him deeply. Yet daily, I eagerly anticipate the next time I will listen to a tape or attend a worship service knowing that my son also found comfort and joy in music.

Have you experienced a deep loss? Have you found that you were unable to sing? God, in His gentle way, will restore the joy of music to your wounded soul, in His time. Seek His face always. Be patient!

Steps of Faith

Father in heaven, thank You for loving my children, just as You love Your Son. Thank You for the knowledge that one day all of Your children will praise You together in heaven. Thank You for the music that comforts during grief. But thank You, too, for giving me back the song.

Never Forsaken

*I lie awake; I have become like a
bird alone on a roof.*

PSALM 102:7

*R*amona sat curled up under a blanket. It was a frigid Saturday night, but her flannel pajamas and beloved cat, Tinker, provided extra warmth. Ramona was near the conclusion of the movie when this scene flashed on the screen: The leading lady is alone at a crowded New Year's Eve party. She begins to cry and tells her friend, "I can't stand not being kissed on New Year's Eve." Right then, the leading man, who has sprinted across the city to reach her, bursts into the room, kisses her, and presto—happy ending.

Up until that scene, Ramona had enjoyed the movie. "Oh *puh-lease,* give me a break!" she practically snarled as she flicked off the television and VCR. But when she plopped back down on the couch, she broke into sobs. That last scene had struck a nerve. Tinker climbed back into her lap, but her nuzzling and purring didn't ease the pain of this new loneliness.

Just last weekend, Ramona had attended the singles' New Year's Eve party at her church. *What am I doing here?* she asked herself. *I should be with Norm and our married friends. I don't know anyone here.* But the awkward loneliness came crashing in when the clock struck midnight. Norm, who had kissed her at midnight a year ago, had left her for another woman. Now he was probably kissing "her." She wanted to scream.

"What am I going to do, God?" she cried, as she stroked Tinker. "I know I can't expect the Hollywood version of life, but I also know nothing's impossible with You. Please give me peace. Heal my heart. And please send me a friend."

Have you ever been lonely in a crowd? Then you can have mercy on the person you see standing alone in a group of people. Make an effort to speak to her, asking her questions about herself. If she's too shy to talk, tell her about yourself! If crowd-loneliness haunts you, arrange in advance for a companion, even if it's a family member or a neighbor.

Steps of Faith

Lord, as often as I read that nothing can separate me from Your love, there are still those times when I feel so alone, even when I'm with friends and family members. Open my eyes to Your steadfast companionship. I trust that You will never leave me or forsake me (Joshua 1:5).

The Seesaw

*Make every effort to live in peace
with all men and to be holy.*

HEBREWS 12:14

J've always been the one to keep the peace in our family. I smooth things over when Mom gets her feathers ruffled. I humor Dad when his arthritis makes him grouchy. I change the subject when anyone starts talking politics over a family dinner.

Of course, the hardest job for a peacemaker comes when both parties believe they were wronged, that it's the other person who needs to apologize. That's when I remind my family about the cross and the seesaw. I heard a pastor preach on this one time, and I've never forgotten the principle. It changed my life as a peacemaker.

You remember how a seesaw operates on a playground? One person sits on each end of the seesaw and, if their weights are about the same, they go up and down with ease. However, if their weights are different, the heavier person must move closer to the center so that the seesaw balances. Then they can go up and down, up and down.

When two people are locked in an argument and neither will budge an inch, this principle of the seesaw can help them to understand how to break the stalemate.

Imagine the cross in the center of the seesaw. The spiritual person must move closer to the center—to the cross. The closer any of us gets to the cross, the more rights we relinquish. In effect, the more mature Christian will be the one to give up the right that is causing the stalemate: the right to be right.

Little is gained by a continuing, bitter argument. Some things are not worth the risk of hurt feelings and broken relationships. Does it really matter who says "sorry" first? Keeping the cross central in our lives is the answer to keeping peace in the family. Jesus laid aside all rights and took on the form of a servant to make peace between God and man. Do you really have the right to hold on to your rights?

Steps of Faith

Dearest Lord, help me to be a peacemaker in the lives of those I love. Teach me to model giving up those rights that separate me from family and friends.

Put on Love

Clothe yourselves with compassion, kindness,
humility, gentleness and patience.

COLOSSIANS 3:12

For so many of us, spending time over Christmas with our extended family is anything but peaceful and joyous. Even in Christian families, where almost everyone has a relationship with the Lord, sinful attitudes creep in. It's difficult not to fall back into old patterns of behavior when we get together with our parents and brothers and sisters. It seems inevitable that someone asks aloud, "Just what do you mean by that?" and then it's all downhill. However, just as we put on festive attire for holiday gatherings, there are some Christlike attitudes we can "put on" that will truly help make the occasion what it ought to be.

Put on grace. Realize that you only have one set of relatives, and you need to accept them as they are, not as you'd like them to be. If there are members of your family with whom your relationship is particularly bad, pray about visits with them in advance. Ask God to make an opportunity for peace and healing, and be willing to take the initiative in putting aside grievances.

Put on forgiveness. You can do this even if the offender refuses to acknowledge that he or she has given offense. Let go of bitterness and resentment because of things said and done in the past. Try to focus on creating pleasant memories for the future instead.

Put on love. This is the greatest way we can imitate the Prince of Peace. The fact that we ever come to love anyone or that anyone loves us defies all human reasoning. We love others because God first loved us, and that is as close as we can come to understanding love. Through love, God can and does bring peace in even the most troubled family relationships.

One vital step toward mending a relationship is resolving to put the past behind you and refusing to nurture old grievances. Don't let your peace be destroyed by dwelling on painful memories from your past.

Steps of Faith

Father, help me remember that peace within my family means that I must first die to self—that my pride, my rights, and my expectations must be laid down. Make me willing.

Faithful Stewards

*To everyone who has, more will be given, but as
for the one who has nothing,
even what he has will be taken away.*

LUKE 19:26

*I*n most marriages one of the partners is the money manager. He or she is organized and thrifty, pays the bills on time, and keeps a sharp eye on the bottom line. But Bill and I are both financial illiterates. We had hoped marriage would straighten us up, but it only made matters worse. We finally had to get some help.

We decided to attend an eight-week seminar sponsored by a Christian financial management firm. During the series we learned that 16 of Jesus' 38 parables center on money; more is said in the New Testament about money than is said about heaven and hell combined; and there are more than 2,000 verses in the Bible dealing with money and possessions. It became obvious to us that how we manage our money is important to God.

As Bill and I worked together, four biblical principles of money management began to solidify in our minds. The first is that God owns it all. If this principle is true, Bill and I reasoned that we have no rights to our property, just the responsibility to be good stewards.

Second, we realized that the way we spend our money is an indicator of our spiritual growth. Money in the hands of a Christian is a tool, a test, and a testimony. Third, the amount of money we have is not important; it is how we manage that amount that has eternal consequences. And fourth, in the parable of the talents (Matthew 25:14-30), we learned that faith requires action. We had to trust God to do what is right with His money.

Bill and I have just started implementing these principles. It's been an adjustment, to say the least. But it works.

In his book, *Master Your Money*, Ron Blue writes, "Stewardship is the use of God-given resources for the accomplishment of God-given goals." Honestly evaluate how you use your resources. Then ask God to direct you in how you can be a better steward of His property.

Steps of Faith

King of kings, I acknowledge that You own it all. Give me wisdom as I attempt to use Your resources to fulfill Your objectives. Help me keep in mind that the way I use those resources is a testimony to my faith in You.

Self-Sufficient

Since no man knows the future,
who can tell him what is to come?

ECCLESIASTES 8:7

*W*hen I was a senior in high school, my best friend's father died suddenly of a heart attack. Her mother was left with a mortgage, property taxes, investments, and not the slightest idea what to do with any of them. Twenty years later, I realized the same thing could happen to me.

My husband, Mac, has always managed the money, while I managed the household and family. It was a tidy arrangement. A few months ago Mac had to go on a 30-day business trip to Germany. As the trip drew nearer, it occurred to us that I was going to have to manage both the household and the money. That's when I began to panic.

A week before he left, after the children were in bed, Mac and I started with the basics—the checkbook. (I hadn't balanced one since before our wedding day.) The next night we reviewed our budget. In one column he listed our monthly expenses, including tithe and savings, and in another column listed our estimated income—his salary, along with some stock dividends and earned interest.

The month of his trip happened to be the month the property taxes were due. He wanted to pay for them out of a certain account but at the end of the first quarter. This way we would earn the maximum amount of interest. He wrote a reminder on a note and placed it on the computer with a smiley face!

By the time Mac left, I had a basic idea of what we earned, what we owed, when it was to be paid, and where it went. And though I pray Mac and I will have a long, healthy life together, I am thankful that he has encouraged me—and prepared me—to manage our finances in case a tragedy strikes.

Who manages the money in your family? If you don't, and something were to happen to the person who does, would you be able to take over? If you are overwhelmed by that prospect, remember that God promises to be with you, guiding and protecting you in all that you do (Psalm 73:21-28). Do what you can to prepare for that situation.

Steps of Faith

Glorious Lord, I am grateful that I have not had to make all of the
financial decisions for my household, but I know one day I may have
to. If and when that day comes, Lord, empower me with wisdom and
faith to manage our resources in a way that is glorifying to You.

"Highly Favored"

*The angel went to her and said, "Greetings, you who are
highly favored! The Lord is with you."*

LUKE 1:28

*O*n the surface she was probably a typical young Jewish girl.
She probably had the same dreams as other girls of her culture: getting married and being a good wife and mother. But Mary was far
from typical.

One day, in a matter of minutes, Mary's life was transformed from
ordinary to extraordinary. And the world was never the same.

An angel suddenly appeared in her home, and if his appearance
wasn't troubling enough, his greeting was even more disturbing. Just
as Mary was recovering from the shock of being addressed as "highly
favored," the angel told her that she would become pregnant by the
Holy Spirit and give birth to the Son of God.

Questions must have clamored in Mary's mind. The most obvious
is recorded in Scripture (Luke 1:34). But Mary also must have wondered about Joseph's reaction, not to mention the gossip, the speculation, the questioning of her virtue. And if she tried to explain who the
Father was, some would definitely question her sanity!

In spite of her questions and fears, Mary submitted to the will of
God (Luke 1:38). As one who was "highly favored," Mary trusted
God to take care of her. Though she had no way of knowing how
much pain would accompany her special calling, she knew God's
love would give her the strength she needed.

Have you ever tried to imagine the Christmas story from Mary's
perspective? What would you think if an angel told you that you were
"highly favored"? You might think life would be a breeze—no problems, no pain. Not according to Mary. Her life demonstrates that God
works out His eternal, universal purposes in our finite, private questions and pain. There is a higher purpose. If you are wrestling with
painful questions today, draw strength from Mary's life.

Steps of Faith

*God my Savior, I praise You for Your glorious works. I praise You for
Your eternal plan. I am filled with awe and wonder that You would
choose to use a sinful creature like me to work out that plan. When
I get discouraged, remind me of Mary. I want to respond with a
heart like hers.*

Letting Go

When his parents saw him, they were astonished.
His mother said to him, "Son, why have you treated us like
this? Your father and I have been anxiously searching for you."

LUKE 2:48

$\mathcal{T}$he caravan creaked through the ancient gates of Jerusalem, beginning its hot, dusty journey back to Nazareth. The Passover Feast had concluded, and it was time to go home. Mary was at the front of the procession with the other women and children. Since Jesus was now 12, Mary assumed He was with Joseph and the other men, bringing up the rear.

It was probably later that night, at suppertime, that Mary became aware of Jesus' absence. Sure, He was known to spend a lot of time alone, but lately His growing body was demanding more food, not less. It was not like Him to miss a meal. Then Mary's worst fears were realized: no one had seen Him all day.

During a restless night, Mary, like most mothers, probably blamed herself. The next day, as she and Joseph made their way through the crowded marketplace, along the narrow streets to the courtyard of the temple, Mary must have prayed earnestly. Then they saw Him! He was standing with a group of men three and four times His age—and they were spellbound by His words.

With a mixture of relief and irritation, Mary questioned Jesus about His behavior. His reply was the first defining line that separated Jesus as a person apart from her and Joseph (Luke 2:49). Jesus was becoming a man. And Mary knew that one day the baby she had held to her breast in Bethlehem would break away from her care into a life and purpose of His own.

One of the most painful aspects of parenting is letting go of our children. However, preparing children for independence is the ultimate task of parenthood. What concrete steps are you taking to prepare your children to be on their own? Ask God to help you discern how best to meet their needs.

F R I D A Y

Steps of Faith

Heavenly Father, there are so many emotions involved in parenting—some of them positive, many of them negative. Sometimes it's downright painful. Give me grace, Father, when I am challenged with the changes that are certain to come in my children. Help me to let go.

The Birth

So [the shepherds] hurried off and found Mary and Joseph,
and the baby, who was lying in the manger. . . . Mary treasured
up all these things and pondered them in her heart.

LUKE 2:16,19

W
E
E
K
E
N
D

*S*hortly before Mary was to give birth, she traveled about a hundred miles on the back of a donkey (try to imagine that!) to Bethlehem for the census. After three or four days of travel, she and Joseph arrived in Bethlehem to find that there were no rooms available at the inn. Their only option was a barn or cave where animals were kept. And this is where this "highly favored" woman bore her child, the Son of God: in the midst of filth and stench, far from the support of friends and family.

Then, even before she could begin to clean up, get comfortable, and rest, a throng of excited, noisy shepherds converged upon them. They exclaimed something about angels appearing to them in the night and announcing "Peace to men on whom his favor rests."

Possibly Mary thought to herself, *Hmmm. Peace and God's favor. That rings a bell. Hey, I could use some peace and quiet right now.*

If it weren't for her faith, Mary's life would have seemed totally out of control. Did she get angry or discouraged? Maybe she was tempted to shake her fist at God and tell the shepherds to go away. But we don't see that. Instead we see Mary's faith transcend the chaos swirling around her and bless her with peace and strength. She could handle whatever God had for her that day and trust Him to make sense of it in the future.

How would you have reacted if you had been Mary? After all, people who were not highly favored were sleeping in a bed, not a barn. Women who were not highly favored gave birth in their homes with their sisters, mothers, and grandmothers at their side. If you get discouraged when you see the evil prosper and the righteous suffer, remember Mary. She chose to trust God in the most incredible situation in the history of the world.

Steps of Faith

Prince of Peace, when I think about how Mary reacted to her circumstances I am ashamed at how I complain about mine. You know what I am struggling with right now, and I know You want me to trust You with it, because doing so is the key to a peace that exceeds my comprehension.

The Grudging Giver

God loves a cheerful giver.

2 CORINTHIANS 9:7

*O*h no, not another sermon on giving. I immediately tuned out as the pastor began to expound on the marvelous virtues of tithing. But this teaching was different: if God loves a cheerful giver, what does He hate? An uncheerful one, a grumpy one, a resentful one—one just like me!

The Holy Spirit's conviction was so complete I wanted to hide under the pew. I had been obedient to tithe all of my Christian life but there was one problem. I hated doing it. I was angry that I couldn't use the money for some things for my family, to pay off bills, to take a trip, to. . . .

But now I was seeing that God was not only interested in my tithing, but also the condition of my heart when I tithed. Why did I find it so difficult to cheerfully give? Did I think that God couldn't supply all my needs according to His riches in glory? Did I think He was a stingy God? Did I think He was going to punish me if I didn't do it?

I heard within a resounding "Yes" to all of the above. As I started dealing with my ungrateful attitude, I felt that peace that passes all understanding sweep over me. There was no condemnation. He gently corrected me and asked me if I wanted to change. After I confessed my sin and told Him I did want Him to change my heart, He began to show me the hidden resentments that kept me from cheerfully giving. And He showed me how to overcome them.

God is good. He wants only what's best for us. He wants our hearts to be purified from the pollution of the world's mindset. By tithing, we are telling ourselves that His purposes are higher than our own.

Steps of Faith

Dear God, forgive me for not trusting You to do good by me. Thank You for searching my heart and showing me those dark places where my resentments hide. Bring everything to light so I may joyfully and cheerfully give everything that I am and have.

Delayed Gratification

The end of a matter is better than its beginning,
and patience is better than pride.

ECCLESIASTES 7:8

*A*bout the time I started bugging Kenny to buy me a new car, we attended a financial seminar. The facilitator touched on the subject of paying cash as opposed to financing and paying interest. *Oh brother,* I thought. *Another tiresome lesson about delayed gratification.*

I decided to dream about the red convertible I had my eye on. *So what if the payments will be $525 a month for six years? I can just see myself tooling down the road with the top down, catching some rays, my hair waving in the breeze. . . .*

Later that night Kenny wanted me to look at a list of financial goals he'd put together—boring stuff like saving for a down payment for a house, paying off our credit card debt, eventually purchasing a new car . . .

The new car got my attention. When I asked him why we couldn't just finance the one I wanted now for six years, he showed me how much money that car would cost us in real dollars, counting the interest. And since my present car would probably last another five years, he wanted us to put the money we would have spent on the car payment in savings, earn the interest from it, and buy a new car with cash.

I pouted. I whined. I teased him about being a wet blanket. But inside I knew what he had proposed made sense.

Six years later I know what a smart guy Kenny is. Since then we have paid off all of our debt, saved $10,000 for the down payment on our house, and bought a new car with cash. However it's not the little red convertible I had my eye on. It's something much more practical: a minivan big enough to haul around the two of us and our three children!

What tempts you to borrow rather than save? Unless it is an emergency, there is no need to rush. First make sure God approves of the purchase, then save a little each month toward your goal. A little delayed gratification and patience can save you a lot of money in the long run.

Steps of Faith

Almighty God, Your Word speaks often about the value of patience and the vanity of worldly goods. Help me to maintain that perspective as I make decisions about how I spend my money. Give me wisdom to know that few things are more gratifying than that which has been delayed.

Obstacles?

For Christ's sake, I delight in weaknesses, in insults,
in hardships, in persecutions, in difficulties.
For when I am weak, then I am strong.

2 CORINTHIANS 12:10

The missionary had just returned from visiting some of the underground churches networked across the newly opened Soviet Union. For years attending church had been a violation of the law that carried a hefty fine, loss of privileges, and sometimes beatings and imprisonment. Only the most committed Christians took the necessary risks to worship and praise the Lord with other believers. Now their stories could be told.

One story in particular stood out in my mind. During one worship service, two armed soldiers burst into the gathering, demanding that anyone who was not willing to die for Christ should leave immediately. Of the 100 people who had risked all to be there, only 20 stayed.

The soldiers barred the doors and turned to face the remaining believers. The soldiers then confided that they, too, were Christians and wanted to worship with people they could trust to keep their secret. If the believers would allow the soldiers to worship regularly with them, they would keep the church a secret. The soldiers were accepted as brothers, and they joined in the worship.

The missionary asked us what we would have done. As I pondered this, I grieved over the possibility that I would have fled. (I thought about the petty excuses I dream up for not going to church on some Sunday mornings.) My spiritual complacency made me sick.

I silently prayed that God would renew my spirit and energize my faith. I wanted to be all that He wants me to be.

What obstacles stand between you and serving the Lord with excellence? It may be an obvious one like a physical disability, poverty, or political persecution. But are these really obstacles (2 Corinthians 12:10)? Whatever it is can be overcome by the power of our Lord Jesus Christ.

Steps of Faith

Holy Father, I thank You that I have not been called upon to risk my life and well-being for the sake of Your Son, Jesus—at least not yet. Father, if that day ever comes, give me grace to serve You with excellence. Until then, give me grace to glorify Your name in my daily life.

41

Excellent Christmas

Not that I have already . . . been made perfect,
but I press on to take hold of that for which
Christ Jesus took hold of me.

PHILIPPIANS 3:12

*F*or years I thought a *merry* Christmas had to be a *perfect* Christmas. What can cause a Christian mother of three to think in such a way about one of the holiest days of the year? Maybe it was all the glossy magazines that combined glitz and glitter to market their products. Maybe it was the bombardment of slick toy commercials that sent my children into a frenzy. Or maybe it was just my perfectionist tendencies.

All I know is that a merry Christmas meant my house had to be spotless; every item of food served had to be made of the freshest, finest ingredients; the house had to smell like a pine forest; the kids had to act like cherubs instead of children; and I had to lose 20 pounds in order to dazzle my husband. Every year I set myself up for failure.

Then last year, ten days before Christmas, just as I was transitioning from perfectionism to hyper-perfectionism, God blessed me with a severely broken leg. I was released from the hospital on Christmas Eve. Nothing had been baked, cleaned, decorated, polished, wrapped, vacuumed, or bought. That night we sat by the fire and consumed bologna sandwiches, popcorn, and store-bought cookies. We sang some Christmas carols, and Sid read the Christmas story from the Bible. For the first time in many years I was able to relax and enjoy Christmas with my family. Instead of being perfect, it was excellent—and truly merry.

Do you know the difference between perfectionism and excellence? Perfectionism is legalistic. It robs you of joy and satisfaction because perfection is an impossible goal. On the other hand, excellence is simply doing the best you can. It is a healthy, realistic balance of priorities. And when you strive for excellence, joy and satisfaction are sure to follow.

Steps of Faith

Almighty God, I know that there was only one perfect person, and that was Jesus Christ, my Lord and Savior. Help me, Father, to overcome my perfectionist tendencies and strive for excellence in all I do—that You and I would both delight in it.

Positive Progress

Jesus Christ is the same yesterday and today and forever.
HEBREWS 13:8

"Insomnia and menopause, do they go together?" my friend asked me. After another night of tossing and turning, feeling tired and lethargic, I responded with a resounding "Yes!"

I knew the answer to my friend's question because of two things: my own experience over the past year and a recent radio program. A doctor who specializes in studying menopause had mentioned insomnia as a major side effect. She also said many women actually feel as though they are losing their minds during this process.

Listening to the radio conversation, a light seemed to come on in my mind. I had thought I was too young for menopause, but I certainly had several symptoms. Two weeks later my gynecologist confirmed my suspicions. She told me what to expect over the next few years and what to do as my body changed. We discussed calcium, exercise, estrogen-replacement therapy, and amazingly enough, birth control.

As I left the doctor's office, I remembered my own mother's battle with sleepless nights. When I consider her struggle during her midlife years, I feel very fortunate to be a woman of the nineties.

It's a blessing to know women's experiences are normal and worthy of study, educational efforts, and medical research. Gone is the element of secrecy and shame. My friends and I can support each other as we go through these changes—and we can guard against the behaviors that might make a longsuffering husband feel like popping one of us into an institution! That's real progress.

Are you struggling with emotional ups and downs or sleepless nights? If you think you may be entering menopause, see your doctor and discuss your symptoms. And in the midst of change, thank our Creator God for His constant care and His involvement in our lives.

Steps of Faith

Father, help me cope with the mysteries and dilemmas of midlife and the aging process. As I continue on my journey, I thank You for Your scriptural reassurance: You are the same yesterday and today and forever.

Precious Promises

He has given us his very great and precious promises.

2 PETER 1:4

$\mathcal{M}$y name is Sharon and . . ." My throat closed. I couldn't go on. I buried my face in my hands and cried shamelessly. How could I confess my dark secret to this group of strangers?

I felt like such a failure. I was a stay-at-home mom devoted to the Christian upbringing of my children. So why didn't it work? The promises of the Bible seemed to be mocking me—the ones about "training up a child in the way he should go," "my sons not putting me to shame," and "all my sons being taught by the Lord." I felt betrayed by God.

Today was Steve's birthday. Normally I would be scurrying around buying special gifts, cooking his favorite dinner, and baking the caramel cake he loved so much. But not today. Steve was spending his seventeenth birthday in a drug treatment center far away from home. My parenting goals and dreams were blown to smithereens.

The small support group waited patiently for me to collect myself. When I finally surfaced from my lake of tears, I poured out my symphony of pain and confusion. When I finished, I felt a heavy load had been lifted. I looked at the faces around the table. I saw compassion, not judgment, in their eyes. They understood. Then I knew—so did Jesus.

New hope coursed through my veins. *Maybe God is still in this picture. His promises might still be true. I just need to hang on and wait for Him to finish what He has started.*

Have you ever looked at a situation and wondered what in the world God was doing? When all we see with our eyes are pain and confusion, it is sometimes difficult to stand on the promises of God. But you can always rely on them. God always makes good on His Word.

Steps of Faith

Dear Father, thank You that Your goals for my children are even bigger and better than my own. I'm sorry for doubting You. It's just that this path is so different from what I thought it would be. Thank You for keeping Your promises.

The Bald Spot

And even the very hairs of your head are all numbered.
So don't be afraid; you are worth more than many sparrows.

MATTHEW 10:30,31

$\mathcal{M}$y husband, Paul, had a head of thick hair when we were first married. Then over the years it began to thin out a little in the back. Paul seldom mentioned it, so I assumed it wasn't an issue. In fact, I was proud of him for not getting hysterical about it.

Then last summer his firm had its annual picnic. The following week, after a special all-employee meeting, the lights were lowered and everyone enjoyed a slide presentation of the festivities—everyone but Paul. There was one picture in which the back of Paul's head was in the foreground. Paul said he didn't even realize it was his head until another employee yelled something about the "blinding light" reflecting off the back of Paul's bald spot. Everyone laughed.

Paul was devastated. He started wearing baseball caps all the time. But even worse, he became withdrawn and sullen. Our sex life all but vanished. And anytime I tried to talk to him, he denied there was any problem. So I continued to let him know how attractive he was to me and at the same time searched the Scriptures for wisdom.

When I came upon Matthew 10:30,31, I gasped, then giggled and asked, "Lord, is this what You want me to use to encourage him?" Right then I had the idea to print out the passage and tape it to the bathroom mirror. After doing that, I simply prayed.

Paul never mentioned the verses, but I noticed a gradual change. After a week, he began venturing out without the baseball cap. He wasn't so withdrawn. But I knew he was out of the woods the day he flexed his muscles and asked me to try to get my hands around his biceps.

Things change with the passing of time. If you are married, you must be sensitive to your husband's struggle with changes in his physical appearance. Focus on him, not the problem or how it affects you. Let him know he has your total and unconditional acceptance.

Steps of Faith

Almighty God, thank You for my wonderful husband. I love him so much. Help me to show him that I accept him as he is. I don't want him to feel pressured to be what he is not or cannot be. Instead let him sense my unconditional love and commitment to him.

MONDAY

The Mirror

Now we see but a poor reflection as in a mirror;
then we shall see face to face.

1 CORINTHIANS 13:12

*M*y calculations indicated that at the end of 1993, I had lost a total of 633 pounds over the course of my adult life. I had tried every fad diet known to woman, and they had all worked. . . . temporarily. And alas, at the end of 1993, I was (once again) overweight—this time by 60 pounds!

So my New Year's resolution for 1994 was to lose that weight. However, the thought of another bizarre diet was depressing. I prayed for guidance and wisdom. I sensed God leading me to a balanced diet of healthy foods and moderate exercise.

But what I really wanted was inspiration, something that would excite me about dieting. Then I found the mirror.

This was no ordinary mirror. This mirror could be adjusted to reflect how I would look at any weight. When the counselor at the diet center adjusted it to my weight goal, I stood transfixed. There was the woman all the weight charts proclaimed I was supposed to be.

The mirror became my inspiration. Suddenly the chocolate cookies, ice cream, and cake that had been my undoing in the past were no longer a temptation. I just thought about my reflection in the mirror.

Today I have kept off the 60 pounds for four months. And though the mirror made dieting more exciting, I can't credit it for my success. The truth is that during 1994, I began looking hard into another mirror: God's Word. There I found God's promises to encourage, guide, and strengthen me as I worked toward my goal. And the more I gazed into His mirror, the more inspired I was not only to lose the 60 pounds, but also to be everything else He wants me to be—that year and for the rest of my life.

Have you set any practical goals for the new year? Maybe it's maintaining a healthier lifestyle, managing your time better, getting your closets organized, or recycling. Whatever it is, God will help you do it, and He will see you through it.

Steps of Faith

Oh Father, thank You for Your promise to be near to all who call on You (Psalm 145:18). I am calling on You right now to help me in this area of my life that I can't get under control. You know how I have struggled. Give me the strength, Lord, and I will give You the glory.

True Success

Remember the LORD your God, for it is he who gives you the ability to produce wealth.

DEUTERONOMY 8:18

Lisa and Paul have it all. Not because Paul has his own successful consulting business. Or because they own a big house with a beautiful yard and two nice cars.

Rather, they have it all because after five years of marriage, they are more in love than ever. They're both very busy, but they jealously guard their time together. They eat breakfast together every morning and end it with prayer for the day ahead. They are learning how to allow Christ to be the center of their marriage.

But it wasn't always so for them. In the early stages of building his business, Paul let it run—and almost ruin—his life. He worked six, sometimes seven days a week, late into the night. Lisa rarely saw him. His spiritual life suffered, too. Sunday morning became his day to sleep late, and Lisa went to church alone, often crying through the service. She begged God to show Paul how little money really mattered, because she couldn't seem to get through to him.

One Sunday morning after the service, Lisa found Paul standing in the back. "What made you decide to come?" she asked.

"I turned on the radio and heard 'Amazing Grace.' I felt like I'd been hit with a ton of bricks! I realized how much I'd let my spiritual life suffer. And my marriage, too. Will you forgive me?"

She nodded, her eyes filled with tears. "I'm glad you're back."

"Me, too. Let's go get some lunch."

Lisa squeezed his hand. Her heart overflowed with thanksgiving as she saw Paul embrace true success.

Financial success can distract even the most devoted Christians from their relationships with God and with their families. We must remember that everything we have comes from God—including our families—and praise and thank Him for His provision.

Steps of Faith

Dear Father, You are the Great Provider. Help me to be a faithful steward of all You have given me. Help me remember that my relationship with You is more important than anything I possess.

Welfare Mother

Yet I am poor and needy; may the Lord think of me.
You are my help and my deliverer; O my God, do not delay.

PSALM 40:17

*I*t was a place I never thought I'd be: in line at the Aid to Families with Dependent Children center. I was desperate—so desperate I was willing to become a "welfare mother." Only a year earlier I was a contented mother with two children, a nice home, and a husband named Stan. The day after Christmas 1990, Stan and a paralegal in his law firm ran off to Mexico, where he divorced me and married her. He did not send child support.

My parents and church helped us as much as they could, but I needed a job. Yet it wasn't long before I realized that a 34-year-old woman with two years of college was not in high demand.

I began to formulate a two-year plan to take care of my family while I finished college. The plans involved public assistance. I began applying for everything from food stamps to federal tuition-aid grants and subsidized housing. In six months I moved into a clean, safe, Section 8 apartment near the college and began to live independently.

I knew God was using this experience to break my internalized attitudes about people on welfare. Like me, many lacked the education they needed to earn more money.

In May 1993 I graduated with a degree in education and began teaching the following August. I got off welfare that same month. Every day I thank God for a country that offers help for people like me—people who have high expectations for themselves in spite of their circumstances.

Did you know that most people who go on welfare do so for only one or two years? There are many myths about people on welfare and the working poor that are exaggerated caricatures or simplistic stereotypes. What can you do? Get involved in your church or community outreach to needy people. Listen to their stories. You will never be the same.

Steps of Faith

My Help and my Deliverer, You hold my life in Your mighty hands.
Help me never to fear but always to expect the best from You. No
matter what the future may look like, You always offer protection
and provision—sometimes in surprising places.

Clutter Control

For God is not a God of disorder but of peace.

1 CORINTHIANS 14:33

Bart hung up the phone and looked at me. "That was Bill and Amy from Sunday school," he said. "They're in the neighborhood—"

"So they're dropping by?" I shrieked, looking around the den at the clutter that had accumulated during the week.

"Let's just stuff everything in closets like we usually do," Bart said, grabbing his shoes and running for the bedroom.

"Do whatever you have to!" I called, heading for the coat closet with a basket of laundry. I opened the door and saw the result of the last time we had unexpected guests. No room! *Ah, the bathtub.*

"What about these files you brought home?" Bart called.

"Put them under the sofa," I said, tossing my makeup into the bathroom cabinet. I swiped at the sink with a sponge and hung a fresh towel.

"How does the kitchen look?" Bart called.

"Oh! The kitchen!" I exclaimed as the doorbell rang.

That night, we had a serious discussion about disorder. We both agreed that we had to stop stuffing things under the sofa and into closets. That kind of chaotic clutter control accomplished nothing. Since we both have full-time jobs, we agreed to try to do our parts in keeping the house in order. We would put things away when we had finished with them. We would pick up in each room a little every day. And we would tackle those closets we were afraid to open and hold a big garage sale!

Does clutter accumulate at your house? Try to enlist your family's help. Ask a friend to help you decide what to keep and what to toss. Break big projects into little goals. And if you have unexpected guests, try to focus on them instead of on the dishes stacked in the sink.

Steps of Faith

Dear Lord, it's hard for me sometimes to stay on top of housework. After I set realistic goals for getting my house in order, help me to use the time I spend cleaning to pray or sing hymns.

F
R
I
D
A
Y

The Calling

*"My food," said Jesus, "is to do the will of him
who sent me and to finish his work."*

JOHN 4:34

I sipped coffee from my travel mug and munched on a granola bar as I wound my way down the misty two-lane country road to Hidden Hills Elementary School. As I turned on the radio, I thought about my fourth-graders this year. They were a great class. But then every class seemed to be great. I smiled as I reflected on how fortunate I'd been during my teaching career.

Yet there was still an ache in my heart. As much as I loved children and longed to be a mother, God had not permitted it. And after the hours of prayer and counseling that followed the miscarriages, the hysterectomy, and the rejections by adoption agencies, my calling as a mother still seemed to be on hold.

Just then the radio news reporter announced that several children had been found in an abandoned apartment which had no food or heat. They hadn't seen their mother for six days.

I was overcome by grief and rage. In my car I cried out to God, "Why couldn't You have given those children to me? I would never have done that to them! I would love them with all my heart."

Right then His still voice spoke to my heart: "Then who would teach My fourth-graders at Hidden Hills? I have freed you to minister to them in a way few women can. You are in the center of My will, daughter. You are doing just what I created you to do."

Joy and peace swept over me. Right there in my car I understood my purpose in God's plan. It did not exactly fit with all of my desires, but I knew in my heart that I was answering my calling.

Do you have the peace of knowing that what you are doing today is what God created you for? Maybe you are "just" a mother or "just" a secretary or "just" a housekeeper. If you are trusting God with your life, you need never be ashamed of where He has put you. It is your calling . . . so make the most of it.

Steps of Faith

Precious Lord, forgive me for all the times I complain about my life. So often I fail to look at it from the perspective of eternity. I pray that Your perfect will for my life will take precedence over all those things that seem to beckon me away from Your purpose.

Help! I'm My Mom

*The rod of correction imparts wisdom, but a child left
to himself disgraces his mother.*

PROVERBS 29:15

$\mathcal{A}$s I was growing up, I had a suspicion that I was adopted—
or at least that I was not my mother's biological child. It was incomprehensible that we were blood relatives. We were too different.

First of all, according to the prevailing culture of the early sixties,
my mother was eccentric and uncool. But I was hip and popular (in
spite of all Mom's attempts to destroy my social life). For instance,
while my brothers and I were in elementary school, Mom made us
finish all of our homework right after school, before we could play
with our friends. Television was limited to one hour per night.
Reading, letter writing, and crafts were strongly encouraged.

It was really humiliating when I wanted to go see a movie. Until
I was 18, my Mom would not let me see any movie with anything
above a G rating unless she had seen and approved it. Mom and I
really went to war when I started having boyfriends. She had to meet
each one and his parents, and she strictly enforced curfews. If I was
late, I was grounded for a week.

At times I thought I hated her because I was convinced she hated
me. Why else would she make my life so miserable? I decided that
when I had children, I would show them how much I loved them by
letting them have and do whatever they wanted.

Then I became a mother, or maybe I should say I became *my*
mother! I found myself establishing the same rules for my children,
and then some. It was unsettling at first, but the older I get, the more
I appreciate her wisdom, strength of character, and love for her
family. I thank God that I have matured into a woman so similar to
my "uncool" mother.

A funny thing happens when a woman has a baby. She grows up.
And she usually models the mothering she received. Can you relate?
If so, take time to thank your mother for all she has taught you about
rearing children.

Steps of Faith

*Heavenly Father, growing up is such a learning process. Little did I
know that even as I was playing with my toys and putting on
makeup for the first time, You were constantly preparing me for
motherhood through my own mother. Bless her, Father.*

Behind the Scenes

*Each one should use whatever gift he has
received to serve others, faithfully administering God's
grace in its various forms.*

1 PETER 4:10

*E*very year I have a Beat-the-Winter-Blues party for our Sunday school class. It's a major undertaking because the class grows every year. But I love to give these parties so that people can form new friendships and strengthen old ones, and so that we can all have fun in the Lord. I enjoy playing hostess, but I couldn't do any of it without Loraine.

Loraine has been my dear friend since college, and I admire her very much. She is a behind-the-scenes person. She is truly a master at making other people successful. The leaders of Vacation Bible school always count on her to provide snacks for the kids. The librarian knows that Loraine sneaks in during the week to organize the books. The class-membership committee counts on her to send postcards to visitors, inviting them back. And of course I rely on her to help me with the party.

At her urging Loraine and I start planning when the party is still two months away. She helps me clean my house and prepares most of the food. I decorate the table and plan the entertainment. And when the first guest walks through the door, I am free to be the hostess. I know I can welcome and introduce and mingle while Loraine replenishes and refills. By the end of the night, our class members are a little closer to each other and to the Lord. The warmth we all feel helps us forget it's 20 degrees outside.

As our guests leave, they tell me how much they enjoyed my party. I tell them to thank Loraine, because without her there would be no party. When they turn to look for her, she's not there. She's in the kitchen, humming a hymn as she washes the dishes.

Often people who are not in the limelight are not thanked for their work. Do you know someone who works behind the scenes to make others successful? Take the time to express your gratitude to that person today.

Steps of Faith

Holy Father, Jesus taught us how to be servants by His excellent example. Help me to use my unique gifts to serve You in the way You want. And help me to find areas of service which may go unnoticed or unrewarded and serve there with a joyful heart.

Unanswered Prayers

Three times I pleaded with the Lord to take [a thorn in the
flesh] away from me. But he said, to me, "My grace is sufficient
for you, for my power is made perfect in weakness."

2 CORINTHIANS 12:8,9

*E*very now and then I tune into the country-western radio station. One of these times, during a low point in my marriage, I came
upon a song called "Unanswered Prayers"—and the words stayed
with me for a long time.

The singer crooned about all the fame, fortune, and beautiful
women he'd prayed for during his life. Instead God had blessed him
with a godly woman who was a devoted wife and mother, healthy
children, a steady job, and loyal friends. Each chorus ended with,
"Thank God for unanswered prayers."

Tears streamed down my face as I thought about all the things I'd
asked God for over the years. I thought of the baseball player in high
school I had been so crazy about. I realized God had protected me
from a life with an unbeliever, someone who couldn't hold a candle
to my husband, Jeff.

I also thought about how early in our marriage I'd prayed for children, only to miscarry twice. It was years later that I would give birth
to our two boys, when I was established enough in my job to work
part-time out of my home and spend more time with them.

There were so many other things. But more importantly, the song
made me think about what I was praying for today. Was I still
chasing after my own dreams down Easy Street instead of steadfastly
trusting God to knit my needs and desires into a protective covering
of His perfect will? That's what I want to do. In the meantime I'll join
in the chorus and sing, "Thank God for unanswered prayers!"

Sometimes our prayers are not answered in the way or at the time
we expect. Have you struggled with this issue? Remember that God's
will is perfect and His love for you is infinite. Ask Him to reveal how
He has protected you from the results of some of your most heartfelt
prayers.

Steps of Faith

Omniscient Lord, thank You for all the times throughout my life You
have not given me exactly what I wanted when I asked for it. Instead
You have always saved the best for me. You know what the future
holds. Bless You. Help me to keep my focus on Your perfect will for
my life.

W
E
D
N
E
S
D
A
Y

Stepping-Stones

But thanks be to God! He gives us the victory
through our Lord Jesus Christ.

1 CORINTHIANS 15:57

*F*or years I was convinced my first marriage could have been saved. And it made me feel twice the failure most divorced people feel.

My high-school sweetheart, Ron, and I married when we were 21. Neither of us was a Christian or ready for the commitment and responsibilities that accompany marriage. Ron was content to ignore our problems and ride it out. I wasn't. I just wanted to escape. After two years we separated, and in six months we divorced.

I thought I was finally free. However, I went from the misery of that marriage to an even deeper anguish. What I thought had been freedom quickly turned into the bondage of sin and shame.

Within months I had hit rock bottom. When I had the strength to look up, I saw the hand of God reaching out to me. He pulled me out of the darkness and into the light. I finally began to know freedom.

I ended my relationship with a married man and sought to reconcile my marriage. I poured out my heart to Ron one night, confessing everything and begging his forgiveness. I told him that I knew that our marriage could be healed if we both gave our lives and our marriage to God. Ron wasn't interested in God or me. It was too late.

The time that followed was difficult, even scary. I was alone again. But through prayer and the study of His Word, God was teaching me. Over the next few years I learned to put God first in my life. When I met and married Greg, the lessons from my past mistakes and the lessons of obedience I learned from God's Word helped us set our relationship on the right foundation. We determined from the beginning to have a Christ-centered marriage.

Think of some of the lessons you have learned from past mistakes: a divorce. A spiritual or moral failure. Mistakes in parenting. A career demotion or loss of a job. Whatever it is, there is hope. God can use your life to glorify Himself.

Steps of Faith

Gentle Healer, how grateful I am that my past, no matter how stained, can be wiped clean, restored, and made new through Jesus Christ. Lord, You know each of my failures. Make them stepping stones to a successful life—a life that glorifies only You.

Love Your Neighbor

Love your neighbor as yourself.

MATTHEW 22:39

Shortly before our new house was completed, Sam and I met our future neighbors, Sid and Marge Drew. We were so excited. They had young children, too. Maybe they were even Christians! However, three minutes into our meeting, we were sick. The foul language and the racial slurs about another family on the block offended us. But when their bigotry shifted to our own ethnic background, I almost lunged at them. Sam squeezed my hand, smiled pleasantly, and then excused us.

Our relationship didn't improve after we moved in. During our first year, Sid accused me of thinking he was "after me," suggested I wear a bag with a *pretty* face on it (so Sam wouldn't work so late), and often criticized the way Sam maintained our lawn. Marge called me a snob, even though I repeatedly invited her over for coffee.

One night as Sam and I were discussing the "disgusting Drews," something happened. We both felt shame and looked at each other knowingly. Then Sam said it: "Sid and Marge are disgusting, but that's irrelevant. We need to stop whining about what they've done to us and tell them about what Jesus has done for them."

That's when Sam and I began to pray for Sid and Marge. It didn't happen overnight, but God has given us love for them and also opportunities to minister Christ to them. And we have seen our relationship heal. In fact they just started attending our Bible study group. Sam and I are determined to love Sid and Marge into the kingdom of God.

Is there anyone in your life you simply don't like? Have you ever wondered why God has brought him or her into your life? It's probably because He has an "improvement plan" for both of you. As a Christian you are commanded to love that person, and God will use that unpleasant person to compel you to trust Him for that love. When you do that, it's a win-win situation!

Steps of Faith

Blessed Lord, You know the people in my life that I'm struggling to love right now. Please give me Your love for them. I want to love them the way You love me.

Love Violated

*The LORD said to me, "Go, show your love to your wife again,
though she is loved by another and is an adulteress."*

HOSEA 3:1

Seven years ago when our son, Christopher, was born, I quit my job to stay at home with him. After a few months, I got restless and told my husband, Joe, I wanted to work again. I began selling life insurance, and before I knew it, I was earning twice as much money as Joe.

I was intoxicated with the excitement that came with success. Two years later, as I was preparing to leave for a four-day convention, Joe and I had a terrible fight. We parted angry. During the convention, I went out with a coworker I had fantasized about for months. We ended up in bed. It was too easy to block Joe and Christopher from my mind and yield to the temptation.

The long flight home gave me more than enough time to think about what I'd done. I was sick. I confessed it all to Joe that same weekend, and I have never seen him so angry and hurt. I told him I would quit my job if he wanted me to. He decided that I should move out for a while, at least until he was ready to make a decision.

Months passed. During that time God's Word began to give Joe the strength he needed to forgive me. He read and reread the Book of Hosea. In the meantime we were in counseling at our church and praying more than we ever had—together and privately. We knew the seriousness of the wounds inflicted upon our marriage. Restoration would be a slow process.

The day I moved back in with Joe and Christopher was a little awkward and painful. But as the years have passed, God has restored the precious element of trust to our marriage. Joe and I have learned that love is indeed more powerful than any sin.

Adultery causes tremendous pain in a marriage, and often it will lead to divorce. But it doesn't have to. We are commanded to forgive as we have been forgiven (Matthew 6:12). Adultery is not an exception. If your marriage has been damaged by adultery, get Christian counseling immediately, and ask God to give you His guidance and strength.

Steps of Faith

Merciful Lord, I am awed as I read in Your Word of Your great compassion and love for people who knowingly violate Your decrees. Your love conquers sin, and You willingly forgive all who repent. Thank You, Lord, for Your restoring love. Help me to always love in such a way.

Needy Yet Loved

He has taken me to the banquet hall,
and his banner over me is love.

SONG OF SONGS 2:4

*D*rool slipped down the corner of his mouth. His nose was running and the pungent smell of human waste filled the room. "Momma, Jackson needs to be changed, and I gotta go to school." Lisa hopped up from the breakfast table, kissed Jackson on the cheek, and raced out the door.

I came into the breakfast room to tend to Jackson. After I cleaned him up, we sat together by the kitchen window where we could see the bird feeder. Jackson squealed with delight every time his favorite redheaded woodpecker landed on the feeder. Eventually I cleared away the breakfast dishes and began the daily wash loads. Jackson kept me company all day long with his nonsensical chatter. He was such a blessing to our family.

I'll never forget the day he was born. I woke up in the recovery room to hushed whispers. Immediately I sensed something was wrong. "Where's my baby?" I asked the nurse.

"You just rest now," the nurse said as she left the room.

My husband came into the room with big tears in his eyes. "It's a boy, honey, but he's . . . he's. . . ."

Jackson was born with Down's Syndrome 27 years ago. For all practical purposes, he is severely retarded. My other children achieve wonderful things in their schoolwork and athletics and help me perform many tasks around the house. Jackson does not—indeed cannot—achieve in any of these areas. But I love my other children no more than I love my Jackson. His very neediness is precious to me. Over the years as I've loved and tended Jackson, I have seen very clearly that this is the way God must see and love me—extremely needy yet preciously loved.

Do you feel lovable? Probably not all the time. The truth is that no matter what you have or have not done, God cannot love you any more than He does at this very moment.

Steps of Faith

Dear Jesus, brand my heart with Your iron so that I will never forget whose I am. Please heal that part of me that feels like I have to earn Your love. Thank You for loving me just as I am.

Chocolate Soul Mate

I thank my God every time I remember you.

PHILIPPIANS 1:3

I met Myra the first day on the job. She was the copy editor; I was to be her assistant. I was in my twenties; Myra was in her fifties. She knew so much about editing, writing, literature . . . well, everything. I was almost intimidated, until I discovered that we shared a special passion: chocolate.

We became "chocolate soul sisters." Reese's Peanut Butter Cups were our favorite, so whenever one of us bought one, we'd share. Often other employees found tiny Tootsie Rolls on their desks after lunch, treats left by the Tootsie Roll Fairy.

Then in December 1989, cancer became part of Myra's vocabulary. Then chemotherapy. Then taxol. She was told she might live two years.

Through it all Myra bravely joked about the weight and hair loss. However, the night before her second round of chemo was to begin, while the two of us were alone in the office, she suddenly started sobbing. She was afraid, she said. "I'm not afraid of dying, but I'm so afraid of the pain. The pain is awful." The two of us held each other and cried for a long time.

Myra never came back to work. There were several more rounds of chemo and I'm certain more pain than I can imagine. But she never again showed fear—only the peace and strength that radiate from a woman who has surrendered her life and eternal destiny to God.

Myra died in January 1994. One of the things she left me was a sweatshirt that reads: "Man cannot live by chocolate alone . . . but woman can!" That was Myra. And she will always be my chocolate soul sister.

Do you have a chocolate soul sister? Maybe she's a cross-stitch, shopping, or political soul sister. Shared passions between friends create a unique bond that can last a lifetime—even through tragic times. Thank God for your soul sister today, and then show her how much you love her.

Steps of Faith

Gracious Lord, thank You for my special friend and all the things we enjoy doing together. She is such a blessing to my life. Please show me, Lord, how I can express my gratitude for her friendship. She is someone I want to be close to for many years to come.

Tough Love

Folly is bound up in the heart of a child, but the rod of discipline will drive it far from him.

PROVERBS 22:15

We were the storybook family: a successful husband, three beautiful, healthy children, and a comfortable home. Frank and I were involved in our children's activities, and we taught them right from wrong, encouraging them to encourage others (1 Thessalonians 5:11). We went to church every Sunday morning and evening. Every member of our family sang in a choir.

Looking back I know we did the best we could, but I still don't know what went wrong.

When she was 13, our middle child, Robyn, became moody and withdrawn. *Hormones,* I thought. When she entered high school, her grades plummeted from A's to D's and F's. Teacher conferences and tutors didn't help. She started wearing black all the time and stopped washing and brushing her hair. Whenever I tried to talk to her, she accused me of hating her.

During her sophomore year, we found the drugs in her room, and it all began to make sense. Frank and I prayed for days before confronting her. When we did, Robyn became violent and threatened to kill herself and us.

As painful as it was, Frank and I arranged for Robyn to enter a drug rehabilitation center 1,200 miles away. It was the hardest thing I've ever had to do.

After several weeks, Frank and I were allowed to visit Robyn. We left encouraged. By the time she completed the program, Robyn thanked us for loving her enough to make the tough decision to send her there.

Even the best parents in the world can't control the choices their children make. And when an older child consistently chooses to do wrong, true love gets tough. Have you ever felt like a parental failure? Dr. James Dobson's book, *Love Must Be Tough*, is an excellent resource.

Steps of Faith

Holy Father, You are the author of tough love. You take disobedience so seriously that You sacrificed Your Son, Jesus, to cleanse my sin and give me eternal life. Thank You, Father, for loving me enough to discipline me when I choose to sin. And give me the wisdom to practice that same kind of love with my own family.

W
E
D
N
E
S
D
A
Y

Faraway Friends

May the Lord keep watch between you and me
when we are away from each other.

GENESIS 31:49

*W*hen we moved from California to Hawaii five years ago, I left behind a close circle of friends: Carla, Suzanne, Donna, and Stephanie. Each one handled my move in a different way. Each relationship has changed dramatically.

Carla provided a lifeline by giving me a one-hour phone call each month. "You decide when you are desperate and need to talk. Call me collect and I'll call you right back." She was right. I needed that long talk every month for more than two years. She provided balance, perspective, long-distance love. Carla also sent "CARE" packages from time to time.

A gifted writer, Suzanne wrote volumes, wonderful stream-of-consciousness letters with deep reflections and vulnerable insights as well as news of the family. When one of her thick envelopes arrived every few weeks, I'd savor the delicious "visit" ahead. These letters called for a quiet moment by myself with a cozy cup of tea.

Donna visited me twice and kept me part of her daily life with many phone calls. Some were quick chats: "How are you doing today?" Others were long, getting-beneath-the-surface conversations. She always prayed with me on the phone. She always asked how she could help. She provided a haven for my rebellious teenage daughter one summer and helped her turn her life around.

Stephanie sent heaps of Christmas packages and called once a year.

All friendships are not equal, but physical proximity is not necessary to share a deep, abiding love. Each of my friends has proved it.

Having a successful long-distance friendship requires the same attention, although perhaps not as much time, as any friendship. It's the commitment to "stick closer than a brother" that makes the difference.

Steps of Faith

Dear God, thank You for giving us friends who are kindred spirits. Help us to nurture the special gifts of long-distance friendships. Give us creative ways to love a faraway friend that will reflect Your lovingkindness as well.

The Saint

Many waters cannot quench love.

SONG OF SONGS 8:7

*O*ccasionally a total stranger will approach me with a look of awe and declare reverently, "You must be a saint!" The reason is that I'm married to a quadriplegic who is paralyzed from the chest down. When people who don't know Scott and me see us together, they seem to assume many things about both of us—most of which are probably not true.

Sometimes it really gets to me. I want to say, "Look, I married Scott 11 years after his accident. There have been few surprises. He was established in a successful career as a CPA. He is almost too independent and very strong, physically and emotionally. Frankly, I need him more than he needs me!"

Then I'm tempted to tell them about our friends Tom and Marie. Talk about committed love. Tom had been the star quarterback in college and graduated cum laude in engineering. Then, two weeks after their wedding, Tom was in a freak accident during a survey expedition, which left him paralyzed from the neck down and with minor brain damage.

Tom and Marie were devastated at first. It took them years to adjust to their situation. Every day Marie bathes, shaves, dresses, and feeds Tom. He has no control of his bladder and bowel functions. But neither one lost faith in God or in each other. Marie once told me that her love for Tom had always been grounded in the reality that God had chosen them for each other and had made them one. She said she would never allow their union to be "put asunder."

Now that's a saint!

Remember when you vowed "to love and to cherish until death do you part"? But did those vows mention a crippling disease, financial ruin, or a tragic accident? Committed love endures anything— just as God's love does. And no matter what disaster you and your spouse may face, God promises it is not beyond anything you can bear (1 Corinthians 10:13).

Steps of Faith

Faithful Lord, I trust that whatever is going on in my life is no accident, that You have already prepared me for it, and that You are preparing me for whatever the future holds. Thank You for Your faithful love. Help me to model that love every day of my life.

Eternally Valuable

My sheep listen to my voice; I know them,
and they follow me.

JOHN 10:27

Ruth was buying lunch when she noticed Carrie, her new coworker, eating alone. Ruth had said hi once or twice but never really talked to her. Carrie seemed shy. And she looked lonely right now.

Ruth walked over. "May I sit down?" she asked. Carrie nodded. "Thanks. I hate to eat by myself."

Ruth bowed her head for a quick blessing and prayed also for guidance. She felt suddenly that the Lord had led her here. Munching on a pickle, Ruth asked Carrie about herself and began sharing about her own life. She talked about singing in the church choir.

"I was in chorus in high school," Carrie ventured.

"Me, too! It was my favorite class. Are you in a choir now?"

"Oh, no," she said. "I sing at home but not in front of anyone. I'm not very good."

"I'm sure you are. Maybe you could sing with my choir! Do you go to church anywhere?"

"No," Carried mumbled. "We spend most weekends on the lake."

"Well, if you stay at home one weekend, maybe you could come to my church. You can tell me what you think of our choir."

For the next few months, Ruth and Carrie ate together often. Ruth felt a burden for her friend's spiritual life. She was saddened, too, by her lack of confidence. Ruth's heart ached when Carrie spoke of her failings. She told Carrie that she was God's unique and wonderful creation and that He loved her very much. Carrie soon began asking Ruth to tell her more. She desperately wanted to hear that she mattered, that her life had value beyond this temporary world.

And one day, over her ham sandwich, Carrie prayed to receive Christ.

Is there someone at work who is desperate to know that she is eternally valuable? Invite her to lunch. Send a note of encouragement. Pray for her and share God's love just as someone shared it with you.

Steps of Faith

Father, help me be sensitive to those who ache to know Your love. Help me show them that they have worth in Your eyes. Thank You for Your promise of eternal life to all who know You.

W
E
E
K
E
N
D

The Out-laws

*Love your enemies, do good to them, and lend to them
without expecting to get anything back.*

LUKE 6:35

*T*oday I can honestly say that I love my mother-in-law, Arlene.
But I couldn't have said that two years ago. Blame it on my immaturity or her insecurity, but shortly after Tony and I married, Arlene
and I had a showdown. We were the dirt-slinging out-laws, and the
family "just wasn't big enough for both of us." Or so we thought.

Amazingly, Arlene and I were both Christians. She had to know
that her behavior wasn't appropriate, because I definitely knew mine
wasn't. Then about two years ago I told a very wise friend, Linda,
about my mother-in-law problem. I slowly began to take her advice,
and God worked a miracle.

Linda pointed out that I would never change Arlene, but I could
change myself and how I responded to her. I needed to ask God to
help me love and accept Arlene as she is. I shouldn't even expect her
to change.

Second, Linda said I had to forget the past and forgive Arlene, the
way God had done for me. Then I should concentrate on healing
one small area of our relationship. I decided to focus on Tony. Arlene
and I certainly loved him, and I would let her share more in our
lives, instead of trying to block her out. Frankly, I just needed to
show her some common courtesy and take a more active interest in
her life.

After putting my ugly pride on God's altar, I experienced a transforming miracle. God poured love for Arlene into my heart. And as
God was doing this to me, I could see Him working in Arlene. Today
we're no longer the "out-laws." By God's grace, we've decided to
allow each other in.

How healthy is your relationship with your in-laws? When God's
love is allowed into the situation, miracles take place. Maybe it's time
for you to take an active role in healing a relationship. God will
amaze you when you utilize the power of His love instead of the
poison of animosity.

M
O
N
D
A
Y

Steps of Faith

*My Father in heaven, it's true that when I married my husband, I
married his family. You chose them for me just as much as You chose
my husband for me. Bless and protect my relationship with my in-laws, especially my mother-in-law. Give me Your love for her.*

Faith Building

Share with God's people who are in need.

ROMANS 12:13

I busied myself in the kitchen preparing trays. I prayed, "Oh God, please don't let her ask me. You know what a queasy stomach I have, and I know You don't want me gagging while trying to feed him."

About that time, Sarah, our volunteer director, came in and asked, "Karen, would you feed Greg today?"

"Oh . . . sure. I'll be glad to," I heard myself saying.

As I fixed his tray, I prayed for strength. Greg had arrived at the hospital just last week. He was 17. He did not have a spinal injury like the rest of the patients in the wing; he had suffered a cerebral hemorrhage while lifting weights in his school gym. His hands were twisted, and he could not lift his head off his chest. I almost cried looking at him. Maybe I was not cut out to do this kind of volunteer work after all.

I brought the tray in and sat next to Greg. "How's it going, Greg? You ready to eat this delicious gourmet hospital food?" I teased.

Greg said very slowly and deliberately, "Yeah, give me the slop." I laughed and he grinned lopsidedly.

We became fast friends. Over the next six months we found we had a lot in common. Jesus, for one thing.

Though his prognosis was grim, Greg insisted that he would be walking by his graduation, just two months away. Everyone knew that walking was a huge stretch for this spastic young man in a wheelchair. But we persevered in prayer. One day I came into the therapy room and looked at Greg. Something was different. His head was up. "What's happened?" I asked.

"They changed my medication," he replied with a smile. "I feel stronger now."

That June, I watched Greg walk onto the stage to receive his high-school diploma. I was witnessing a miracle.

Have you given of your time lately to someone else? We can miss out on many blessings if we don't reach out to others in need.

Steps of Faith

Dear Jesus, thank You for the privilege of ministering to others—and for the ways they minister to me. Watching You work miracles in so many different ways has increased my faith in You. You really are the same yesterday, today, and forever!

Pen, Pad, and Prayer

I have the desire to do what is good, but I cannot carry it out.
For what I do is not the good I want to do.

ROMANS 7:18,19

*D*uring the past 20 years, I have failed at every imaginable diet gimmick. So when I finally decided to get serious about losing my extra 40 pounds, I sat down with a pad and pen and prayed for wisdom. I knew I couldn't do it without some divine insight.

Before I began counting calories and fat grams, I simply recorded what I ate and when I ate it. This was an eye-opener. I ate the most junk food while watching television between 8 P.M. and midnight. It occurred to me that if I went to bed earlier, I might consume a little less food. So the next week I started retiring at 11:30 P.M. Soon I was going to bed at ten o'clock (and consuming a lot less food) and waking up at six, giving me plenty of time to—you guessed it—take a short walk. In the meantime I was still tracking my diet, which hadn't changed much so far.

Then I decided to prepare my first low-fat meal. The pressure was off because I wasn't trying to convince myself that I would eat that way for the rest of my life. Soon I was eating a low- or no-fat meal once or twice a week.

As time passed, I began to notice little changes. The most obvious were the pounds and inches I'd lost, but there were others. The junk food was no longer appealing, and the thought of sleeping in and skipping my walk actually depressed me.

Since I began my diet, I've lost 34 pounds. I'm almost there! And every time I look at my leaner reflection in the mirror, I thank God for giving me the strength to do something—even just picking up a pen and saying a prayer—to begin getting in shape.

Do you get overwhelmed at the prospect of trying to lose 10, 20, 50 pounds, or more? If you need to get in shape, do something, anything to get started, even if it's simply pushing away from the table. Then progress at your own pace. Soon you will overcome those habits that make you overeat, and you'll begin to enjoy all the benefits of a healthy lifestyle.

WEDNESDAY

Steps of Faith

Lord, when I look at the body You've given me, I grieve over the way I've abused it over the years. Give me the strength to get started on the path of healthy living through the discipline of proper diet and exercise.

The Sacrifice

Do not let your hearts be troubled. Trust in God;
trust also in me. In my Father's house are many rooms . . .
I am going there to prepare a place for you.

JOHN 14:1,2

*K*elly was divorced and had two children of her own, Ian and Emily, when she met my ex-husband, Frank, and our daughters, Lauren and Heather. Kelly and Frank married two years ago.

Frank and Kelly live in the house she inherited from her grandmother. It's not big, but it's filled with antiques and tasteful decor. Ian's and Emily's rooms have been designed to suit their personalities, tastes, and learning styles, and are furnished with antique beds, dressers, chairs, and desks.

Lauren and Heather were charmed by Kelly's house, but there was no place for them when they stayed on weekends. One had to share a bed with Emily; the other had to sleep on the sofa. They felt like visitors instead of family. I told the girls to trust God to make a place for them.

I tried to explain the problem to Frank, to no avail. So I took a deep breath and called Kelly. She reassured me that she was aware of the problem and was working on a solution. She didn't say what she had in mind.

The following Sunday night, Lauren and Heather returned breathless with excitement. Kelly was going to convert her grandfather's den into a room for the girls. Together they would pick out paint and wallpaper, along with some furniture from her mother's attic. It would be their room.

Frank mentioned later that the den had been Kelly's favorite room. She would spend hours in there reading or just remembering the grandfather she loved and admired so much. But she gave up that room for my girls.

She made her house their home.

Trying to blend a family only on the weekends causes stress for everyone involved, but especially for the nonresident children. Giving them a place of their own tells them how much you care and can be the foundation of a wonderful, lifelong relationship.

Steps of Faith

Glorious Lord, how wonderful it is to know that You have a place prepared for me in Your Father's house. I can't wait to see it, but until then, keep my eyes open to those for whom I may need to prepare a place—either in my home or in my heart.

Picture Perfect Kids

*Trust in the LORD with all your heart and lean not on
your own understanding.*

PROVERBS 3:5

Sam and Becky Bailey were our heroes when Rick and I were first married. They had six beautiful children, whom they homeschooled and prayed with every day. Everyone admired them. We wanted our future offspring to turn out just like the Bailey kids: picture-perfect.

That was eight years ago. Today Rick and I have three children, and we almost destroyed them and our relationship with God in our zeal to be "Bailey clones." Our expectations were too high, and whenever a child disappointed us (which was often), we took it personally. (*What if this child doesn't turn out right? What will people think about us?*)

Our children were miserable. Rick and I were stressed out, on the brink of bitterness. We had sacrificed socially, financially, materially—and spiritually—for these kids. We felt like parental failures.

Then one Sunday Jennifer Bailey, age 17, walked into church dressed in black with spiked blue hair. Three hundred pairs of eyes were glued to what had once been cute little Jennifer Bailey. Sam sat with his arm around her throughout the service.

Later Sam said all that mattered was that Jennifer knew that he and Becky loved her unconditionally. Jennifer was God's child, too, and they trusted Him to guide and protect her.

I realized then that Rick and I weren't trusting God with our children, and our children certainly didn't know our love was unconditional. Because of our fear and insecurity, we had put our family ahead of God.

Are you plagued with fears about your children not "turning out right"? Certainly in today's culture, there are reasons to be concerned, but God hasn't changed. He's still in control, working in the lives of each of your loved ones. Entrust them to His care. Then praise Him for being the almighty God of the universe.

Steps of Faith

Dear Father, forgive me for the times I've allowed my family fears to consume my love and trust. That makes everyone miserable. I know in my heart that You are God, the one and only God. You gave me this precious family. Now I give each person back to You. There is no safer place.

The Teddy Bear

I have been reminded of your sincere faith, which
first lived in your grandmother . . . and, I am
persuaded, now lives in you also.

2 TIMOTHY 1:5

*F*our-year-old Pammy crawled into my lap for a bedtime story. The blonde ringlets framing her angelic face were still damp from her bath and she smelled sweetly of baby powder.

"Grandma, tell me the story of Jesus and the little boy with the fish."

The wide old rocking chair easily held the three of us, for Pammy had begged to include Rockford in the nightly ritual. Rockford was my teddy bear. Usually, this dapper-looking brown bear sat on the bookshelf in the guest bedroom and tried to appear nonchalant. But he was fooling no one. When Pammy came to visit, Rockford came alive. He went everywhere with her.

"After the meal, the disciples collected 12 full baskets of leftover bread and fish," I said, finishing the familiar Bible passage and closing the book. I cuddled my only granddaughter close to me. "Pammy, why is this your favorite story?"

She thought for a moment, then said, "It's because the little *boy* helped Jesus. The other stories are about *grown-ups* helping Jesus." I knew what was coming next. "Grandma, tell me about when my daddy was a little boy in your house! Way back when Rockford was *his* teddy bear."

Like me, Rockford was a constant in her life. I knew she talked to him, telling him important secrets, especially since her daddy was no longer living at home. I wished John would find his way back to his family, but at least I could share good things about my son with Pammy and teach her to pray for her daddy every day.

Grandparents are important influences in helping grandchildren grow in their faith and in bringing a loving stability to the family. In instances where one of the parents has left the home, a caring grandma can make a big difference.

Steps of Faith

Dear God, help me to be the link between my grandchildren and You. Give me patience to teach them Your ways and humor to lighten their problems.

Loving God

*"Love the Lord your God with all your heart and
with all your soul and with all your mind." This is the
first and greatest commandment.*

MATTHEW 22:37,38

*S*everal years ago, my husband, Hugh, and I were trying to have a baby. I had miscarried twice, and from then on it seemed I would never get pregnant again. I was brokenhearted.

Some relatives suggested that I didn't have enough faith to get pregnant, that I had to really *believe* God would give me a baby. From then on my prayer life became focused on having a baby. Eventually I was praising and worshiping God, not out of love or reverence for Him, but out of desperate hope that somehow these words would coax a baby out of God's arms into mine. But deep inside, I hadn't forgiven God for the deaths of my babies.

Then one Sunday after church, Hugh and I walked to our car with our friends Max and Libby. They told us that the latest round of chemo had failed to inhibit the spread of the cancer in Libby's body. Hugh and I listened in wonder as Max and Libby took turns praising God for His tender love and mercy during these dark days. And their love for Him was so real; it was as though they knew Him intimately.

As we drove home, it became clear to me: I had put my love of a baby ahead of my love for God. I was harboring unforgiveness toward Him, and I was trying to impose *my* will upon *Him*! No wonder I was so miserable. That night I told Hugh everything. As I cried, he held me and prayed, "Father, heal my dear wife. Let her love You because of who You are, not because of what You can give her."

Since then the focus of my prayers, praise, and worship has turned exclusively to God. I know my love for Him is real. I still haven't had a baby, but I have a God who fulfills my deepest longings every day.

Do you love God more than anything or anyone else in the world? That is His greatest commandment, and He will help you to obey it. Ask Him to reveal any other gods in your life and then let them go. No other god can love you like your heavenly Father.

*M
O
N
D
A
Y*

Steps of Faith

*Father, I long for an intimate, loving relationship with You. Show me
how. Fill my heart with no other longing but to love, serve, and obey
You.*

A New Beginning

> Hope does not disappoint us, because God has
> poured out his love into our hearts by the Holy Spirit,
> whom he has given us.
>
> ROMANS 5:5

*P*auline adjusted the orchid and plumeria lei around her neck and smoothed the Hawaiian wedding dress over her slender hips. Outside the window, she could hear the pounding surf competing with the music. Guests were waiting. Jim was waiting. Her new life was ready to begin.

From the nightstand she picked up the framed photograph of Mickey, taken shortly before he died. How many nights had she cried herself to sleep holding this very picture in her arms? They'd been married 12 years when he was killed in a fiery car accident, leaving her a young widow with two sons to raise alone. Todd and Mark were five and eight years old. That was four years ago.

Pauline gazed lovingly at Mickey's smiling face and knew he would understand why she was moving his picture to the den. Last night, Jim had confided in her that he had moved Maureen's photo from beside his bed to the living room. Maureen passed away two years before after a long battle with leukemia. Their daughter, Jenni, was six then.

As she walked through the garden, Pauline saw Todd, Mark, and Jenni ahead of her, sprinkling her path with orchids. The children had been tentative at first about Jim and Pauline getting married, but now their enthusiasm thrilled her heart.

They had prayed together and asked God to truly blend the two families into one and to give them unity. Today was a new beginning for all of them.

Only God can redeem families like Pauline's and Jim's. Their three children had each lost a parent, leaving a deep wound in their young hearts. Now He was bringing these two broken families together to love and support each other. No matter what has happened in your past, God can give you a new beginning, too.

Steps of Faith

Dear Lord, heal the wounds and hurts of my past and redeem my life for Your purposes. Give me a brand-new beginning with You in control.

The Good Life

*Be careful, or you will be enticed to turn away and worship
other gods and bow down to them.*

DEUTERONOMY 11:16

*V*ickie and I had been best friends since the eighth grade.
During our junior year, Vickie started dating Scott, and by that time,
Danny and I were going steady. We were the "Big Four" in our
church's youth group and in our high-school class. One of us was
always being voted "Most *Whatever.*"

After high school, we all attended the same university. Danny and
I were married the June following graduation, and Vickie's and
Scott's wedding was that August. Scott's new career took them immediately to Chicago, where he began working as an assistant to a successful commodities broker. Danny turned down an engineering job
offer from a big firm in Memphis, and accepted one with a smaller
firm in our hometown. We wanted to raise our children close to our
families.

Before the children came, Danny and I visited Vickie and Scott
twice a year. They had a charming condominium filled with beautiful furniture. They knew all the hot spots, and we padded behind
them wide-eyed, so impressed with all the people and places they
knew.

Then, during one visit, Danny and I proudly announced that I
was pregnant. To our surprise (and my disappointment) Vickie and
Scott received the news coolly but politely. Then it really hit me how
different we had become. We had different priorities, different goals.
Vickie and Scott were interested in image and careers, at any cost.
They were having too much fun to "let a bunch of kids spoil it."

I placed my hand on my growing tummy and silently thanked
God for our child. I knew at that moment we were living the good
life, even without all the outward trimmings. We valued what God
valued: family, love, and relationships. We would have no regrets.

Through television, movies, and magazines, women are bombarded with images of what the world considers success, happiness—the good life. Think about your definition of the good life. If
it removes God from the throne of your life, then the good life has
become your god.

Steps of Faith

*My Lord and my God, thank You for the good life You have given
me. It may not impress the world, but I know You are first in my
heart. That's all that matters.*

Your Best Interest

*The rich rule over the poor, and the borrower is
servant to the lender.*

PROVERBS 22:7

*J*udy stared at the column of figures. *This can't be right! I had better get the calculator,* she thought. Carefully, she wrote down the minimum monthly payments for each of the four credit cards: $95, $160, $31, and $204. Total: $490 each month.

Next, Judy looked at the interest she was paying. She was surprised to see that the percentage rates varied from 9.9 percent to 18.9 percent! Taking a deep breath, she added up the dollars she was paying in interest each month. Total: $265.

Good grief, that's more than half of my monthly payments just for the interest! What a waste! She felt sick inside.

Pouring herself a fresh cup of coffee, Judy sat down at the kitchen table where she had spread out her bills and her budget book. *No wonder I can't get those balances down on the credit cards. Every payment I make is cut in half!*

Judy thought of all the things she'd rather do with that extra money each month. She could get the car repaired, save for a nice vacation, or help that young family at church heading for the mission field.

Suddenly, she was on her knees asking God for help. "Lord, those plastic credit cards are like iron chains holding me captive. Please set me free."

Like Judy, many of us are prisoners to our credit cards. Are you working hard to earn an income, only to see a portion of it squandered on high interest rates? Are you willing to sacrifice to get out of debt? Will you allow God to change your heart so you can become a better steward?

Steps of Faith

Heavenly Father, I want to be a wise steward of all the resources You've given me. Please help me to break the cycle of charging things on credit cards and paying high interest rates. Help me make a budget plan and stick to it. Teach me to honor You in my spending and giving habits.

Fragrance of a Home

If the home is deserving, let your peace rest on it.
MATTHEW 10:13

La casa de hermano y hermana Ortega! How I loved coming to visit this special family who lived in an adobe house by the seacoast. Hermano Ortega served as deacon of a small church where my husband and I worked as missionaries in Mexico.

After rounds of hugs, kisses, jokes, and greetings, the Ortegas led us to the large wooden table in the center of the kitchen. A petroleum lantern swung over our heads and pink roses were printed on the vinyl tablecloth.

As usual, we brought a food item to share, knowing that Señora Ortega would insist on feeding us the moment we walked through the door. The menu was always the same: boiled pinto beans flavored with bacon and cooked over a woodstove. Next, handmade tortillas were cooked right before our eyes and served to us hot and fluffy from the griddle. The supply of these two items was always plentiful. The Ortegas' three well-behaved children brought us their best chairs and joined their parents in making us feel welcome and special.

I looked around at the happy faces of these dear friends. They were to be envied for the joy and camaraderie they shared. The plain, unmatched metal dishes and bare walls spoke of poverty, but the attitude of gracious generosity shouted a wealth of love and service that few families possess.

We've been missionaries now for 20 years, and my family, too, lives a simple lifestyle. I thank God for the model of sincere hospitality shown us by the *familia Ortega.* I endeavor to instill in my own children the value of having a home, no matter how humble, filled with the fragrance of love, generosity, serving, and even a pot of beans.

What does the aroma of your home say to your visitors? Does it welcome them to a family who rejoice in the little pleasures of life? The fragrance of your home can add more beauty and joy than a fortune invested in interior decorating.

Steps of Faith

Father, as Your eyes look upon the earth, may You look on our home with favor. Help us welcome others as You Yourself would be welcome if You visited. Amen.

F
R
I
D
A
Y

73

Romantic Notions

Let him kiss me with the kisses of his mouth—
for your love is more delightful than wine.

SONG OF SONGS 1:2

*M*arge, I'm telling you the truth!" I said. "There's not a romantic bone in that man's body! He watches me swoon when flowers arrive at the neighbor's. He receives my sentimental Valentine cards and says, 'Mushy again? You know I like funny!' He knows I crave affection and attention. Still, nothing. Zero. Blank."

"Listen, I was standing in line at the grocery store yesterday and picked up a woman's magazine with a list of tips for creative romance. You interested?" Marge was a loyal friend, and I trusted her judgment.

"I'm more than interested. I'm desperate!"

She flipped open the magazine and began to scan the columns. "Sheila, this might help! One idea is to keep candles near the bed. You can create a romantic glow any night. So what if it's your idea? Who cares who lights the candles?

"The husband in this article sounds a lot like Stan," Marge continued. "The woman calls herself a 'hopeless romantic,' but her husband didn't care. In the end she says, and I quote: 'So I light the candles for myself because I enjoy a candlelit room. He can choose to enjoy it if he wants, but I learned that he doesn't have to light the candles for me to enjoy the romantic atmosphere!'"

Hmmm! I was thinking. That's so true. There are lots of little things I can do to fulfill my need for romance . . . and who knows? Maybe Stan will catch on eventually!

Perhaps it's time to redefine romance in your marriage. Your husband may be doing all he can to be tender and loving, but if your expectations for romance are unrealistic, you are setting yourself up for disappointment.

Steps of Faith

Dear Father, help me to appreciate the husband You've given to me. I don't want to be critical of him in this area. Instead, give me creative ideas for bringing romance into our lives. Teach me to affirm the loving things he does for me every day.

The Crisis

For the eyes of the LORD range throughout the earth to
strengthen those whose hearts are fully committed to him.

2 CHRONICLES 16:9

J knew my husband, Craig, was careening into a midlife crisis the day he traded in his pickup truck for a red sports car. How long was this phase going to last, I wondered, and what was life going to be like in the meantime?

I never used the term "midlife crisis" around Craig, because no man suffering from one thinks he's in one. And even though the terms "midlife crisis" and "male menopause" have become comical clichés, I knew there was nothing funny about them. I'd seen more than one marriage flounder in the wake of a seemingly harmless midlife crisis.

I realized Craig needed more encouragement and patience than at any other point in his life—even adolescence! So I just watched while he changed his wardrobe and worked on regaining his "washboard abdomen."

I decided to pray for him more diligently. Paul's prayer for the Ephesians (Ephesians 3:14-21) seemed appropriate.

I also began to determine how I could encourage him more practically, obviously—in ways that he could see, hear, and touch. I put love notes in his lunch every now and then, tried to look a few degrees better than "death warmed over" at the end of the day, and began exercising in the mornings to tone up.

I then began to pray specifically that God would bless our marriage and create a more intimate relationship both spiritually and physically. From time to time I even initiated our lovemaking, which pleased Craig tremendously. So did my admiration of his lovemaking.

The crisis lasted about three years, but with love, prayer, and a lot of encouragement, our marriage survived and is better for it.

Is your spouse experiencing a trial? Prayer is a vital key to encouraging his spirit and knowing how and when to encourage him in tangible ways. No one, next to God, knows or loves your husband like you do. Be willing to make the sacrifices necessary to help him through a tough time.

Steps of Faith

Lord, You know I love my husband, but sometimes I forget how much love and encouragement he needs. He carries such a burden for the family. Help me reach out to him and show him how much I admire him.

Made New

Inwardly we are being renewed day by day.
2 CORINTHIANS 4:16

*L*isa seated herself at my breakfast table. She had called early that morning to ask if we could meet later that day. As I hung up the phone, something told me I had a divine appointment with this young woman. I began praying immediately.

Lisa was getting married that Saturday. She is the eldest daughter of our music director, so the wedding would be quite a production. My husband, Leon, and I counsel couples before they marry. We talk about communication, finances, raising children, spiritual partnership, and, of course, sex. We had already met with Lisa and Brett.

Before she even began speaking, the tears were running down Lisa's face. Then she blurted out, "I'm not a virgin, Mrs. Keyes. Neither is Brett. We haven't had sex with each other; but we both got involved with the wrong people in college. I know God has forgiven me, but I am so grieved that I'm not going to be a virgin on my wedding night."

She nervously sipped her coffee. I listened quietly.

"I feel so ashamed—like I'm going to be the biggest hypocrite in the world walking down the aisle in a white dress and veil."

I took Lisa's hand. "You can't undo the sin you committed, but you can accept God's forgiveness and the truth of His life in you." I opened my Bible to 2 Corinthians 4–5 and read several verses to her. After reading 2 Corinthians 4:16, I explained that in Christ we are made new—daily. On that basis Lisa could reclaim her virginity in the name of Christ.

At first Lisa was incredulous. But by the time she left, she was beaming, just like an excited bride-to-be.

The sexual revolution has left millions wounded in its wake—including Christians. Are you, or someone you love, one of its victims? Sexual sin is never to be taken lightly; however, in Christ there is hope for forgiveness and restoration. He makes *all* things new when you repent of your sin and make Him Lord of your life.

Steps of Faith

My Counselor and Redeemer, how often I get mired in guilt and shame of sin, when in reality I am being made new every day. Thank You, Lord, for Your precious blood that continually washes me clean. Give me grace to share this truth with others.

Very Blessed

*The Lord bless you and keep you; the LORD make his face
shine upon you and be gracious to you; the LORD turn his
face toward you and give you peace.*

NUMBERS 6:24-26

Several years ago, I began blessing my husband. Before he leaves for work every morning, I lay my hands on him and recite Numbers 6:24-26.

At first Steve was a little overwhelmed by the blessing, but eventually he was blessing me as well. As the children came along, the blessing was part of their morning routine. They wouldn't let me forget it.

Over the years I realized how the blessings were affecting my family, but I hadn't thought about their effect on the spiritual essence of my home. Then last summer Norma Boatwright stepped into my house.

I had always been a bit intimidated by Norma. She comes from a very wealthy family in the northeast. Her husband, Howard, is a successful banker in town. They both had dramatic conversions a few years ago and joined our church. Soon Howard and Norma were in leadership roles. I had heard that they had been blessed with an extra measure of wisdom and discernment—but I didn't know them.

Last August I hosted a baby shower for a friend of mine from church. Norma was on the guest list. As the day of the shower neared, I began to panic. *What will Norma think of my little house? She certainly won't be impressed.*

Norma was one of the first arrivals. As I escorted her to the family room, I sensed that her attention was focused entirely on my house. Just when I was getting a little uncomfortable, she turned to me with a bright smile and said, "Oh, what a sweet spirit there is here. So much peace, joy, and love. Your family is very blessed, my dear."

"You can say that again," I said smiling, as I handed her a cup of punch.

No interior decorator or architect can achieve the beauty and grace that a home filled with love, joy, and peace exudes. It's God's blessing on a household that is faithful to His Word. Pray that your home would reflect your faith in Him.

Steps of Faith

Father, I want to provide my family a home full of the beauty of Your presence. Let it begin with my commitment to Your Word. Give me the discernment to remove from my home those things that don't honor You.

Tears of Exhaustion

*In my anguish I cried to the LORD, and he
answered by setting me free.*

PSALM 118:5

T
H
U
R
S
D
A
Y

I awoke suddenly, hearing a pitiful cry from the baby monitor. I bounced out of bed and ambled across the hall. My sweet seven-month-old was wide awake at one A.M.

First I tucked her covers tighter. Then I spoke in a very low voice to comfort her. Neither was working. Then I realized she must be hungry. (Motherhood is a multiple-choice test!) I walked downstairs to the kitchen and propped her on one hip while I made the bottle. Surely this would work.

I lowered myself with my precious bundle into the recliner rocker and put the bottle in Emily's mouth. I was so very tired, yet every muscle was tense. I had been playing Superwoman recently, balancing a full-time job, trips to the babysitter that ultimately resulted in guilt ("You should be at home with that child!" pounding in my head), and a sweet but somewhat resentful husband who was feeling very neglected. I felt physically exhausted and emotionally drained.

The quietness of the hour gave me to time to reflect on how I was trying to handle everything myself. I had not made a conscious decision to leave God out of my life. I certainly wanted His will and His guidance. I simply had no mental energy left for Bible study or concentrated prayer times. Again, I felt guilty. But as tears of exhaustion rolled down my face, the Holy Spirit revealed to me that I was not alone. Emily had cried out in the darkness for comfort, security, and food, and I responded immediately. In the same way God responds to His hurting, frightened, and hungry children in all the seasons of their lives. And at that moment I realized this was a season—these circumstances would not go on forever. Life's demands would change, but He would remain constant.

What season of life are you experiencing? Are you trying to cope with all it demands in your own strength? God wants to help you balance the demands of your life. Take His yoke and let Him teach you. You can trust that His burden is light and that you will find rest (Matthew 11:28-30).

Steps of Faith

Dear Lord, forgive me for not trusting You with every aspect of my life. I give each one of them to You. Take all that I have so that You will be all that I need.

Snow and Fire

*Now to . . . the widows I say: It is good for them
to stay unmarried, as I am. But if they cannot control
themselves, they should marry, for it is better to
marry than to burn with passion.*

1 CORINTHIANS 7:8,9

*C*ertainly you don't expect me to believe this, Mother," I said with stunned incredulity. "You're joking, right? *Mother?*"

Mother sat silently, at perfect ease, on the couch. Snow-white, soft curls framed her serene smile. It's a smile I know well: it's the one that appears after she's dropped a bomb and is waiting for the smoke to clear. She wasn't joking.

I shuddered. "This is too awful, Mother. It makes me sick!"

"Now, dear. Don't get hysterical," she said calmly. "Milton and I are adults, and he's going to move in with me. And I told you the problem: if we marry, I lose all my benefits. It's that simple."

My face dropped into my hands, and then I tried another approach. "Mother, what are Nicole and Adrian going to think about their grandmother living in sin? I've been on my knees for years praying for their chastity, and it's their grandmother who's going to lead them into fornication! Haven't you ever heard of AIDS?"

"That's silly," she replied, unruffled. "You have nothing to worry about."

"But Mom," I said, softening my voice and seating myself next to her, "don't you remember what God's Word says about sexual sin? Is that meaningless to you now?"

Mom was silent for a moment, stood up, and as she walked out of the room, declared, "Just because there's snow on the roof doesn't mean there's no fire in the stove! I want to be happy."

Deep inside we both knew she wouldn't be.

Sexual promiscuity is spreading at epidemic proportions among the older generation. There are several reasons: longer life expectancy, benefits programs that penalize the widow or widower who remarries, and a culture that is obsessed with sex. Decide now that whatever your age or circumstances, you will obey God's Word.

Steps of Faith

Eternal God, I am so grateful for my parents and grandparents. I understand that, even at their age, sexual temptation can be a problem, especially in our society. Protect them, Father. Give them Your wisdom.

Loving the Father

Anyone who has seen me has seen the Father.

JOHN 14:9

$\mathcal{D}$ad, what was your dad like?" As a young girl, I must have asked that question a hundred times. His father had been killed in a hunting accident when Dad was 13 years old. I'd seen some pictures and heard some stories, but that was it. My grandfather seemed more like a ghost than a real person. My brothers and sister and I have grown up with the heartache of knowing that someone we loved dearly had lost someone he loved just as strongly.

As I matured into adulthood, my longing to know my grandfather grew. During one visit to my father's hometown, I inquired again. Dad and his mother told me some stories I'd heard before as well as some new ones. A portrait of my grandfather began to take shape. He was a quiet man with a dry sense of humor. He had been the chief engineer for a bridge that crossed a major river in the city. During that project a contractor tried to bribe him with $2,000. It was 1938 and he was not rich, but he refused to accept the "bonus."

Then Dad began to tell me how each of us reminded him of his father in one way or another: one brother is built like him; the other has his temper; and I have his sense of humor. Then he said, "If you really want to know what Dad was like, look at your sister, Susan. See the person she is. If you know her, you know my dad."

That insight really helped, but it wasn't until I read the letters that I began to love him. My grandmother had saved his correspondence to her during World War I. As I read each letter, I could see the man, hear his laughter, and sense his understated charm. He had put his heart on paper, and I was getting to see who he really was.

Do you love God as a person? Does He seem more insubstantial than real? Jesus told His disciples that if they had seen Him, they had seen the Father. Get to know God through His written Word and the ultimate Word, His Son.

Steps of Faith

Precious Father, the more time I spend learning about You through Your Word and the testimony of others, the more my love for You grows. Thank You for making me a part of Your forever family. I long for the day when I will be able to fellowship with You in eternity, face-to-face.

The Blessing

For I am the Lord, your God, who takes hold of your right
hand and says to you, Do not fear; I will help you.

ISAIAH 41:13

*J*n 1972 my husband, Jack, and I were expecting our second child. I was healthy and the pregnancy seemed normal. But after Dawn was born, my doctor told us she wasn't "normal"—she was a Down's syndrome baby.

The shock that had set in at the hospital quickly diffused after we got home. I cried for days, telling God, my husband, and myself that I couldn't handle it. I didn't know how or why this had to happen to me. I wanted answers to my questions.

There was a mixed reaction from neighbors, friends, and family members. Some felt awkward and hung back. Many wanted to reach out but didn't know what to say. I understood, and struggled for the words to comfort them—but I didn't have them.

God sent a woman who had those words for me. Arlene was a member of my church, but I didn't know her well. She wrote me a note right after Dawn was born. I still have it.

Arlene said that God had blessed us with one of His very special children, a child who would need an extra amount of love and patience, but one who had the capacity to give an extra measure of love and joy in return. "Normal" parents couldn't handle this task; it would take a very special couple. Our all-knowing, all-powerful heavenly Father had chosen Jack and me to be a vessel through whom He could love and nurture Dawn during this lifetime.

Arlene was right. Today Dawn is 23 years old and the joy of our lives. She graduated from high school two years ago and has a job. Her sense of humor, along with her love for the Lord (and everyone else), are a testimony to our Father's wisdom and sustaining grace.

Have you ever known someone who gave birth to a child with a disability and you didn't know what to say? You can encourage your friend simply by letting Christ live through you. Give her your time in phone calls, notes, visits, meals, outings, and lots of prayer. Remind your friend that God knows her fears and has promised to help her—and so have you.

Steps of Faith

Almighty God, You bless us in so many different ways. Some are difficult to spot immediately. Continue to bless and strengthen those families with special children. Show me how I can be a blessing to them.

Encouraging Word

The Lord is not slow in keeping his promise,
as some understand slowness. He is patient with you,
not wanting anyone to perish.

2 PETER 3:9

*S*econd Peter 3:9 is the first verse I remember reading in my Bible all those years ago. I don't know how I found it. I didn't know a verse like that was in the Bible. God simply gave it to me, and I began to have hope.

Over the past several years I had really blown it as a Christian. My life up into my twenties had been a saga of rejection and verbal abuse. I married a man I didn't love because I thought no one else could love me. When that marriage disintegrated, I became involved with a married man, convinced that I wasn't worthy of a decent, God-fearing man. Then this man's wife discovered the affair—along with the rest of our town. It was devastating.

My spirit was screaming in anguish. The pain—emotional, mental, and spiritual—was crippling. I spent entire days sitting in my bed, crying and trembling. The only reason I didn't commit suicide was that I was terrified of going to hell. I thought I had pushed God too far.

Then God gave me 2 Peter 3:9. At first I read the verse, then the chapter, then the whole book. Snatches of the Sermon on the Mount came to mind, and I finally found it in Matthew. Someone said, "Just read Ephesians. All you need is Ephesians." And I read it repeatedly for weeks!

In one year the Word of God had strengthened and encouraged me so much that I hardly recognized myself. God was filling me with peace and courage. However, it wasn't until I read Psalm 51 that I could joyfully accept the truth of God's forgiveness. King David had blown it badly as well, and his words echoed my heart's longing for restoration.

Whenever I need a little encouragement, I open my Bible. Only the Word of God has the power to give me the strength and wisdom I need.

How do you encourage yourself? Listening to praise music, calling a friend, and positively affirming yourself certainly can help. However, God's Word works miracles. Wherever you are lacking courage, God will replenish it with the power of His Word.

Steps of Faith

Father, thank You for the power of Your Word to encourage me, no matter how badly I've failed. Even though You have repeatedly demonstrated Your love in profound and mighty ways, I need to be reminded.

Choosing Chastity

*Flee from sexual immorality. . . . Do you not know
that your body is a temple of the Holy Spirit, who is in you,
whom you have received from God?*

1 CORINTHIANS 6:18,19

Lauren's mouth contorted as she futilely fought the tears. "Oh, Mom, Ashley's pregnant! She just told me," she sobbed.

My mind raced as I held my weeping daughter. *Ashley? Lauren's friend from school?* I felt sick.

For the next couple of hours Lauren and I talked about the obvious consequences of Ashley's behavior—and the not-so-obvious. We discussed sexually transmitted diseases (some resulting in death), abortion, postponement or loss of education, and financial problems. However, I wanted to stress to Lauren that chastity was more than a pragmatic choice—it was a spiritual one as well.

"Lauren, do you understand the spiritual consequences of premarital sex—or any type of sexual immorality?" She said she knew it was sin but wasn't sure about the consequences. So I asked her to read aloud 1 Corinthians 6:12-20 and 1 Thessalonians 4:1-8.

When she finished, we discussed how the body of a believer is the temple of the Holy Spirit. When we sin, especially sexually, we grieve Him because we're subjecting Him to that very sin.

Then I told Lauren the joy her father and I experienced on our wedding night. We were chaste, and our bodies were our wedding gifts to each other. "From the day you were born I've prayed that you and your husband would experience the same joy."

I was smiling, and Lauren was blushing.

Do your children and teenagers understand the importance of remaining chaste? Your son or daughter is being bombarded with sexual pressure unlike anything you might have experienced 20 or 30 years ago. Talk openly with your children, and let them know you're praying for them.

Steps of Faith

Dear Father, please protect my children from the powerful influence of the world. They are living in a culture that sneers at chastity and moral purity. I trust their well-being to You, Lord, but at the same time give me the wisdom to be a sensitive and loving parent even if they fail.

Filling the Shoes

As a mother comforts her child, so will I comfort you.

ISAIAH 66:13

*B*eing the only daughter in a family of four children was a great way to grow up. I got a lot of attention. My father adored and spoiled me. My older brothers teased me until I was of dating age, when they became extremely protective. But best of all, I had a special, almost exclusive relationship with my mother. She was my best friend.

Then in 1992 Mom died of breast cancer, and my life changed in ways I could have never imagined. By this time I was a wife, a mother with two young children, and an attorney for a large firm. That's why I appreciated my parents always opening their home for all the holiday meals. Mom would cook the big items, while my sisters-in-law and I would contribute desserts or salads. All I really had to do was get my family there.

Thanksgiving was the first holiday after Mom's death. We decided to have it in my home. It was a disaster! My turkey was dry and my stuffing had the consistency of clay. I tried to do it all—just like Mom—but I almost collapsed!

Then my father started calling me about little things Mom used to do. Even my brothers began asking me for "motherly" advice! I finally called a family meeting and gently explained that I couldn't be Mom. We needed to help each other. Mom's absence was an adjustment for all of us, and it would take time.

In the meantime I have tried to deal with the void her death left in my life. I cried every day for the first year. How I miss her. Yet it is in those times that I feel closest to God, as He strengthens me with the memories of all she has taught me. Maybe one day I'll be able to fill those shoes.

Have you had to deal with the death of a loved one? Think about how that loss changed your life. Did you have to assume any new roles? Death is the ultimate change. It is traumatic for everyone. Ask God to comfort and strengthen you during that difficult time.

Steps of Faith

Lord, I praise You for Your never-changing love and faithfulness, especially during the trials of my life. Thank You for the comfort You give. And Lord, the next time I face the death of a loved one, help me adjust to the changes that are sure to follow.

Possessed

*Seldom set foot in your neighbor's house—too much of you,
and [she] will hate you.*

PROVERBS 25:17

$\mathcal{M}$y first impression of my neighbor Beverly was very positive. She looked like she could have been a model for *Working Woman* magazine and exuded confidence and charm. She seemed to have it all together.

At the time Beverly and I were becoming friends, she was engaged to Burt, a man she'd been seeing for years. Then six months ago, without explanation or warning, Burt called off the engagement. Beverly was devastated. She was 34 and thought her life was over.

When she called me late that night, she was crying hysterically and talking about suicide. I urged her to come over, and when she left in the wee hours of the morning, I encouraged her to call me anytime she needed to talk. That was a mistake.

Soon Beverly was calling me every day, sometimes three times a day. She would cry most of the time, telling me that I was the only person who cared about her. Then she began showing up at my house in the afternoons. She would stand in the kitchen and cry while I tried to prepare supper and tend to my family. She totally dominated my life. Something had to change.

Firmly, but with love, I told Beverly she could no longer drop in every night; I invited her to visit on Friday nights, when the kids were usually out with their friends. I also suggested that she talk to a counselor. As much as I wanted to be her friend, she needed someone better qualified to help her work out her problems.

Beverly is doing much better today. We are still friends, and Beverly has made some new ones—including a very nice man she met at church!

Have you ever had a possessive friend? Did you feel helpless and ultimately resent her because you didn't have the heart to tell her to give you some air? Next time, you set the rules and force yourself to say no when it's necessary. It's the healthiest response for everyone involved.

Steps of Faith

Father, it's pretty overwhelming when one person latches on to me and thinks I have the answers to all her problems. I want to help any hurting friend, but I know my family must come first. Give me strength and wisdom, Father, the next time a friend becomes possessive.

85

Shaken, Yet Content

I have learned to be content whatever the circumstances.

PHILIPPIANS 4:11

*T*he year of 1993 was painful and difficult for my husband and me. Within six months, both our fathers died. Due to the trauma of the funerals and months of grief, I experienced a relapse of a chronic illness I had been battling for eight years. Our entire family was looking forward to the new year of 1994.

Then, in the dark early hours of January 17, 1994, our lives took a sharp turn that changed us and our perspectives forever. At exactly 4:31 A.M. our city experienced a violent, terrifying earthquake. The shaking was so powerful that our bed literally lifted off the floor. Once our family was huddled together under our hall doorway in the total darkness, we began to realize how bad the quake was. We crawled over toppled furniture to get outside and simply sat in our front yard until daybreak. Then we were able to see the damage and assess our losses.

Our home, our sanctuary of safety, had been virtually destroyed. Later that morning our oldest daughter arrived home in tears but unharmed, and eventually we located our family cats, also alive and well. We had come through with our lives.

You learn a lot about yourself and what you value while shoveling piles of shattered belongings into trash cans. Those broken objects were once treasured birthday gifts, my grandmother's heirloom china, all our family mementos. Very little was salvaged. During the next few months as we stayed in hotels and in friends' homes, I discovered what I truly treasured—my family, our friends, and my faith in God. The earthquake taught me two profound lessons. First: don't hold too tightly to material things. They can vanish in a moment. And next: be content with what really has value—the people we love!

Evaluate what really matters most to you. Adopt a grateful attitude and maintain an open-hand policy about your possessions: see yourself holding all your possessions loosely on the palm of your hand so they are available to God at all times. They belong to Him anyway. Then you will be content with what you have—and what you don't have.

Steps of Faith

Dear God, thank You for teaching me what is truly precious in this life. You have taught me how to be content.

THREADS OF SPRING

Refreshing

Refreshing

Every spring I get the urge to dig in the dirt. I can remember my first garden—a plot 24" x 36"—yes, inches. My husband defined the space for me in the tiny backyard of our first home in Oregon. Even in my inexperience I knew I should decide on only one vegetable. I selected asparagus. I could see myself serving this elegant vegetable to our friends. But no one told me about the two-year growing cycle of asparagus. My disappointment was tremendous. But I persevered and gave that tiny plot more attention than ever.

Year two arrived and the asparagus began to look strong and edible. I was ecstatic. How grand it would taste served with a light lemon-butter sauce. My taste buds tingled. And I was completely unprepared for what happened next. Before the asparagus was ready to harvest, we had to move. I cried over leaving the asparagus.

Over the years I've had many successful gardens—much larger and very bountiful. But never did I forget what I learned from that first tiny patch: We are not in charge of our lives. Circumstances weave together both joy and sorrow. Sometimes we will see the fruits of our labor; sometimes we will not. The Master Gardener, who is tending the garden of our lives, never moves away. He knows our lifecycles, and in all circumstances He is there tending, pruning, watering, feeding—and yes, even weeding.

What a refreshing thought!

My New Life

*These should learn first of all to put their religion
into practice by caring for their own family and so repaying
their parents . . . for this is pleasing to God.*

1 TIMOTHY 5:4

*H*eather, my youngest, had just married and moved to another city. My three other children were scattered across the country. What had once seemed like a tiny house crammed with people and furniture now echoed with emptiness. My nest was empty, and I sensed a new life was about to begin.

Because of my husband's death 12 years ago, I had become the sole provider for the family. It hadn't been easy to juggle the responsibilities of four children and a job, but God blessed me and gave me wisdom to be both father and mother. Now I was in middle management, making four times my beginning salary.

A few months ago I was offered an upper-management position, which was the next step to my dream of becoming a vice president. It included all the executive perks and a big, fat raise.

Was this the beginning of my new life? The only drawback was I'd have to move almost 900 miles away. My empty nest would have been easy to abandon; but it was my parents. They weren't as well as they should be, especially Mom. The more I prayed about them and the job offer, the more I knew God wanted me to stay.

It was one of the easiest yet most difficult decisions of my life. My parents had sacrificed so much for me over the years; now it was my chance to return the love. It wasn't long before the three of us were living under the same roof again—but it was my roof this time.

God continues to bless my work and grants me the wisdom to care for my parents. He meets me every day at my point of need.

Pleasing God is our priority, but often that means sacrifice. The Bible tells us that repaying our parents for what they've done pleases God. Is God calling you to a special sacrifice for your parents? If so, let Him make a very difficult decision a little easier.

Steps of Faith

Father in heaven, only You have sacrificed more for me than my parents. I want to live a life that pleases You. Show me how I can honor You by honoring them.

The Counselor

But the Counselor, the Holy Spirit, whom the Father will send in my name, will teach you all things and will remind you of everything I have said to you.

JOHN 14:26

*B*eing a support-group facilitator in a church counseling ministry exposed me to many brokenhearted, divorced people. The training equipped me to compassionately and realistically deal with each person. It was a great formula of Scripture, probing questions, and Christian counsel.

I confess, however, that I sometimes grew impatient because the formula didn't work for some people. They seemed to *wallow* in misery. I wanted to yell, "Get over it! It can't be that bad!"

Then the unthinkable happened. Kirk, my husband of 18 years, came home from work one day and announced he didn't love me anymore. Our marriage was over. He'd found a lawyer and an apartment. *Goodbye.*

Even the death of my parents hadn't prepared me for the overwhelming pain and sense of loss that came with our separation. I felt trapped in a dark tunnel of anger, fear, grief, and bewilderment. I didn't know how to pray. All I could do was cry.

It was agreed that I should take a break from the counseling team. I returned a year later—a completely different woman. During that year God used all those hours I'd spent listening to victims of divorce to teach me about my own divorce. I thought I'd been a compassionate counselor before, but now I understood the pain firsthand.

I've also learned that the light at the end of the divorce tunnel isn't a train—it's God illuminating my way with His Word, guiding me out of the darkness through prayer, and constantly drawing me closer to Him.

In some ways divorce can be more emotionally, mentally, physically, and spiritually devastating than a death. Has a divorce affected your life? Pray that God will transform that loss into a mighty testimony of His love.

Steps of Faith

Counselor, only Your wisdom and power can bring good out of the tragic destruction of a marriage. Strengthen my loved ones who've been hurt by divorce and bless and protect those marriages around me from it.

The Begonias

The owner's servants came to him and said,
"Sir, didn't you sow good seed in your field? Where then
did the weeds come from?"

MATTHEW 13:27

*E*ven though I had no experience gardening, I decided to work the bed along my front walkway. After what seemed like weeks of watering and fertilizing, tender green shoots began to appear. I was ecstatic, but my sister-in-law, Kay, asked warily, "What kind of flowers are these?" When I told her, she almost shouted, "Begonias! They don't look like begonias." I quickly explained that my mother, a gardening expert, had told me over the phone that not all begonias look alike.

Over the weeks the tender green shoots grew and multiplied until they had taken over the flower bed. Some were eighteen inches tall, but none of them had bloomed. I diligently watered and fertilized. When my mother came into town for a visit, I proudly showed her my flower bed. She said, "Honey, I'm afraid you've got nothing but a bed of healthy weeds."

Some of the best spiritual lessons come at moments of extreme humility. If I'd known what a begonia looked like, I wouldn't have been fooled by the weeds. There have been "weeds" in my Christian life too: astrology, materialism, pride, and peer pressure, to name a few. Each time I put my faith in one of these false gods, I was hurt. The root of the problem was my ignorance of the truth spelled out in God's Word.

As far as my gardening skills are concerned, I've come a long way—now I can tell the difference between flowers and weeds. And I can tell the difference in the spiritual realm as well.

What weeds have you let spring up in your spiritual garden? Can you even tell they're weeds? You may not be able to until it's too late—unless you spend some time reading the Master Gardener's Book. It's what you need to weed out the sin in your life.

Steps of Faith

Master Gardener, weeds in my life have choked out much of my
spiritual joy. Give me discernment to know the difference between
weeds and true spiritual growth.

Sunday Dinner

Practice hospitality.

ROMANS 12:13

$\mathcal{T}$he scene had been repeated many times over the years. After the worship service, friends would ask us out to dinner. My reaction was to say, "We'd love to!" Then Alan would interject, "But we can't. Thanks for asking." Once in our car—out of earshot—the usual exchange ensued:

Me: "Why can't we go out with everyone else?"

Alan: "Because we can't afford it. You know we're on a budget."

Me: "But I really want to visit with our friends."

Alan: "Why don't we invite them to our house for dinner instead?"

Me: "You know perfectly well why. The house is a mess, and the only food I have to serve is leftovers."

Alan: "Well, if eating with our friends is so important, maybe—for a change—we could clean up the house and have a meal planned to include others before we leave for church!"

I finally realized Alan was on to something. All it took was planning. I began doing most of the dusting and vacuuming on Saturdays. Alan agreed to mop the kitchen floor, and he made sure the dishes were washed and put away by Saturday night. When we left for church on Sunday morning, I knew the house was in decent shape.

Casseroles, Crock-Pot, or cookout began to be the typical Sunday dinner fare. And in case I didn't have time to prepare something ahead of time, three or four cans of soup were always in the pantry—just in case.

Am I this prepared every Sunday? I wish. It usually boils down to the choices I make during the weekend. If I'm not prepared, I know Alan and I will be eating leftovers at home, alone, instead of with our friends.

Do your Sundays ever resemble this scenario? They don't have to. Clean your house and plan your Sunday meals ahead of time. Even if you don't have company, you'll return from church to a clean house and the peace of knowing that dinner is practically ready.

Steps of Faith

Dear Father, I know that Christian hospitality involves planning and discipline. Help me as I try to stick to our budget and at the same time open my home to the fellowship of my brothers and sisters in Christ.

Rosie's Boxes

*Is [the kind of fasting I have chosen] not to share your food
with the hungry and to provide the poor wanderer with
shelter—when you see the naked, to clothe him, and not to
turn away from your own flesh and blood?*

ISAIAH 58:7

Life in my home was a continuous lesson in blessing others and being blessed in return. I can't count all the times my mother boxed up clothes, toys, food, and used furniture for someone who had a need. Then, when I grew up, I realized *I* was a needy person! Just out of college, in a strange city, and getting ready to start a new job, I had little money for suitable clothes. I was tempted to charge a new wardrobe on my new credit card, but common sense nixed that idea.

The next day a huge box was delivered to my apartment. My mother's friend Rosie had sent some clothes she'd outgrown. I had mixed feelings at first. I'd never considered Rosie a kindred spirit in the realm of fashion. But my feelings quickly changed after I pulled out several beautiful suits and dresses, plus shoes and purses—my colors, style, and sizes. Rosie's gift probably saved me $600 in clothing expenses.

History repeated itself several years later. My husband and I were planning a two-week "shoestring" trip to Europe. I had few casual clothes, and Mitch said we couldn't afford to buy me any. I resisted the urge to pout. Later that day Mom called, saying that Rosie was sending another box: Her mother, Mrs. Boyden, had died in a nursing home. Once again, my initial lack of enthusiasm was met with a blessing: a box full of cute, comfortable outfits—even a pair of walking shoes.

So what if "Boyden, Room 334" is written on all the tags. It only reminds me that this is one of the ways God recycles His blessings.

Have you ever resisted the urge to buy something you needed because you couldn't afford it—and then had someone unexpectedly give it to you? This is the way the kingdom of God works. Those who bless are blessed, and they continue to bless others—a spiritual form of trickle-down economics. Are you looking for opportunities to bless others?

Steps of Faith

Dear Lord, in Your kingdom nothing is wasted. No one is forgotten. Every need is met. Keep me sensitive to the needs of people around me and those things in my life that someone else may need.

F
R
I
D
A
Y

93

Just Do It

Look to the LORD and his strength; seek his face always.
1 CHRONICLES 16:11

*H*aving a regular prayer time was so easy before I had children. I had a specific routine, time, and place—and if I hadn't covered everything on my checklist, I felt like I hadn't really prayed. Then the babies started coming, and my prayer routine disintegrated. Every time I'd start, I'd be interrupted. By the time the third baby was born, my prayer life was nonexistent. I felt like a spiritual failure.

I don't know how long it took me to realize that God doesn't need a routine or a checklist—and neither do I. He just wants me to pray and "pray continually" (1 Thessalonians 5:17), no matter where I am, what time it is, or what I'm doing.

This was a radically new concept to me, but I tried it. The first time was at about 1:15 A.M., when I was feeding Benjamin. In those moments of quiet I began talking to the Lord, unloading my burdens and giving Him praise. I sensed His presence and peace, even though I wasn't on my knees and reading from my Bible. Wow!

Soon I was praying while folding the laundry, loading the dishwasher, changing diapers, or shopping for groceries. It's added a whole new dimension to my relationship with the Lord and has been my source of strength as I'm rearing three children. Even more amazing, the women in my Sunday school class consider me a real prayer warrior and often call me with their requests.

One day my sister, Suzanne, was complaining that she no longer had time to pray. In the past I probably would have consoled her with, "Don't worry about it. God understands." But not now. I said, "Just do it, Suzanne. It's not as difficult as you think." Then I shared what God had shown me.

Do you have a list of excuses for not praying? The truth is, if you're a Christian, there is no excuse. Kneeling and praying Scripture are great, but they're not always necessary. The Holy Spirit constantly and permanently indwells you so you have perpetual access to the Father. Just do it.

Steps of Faith

Eternal God, You are not bound by time or space and neither is my relationship with You. Forgive me for imposing such limitations on my prayer life. Help me to remember that I need to seek Your face always.

Surging Testosterone

*Husbands, in the same way be considerate as you live with
your wives, and treat them with respect.*

1 PETER 3:7

*H*al! Have you lost your mind? Get away from me!" I said as
I broke away from my husband's sudden embrace—and in the
laundry room of all places! I couldn't believe this man. We'd been
arguing off and on all day and now, just because I'd put on that outfit
he likes so much, he couldn't keep his hands off of me! And just a
few minutes ago he had told me I was a sloppy housekeeper! Men!

I marched back into our room and changed into my baggy gray
sweats. Even Hal wouldn't get turned on by those.

Later that night the house was quiet. A fire crackled in the fireplace. Hal was at a hockey game (hopefully yelling off all that surging
testosterone) with our sons. Still in my baggy gray sweats, I was curled
up on the sofa, reading a novel. A scene between the hero and heroine
made me smile. They reminded me of Hal and me. I closed the book
and stared into the fire. Thoughts of Hal and all the sweet, romantic
things he had done over the years played across my memory.

The fire. The quiet. The memories. The time. All these began to
ease my tension and awaken my desire for my husband. Before I
knew it, I could hardly wait for Hal to get home!

Then I remembered what I was wearing. Oh no! I wouldn't get to
first base in my gray sweats! I quickly changed back into one of his
favorite outfits. And later that night I thanked God that my husband
would never be able to work off all that surging testosterone.

Men and women are different—have you noticed? You might say,
"Of course I have!" However, many women get frustrated with their
husbands *because* they think and act differently. Sex is an especially
tricky matter. Just be realistic. Remember that your husband is visually
stimulated and his sex drive can turn on like a light switch. Women
need more time, like a sunrise. And the more romantic, the better.

Steps of Faith

*Dear Father, I thank You that You created men and women to think,
act, and respond differently. It sure makes life interesting. Give me
wisdom as I try to be the best wife You want me to be.*

Pressing On

I press on toward the goal.

PHILIPPIANS 3:14

Mom has always been a goal-oriented high achiever. However, by the time I was six, she could clearly see that I wasn't. Over the years I dropped out of art, piano, horseback-riding, and dancing lessons. I often started a project but never finished it. I was satisfied with average grades and accomplishments. I'm sure it was frustrating for Mom, but in her wisdom she didn't force me to be something I wasn't.

Then in the eighth grade I discovered track. I was the fastest in my class in the 100-yard dash and had the natural speed and endurance for the 440- and 880-yard runs. For the first time in my life I was setting goals and enjoying teamwork, purpose, and accomplishment. (I can still hear Mom cheering from the stands—louder than anyone else.) By the time I graduated from high school, I had won many tournaments, along with a full athletic scholarship to a state university.

Years later I would come to understand that Mom was the type of person who wanted to master everything, whereas I was more selective—but became equally determined when I finally set my goal. For instance, after getting married, I had a difficult time getting excited about saving money until my husband and I started looking at a little house on three acres. Just as in my track days, I eagerly sacrificed "wants" and "pressed on" until we moved in.

Today I encourage my children to set goals and "press on," whether in the physical, financial, educational, or spiritual arena. And like my mother, I keep my frustrations to myself. But no one cheers louder than I do when they succeed!

Setting goals (short- or long-term) sets your course and, when the goal is achieved, gives a sense of joy and accomplishment. If you and your family aren't already setting goals, ask God to show you one to begin with. Then ask Him for the strength to "press on."

Steps of Faith

My Lord, only You know all the goals You have planned for me. Give me the wisdom and strength to know and follow Your will.

Culture Blues

Be not deaf to my weeping.
For I dwell with you as an alien.

PSALM 39:12

$\mathcal{M}$y depression was best described as a vague sense of dread that something was terribly wrong—wrong with me, my husband, my whole life. That was all I knew. Most of the time the feeling passed after a day or so. When it seemed to come to stay, I knew it was time to get some help.

Our church offered a prayer and counseling ministry. It seemed the best place to start. I was fairly certain I knew the source of my problems. I was what some people call a "third-culture kid," a young person who leaves his culture and lives for a long period in another. The result is that he or she develops in a third culture—a combination of the two.

Third-culture children are usually missionary or military kids. Research shows that many of these children have feelings of alienation and confusion upon returning to their country of origin. They feel that there is something different about them that prevents them from ever fitting in with any group, and to some extent this is the case.

Understandably, "third-culture blues" can lead to depression if the feelings are not dealt with, and there are now special programs to help people in this situation. But one thing I learned from the experience is that nothing leads to depression faster than focusing on yourself to the exclusion of other people. If I was ever going to connect, belong, or make friends, it was up to me to reach out to others. Once I accepted that fact and began to spend more time in prayer, I no longer felt overwhelmed by negative feelings. And on my way to forming new friendships, I learned that though cultural differences are profound, people are people no matter where they live. They all desire to have significant relationships.

Depression comes in all kinds of forms and can have innumerable causes. One thing all sufferers of depression share is a feeling of isolation—being unwilling or unable to relate to other people.

Steps of Faith

Father, I know that Jesus understands depression because He was rejected and alienated by His own people. But that didn't stop Him from giving of Himself to others—or from asking His friends for help.

Worn Out

Whatever you do, work at it with all your heart . . .
since you know that you will receive an
inheritance from the Lord as a reward.

COLOSSIANS 3:23,24

All day I'd been busy baking and wrapping presents while Tom lay around watching football. He didn't even like football! Usually he spent Saturdays in his workshop, on the computer, or at the racquetball court. But lately he didn't seem to want to do anything. It wasn't like him at all. And it was driving me crazy.

I grabbed my coat and went over to Martha's. "I'm going to kill him!" I told her. "He just lies around watching TV. He grumbles at me and the kids and complains about his job. He doesn't want to get up in the mornings. He's just not himself. I wish the real Tom would come back!"

"Maybe he's just burned out," Martha commented quietly. "Jerry went through that shortly before he retired."

"Burned out? Of course! Why didn't I think of that before? He has given so much of himself to his work. He pours his heart into it. How did you help Jerry snap out of it?" I asked.

"I prayed and encouraged him to pray for himself and his coworkers. We talked about the job duties that he really liked, and he focused his energy on those areas. That's what helped him the most, I think. That and the Lord, of course."

I put my cup in her sink. "Thanks for listening. You're a good friend. Now I've got a job to do."

If your husband suffers from burnout, you can: be a good listener; build up his confidence; suggest a vacation or weekend away; inspire him to stop trying to control everything; encourage/inspire him to learn a new skill, at work or at home, to stimulate his brain in a different way. And you can let him know you're praying for him.

Steps of Faith

Dear Lord, please make me sensitive to the signs of burnout so I can uplift my loved ones who suffer from it.

Jehovah-Shammah

And the name of the city from that time on will be:
The Lord is There [Jehovah-Shammah].

EZEKIEL 48:35

*W*e've been best friends forever," Rosie explained to Philip. "There's no other choice. Rebecca has to be my maid of honor."

The girls were born one month apart. Their parents were good friends so they spent lots of time together from infancy through high school. Although they went different directions for college, they never lost touch, thanks to e-mail messages and long-distance telephone calls.

One thing they had always had in common was their faith in God. But Rosie had embraced some unbiblical views on issues like gay rights, abortion, and premarital sex. She was currently living with her boyfriend.

Rebecca was the first one Rosie called after Philip proposed. "We are finally setting a wedding date and I want you to be my maid of honor!" Rosie squealed into the phone.

"Congratulations!" Rebecca said warmly. They talked about possible wedding dates and bridesmaids' dresses, color schemes, and invitations. Before the conversation ended, Rebecca asked bluntly, "Is Philip a Christian yet? We promised each other we would never marry a man who didn't know the Lord, remember?"

"I was too young to know any better," Rosie said. "I'd forgotten all about that."

"Sounds like you've forgotten the Lord, too," Rebecca replied softly. "Remember *Jehovah-Shammah?*"

"The Lord is there," Rosie said immediately, recalling the schoolgirl "code" she and Rebecca had made after studying the Old Testament names of God during a summer Vacation Bible school. She knew exactly what her friend would say next.

"Oh, Rosie, how can you marry Philip if the Lord is not there?"

Jehovah-Shammah—The Lord is There—referred specifically to the city which the prophet Ezekiel saw in his vision (Ezekiel 48:35). It's one of the names of God we easily forget, but what a wonderful reminder to us that we are never out of God's care. He will never leave us or forsake us.

Steps of Faith

Jehovah-Shammah, thank You for being there in so many places in my life! Thank You for Your Word, which convicts us of sin and brings us face-to-face with You, the Lord who is always there!

Friendly Nourishment

A friend loves at all times.

PROVERBS 17:17

W E E K E N D

*H*eroes, friends, and guardian angels can appear in all different shapes, sizes, and ages. Mine took the form of a slightly plump, stay-at-home mom named Adele. Adele and her family lived down the block when I was growing up.

I came from a very unhappy, anger-filled family. I became a troubled, hurting, and lonely teenager. My parents had an unstable marriage, and my father would often leave us when he could no longer stand the chaos. During my teen years, my mother was also diagnosed as a manic-depressive. She would frequently explode in outbursts of rage or become terribly depressed and isolated.

My primary method of survival was to seek refuge and comfort outside of my home. That's how Adele came into my life. She opened her heart and her home to me, silently acknowledging the pain and constant fear that I felt. She gave me her soft shoulder to cry on and a place of safety to run to when I was sad and afraid. Adele was not a gourmet cook, but I was welcome to stay for her family dinners. She always listened to me quietly, never interrupting, caring for me without judgment or criticism. With open arms and a heart that understood as well as listened, she taught me how to be available to others. Adele was my friend, my confidante, my counselor, my mentor, and a guardian "angel." I will always believe she helped save my life.

We live in a society that moves at a very fast pace. Many of us feel pulled from so many directions by family, jobs, church, and ministry. We need to remember that love is the highest of all God's commandments, and the greatest gift we can give. Leave your heart open and your life available to those God might send your way to love and care for.

Steps of Faith

I pray that I will be sensitive and available to the needs and feelings of those around me. Father God, never let me forget the love and compassion I have received from kind people in my life. I have seen Jesus in them; may others see Jesus in me.

A Changed Heart

He has given us this command: Whoever loves God
must also love his brother.

1 JOHN 4:21

*A*s my husband and I sat beside the window in the little café in Washington, D.C., I watched the people rushing by. Most of them were frowning, with stress or anger lining their faces. Very few looked happy.

"What are you thinking?" Tim asked me.

"I'm wondering about those people out there. What are their lives like? Do they know the Lord?" I had an overwhelming sense that they were lost. I prayed, asking God to send someone to share the gospel with them.

Back at home, I took my place again alongside loving family and friends. I lived my busy life just as I had for the past 35 years—secure in the knowledge of where I'd spend eternity.

Then, one Saturday afternoon when my daughter and I were eating lunch at the mall, I watched people walk by and wondered, as I had in Washington, if they were Christians. Did they know that Jesus loved them and had died for them? I began to see them not as shoppers in search of a great bargain but as desperate people in need of the Good News.

That afternoon, my heart changed. I began to pray for people I came in contact with, wherever I was: in my car, on the street, in the grocery store, or at the library. I prayed for opportunities to tell people how Christ had changed my life, something I'd never had the courage to do before. Since then, I've shared my faith with many people in my community. Some have accepted Christ, some haven't. Regardless of their decisions, I know I'll never look at nonbelievers the same way again.

In this hectic world, it's easy for Christians to be distracted from our main purpose: sharing the Gospel. Sometimes we forget that non-Christians will spend eternity separated from God. Ask the Lord to fill your heart with love and compassion for those who don't know Him. Pray for opportunities to share the Good News with them.

Steps of Faith

Lord Jesus, give me a tender heart toward people who don't know You. Help me to show them what life is like with You so they won't want to live without You.

Rolling Pin Religion

Why does your face look so sad when you are not ill?
This can be nothing but sadness of heart.

NEHEMIAH 2:2

*M*y Aunt Pearl had what she called "rolling pin religion." Basically it worked two ways. If you stepped out of line at Aunt Pearl's, she had only to pick up her rolling pin and tap it a few times on the wooden butcher's block to get your attention. Order was restored immediately.

The second way Aunt Pearl applied "rolling pin religion" was to bake up batches of her unique pie crusts, then fill them with a luscious pecan mixture, fresh lemon custard, or glazed strawberries topped with meringue.

"The secret's in the crust," Aunt Pearl would tell us, rolling out her pie dough. "My brother Darius, he's ailing, but it ain't nothing physical. It's in here," she'd say, tapping at her chest and leaving flour marks on her dress. "After his Nellie died, well, he just ain't been the same."

Then Aunt Pearl would start praying for Darius. She'd work the dough and ask God to lift his depression. She'd flute the pie rim in that special way she had and implore Almighty God to free Darius from his suffering. She'd go after the devil with the same enthusiasm, imploring God to send him packing "in the name of Jesus."

Later, when her specially made pies were delivered, joy was often restored.

Her faith was simple: "We are the family of God, and it's time we started acting like it. We need to pray and encourage one another. I've always found that a fresh-baked pie has a way of saying, 'You are loved.'"

This Sunday look around your church at the folks who make up the family of God. Some of them are hurting and truly need a helping hand or a word of encouragement. Does someone need a few extra dollars to make ends meet? Or maybe one of these special "prayer pies," like Aunt Pearl used to make, would be a nice way to assure them of your prayers.

Steps of Faith

Dear Father, thank You for people like Aunt Pearl who show us how to love each other in a practical way. Help me set that same example in my family.

Reaching Out

*But if we walk in the light, as he is in the light,
we have fellowship with one another.*

1 JOHN 1:7

*S*usan pulled into the parking space and turned off her car. *Father,* she prayed, *You know how hard this is for me. But I know I need to be here. Please help me.*

Once inside the auditorium, she sat down beside a woman who looked about her same age. But the woman had her husband and three children with her and never looked up.

The service began—prayers, hymns, announcements, the welcome to visitors. Susan hated this moment of enforced friendliness because it was so meaningless. "How are you?"—the end. Maybe this church would be different. She took a visitor's card and when the music began, the woman next to her introduced herself and then turned to greet someone else. A few other people shook Susan's hand but didn't bother to ask her name. No one approached her after the service was over.

Later, on the phone, she talked about her frustration with her mother. "You'd think that Christians would be more friendly. No one at the churches I've visited cares whether I come back or not."

"Honey, if you keep waiting for someone to reach out to you, it may never happen. Why don't you be the one to reach out?"

"But that's not my job! I'm the visitor."

"I know, but you might have to make the first move. Find out if they have a singles class. Sunday school is a great place to make friends."

Susan decided it was worth a try. Tomorrow she'd call the church and get more information.

Do you feel isolated at your church? Be the first to say hello and extend your hand. Talk with a staff member about how you can make a difference. Check out a Sunday school class. Volunteer for a committee or join the choir. The more involved you are, the more welcome—and less isolated—you're likely to feel.

Steps of Faith

Holy Father, help me reach out when I feel isolated, and help me be sensitive to others who might be feeling the same way.

Bart and the Blessing

People will be lovers of themselves, lovers of money, boastful,
proud, abusive, disobedient to parents, ungrateful. . . .
Have nothing to do with them.

2 TIMOTHY 3:2,5

The blessing of our meal is a special time. I open it thanking God for the food and my family, then each child prays, and Mark closes. Mark and I are trying to teach our children that God is a faithful provider, worthy of thanks and praise.

Not long ago my brother-in-law, Ross, was in town for a visit. As we finished dinner, he announced that *The Simpsons* was starting in 15 minutes. A collective gasp was heard around the table: my children in excited anticipation, Mark and me in horror.

"Oh Daddy, please, Daddy, can we watch just this once?" they squealed.

Ross said, "Come on, Mark and Susan, it's a harmless show. It's one of my favorites. You'll love it."

Mark and I had never seen *The Simpsons*, and we had never allowed the children to watch it. But we decided to make an exception that night.

What a mistake! What an eye-opener!

First, I noted the way the show portrayed the family: two idiotic parents with children who understood more about life then they did. But Bart was the worst—obnoxious, disobedient, ungrateful, and unruly. There was a scene in which Bart was asked to say grace before a meal. He said, "We made all this stuff. So thanks for nothing! Amen." What made it worse was that my children laughed.

After Ross left, we had a family meeting to discuss *The Simpsons*, using Bart's "blessing" to underscore our concern. Then our oldest said, "You know, maybe if the Simpsons said the blessing like we do, Bart would know to thank God for everything." That was all we needed to hear.

Are the cartoons and television shows your children watch distorting their view of God? Take an evening to watch television with your children. Make note of the ways in which God is treated or ignored, and then discuss them as a family when the show is over.

Steps of Faith

My Provider, I give You all thanks and praise for Your faithful provision. Forgive me for the times I take Your daily gifts for granted. Help me to instill in my children an awareness and appreciation for all You have done and continue to provide for them.

No One to Talk To

*From now on there will be five in one family
divided against each other.*

LUKE 12:52

*O*ne truth that all family members know (no matter how they may
try to deny it) is that men and women are profoundly different. The
longer a wife lives with her husband and the more intimately she comes
to know him, the more she grasps the realization that there is a kind of
gulf between them that cannot be bridged. One of the ways this
becomes most apparent is in the ways men and women communicate.

She: "He never wants to talk."
He: "She always wants to talk, but she never wants to listen."
She: "He doesn't tell me what he really thinks and feels."
He: "When I tell her what I think or feel, she tells me why I'm
wrong to think or feel the way I do."
She: "When I talk to him, I can't get his full attention. His eyes
glaze over, and I can tell he's thinking about something
else."
He: "She doesn't give me time to think. While I'm still thinking
about the last thing she said, she's gone on to a different
subject."
She: "He won't express himself. He shuts me out."
He: "She invades me. She demands to know everything before I
have a chance to tell her."
She: "He's never available when I need to talk."
He: "She calls me at work and then gets mad when I can't talk."
She: "I wish I had someone to talk to."
He: "I wish I had someone to talk to."

Husbands and wives both desperately need to talk to each other,
but they must learn and appreciate each other's style of communication. Some people readily articulate their thoughts and feelings and
are anxious to do so; some people need more time and space to collect their thoughts.

Steps of Faith

*Father, one of the most exciting things about marriage is that men
and women are different. Keep me from falling into the trap of
resenting my husband because he thinks and talks like a man and
not like me.*

105

Peace Cookies

All this is from God, who reconciled us to himself through Christ and gave us the ministry of reconciliation.

2 CORINTHIANS 5:18

Latitia rushed in the front door, threw her books on the sofa, and screamed, "I'm so mad I could spit!"

Her mother looked up with a concerned glance. "You want to tell me what's wrong? After you cool down just a little, that is."

Rapidly Latitia dived into her tale of woe about her school day. "This girl, this white girl, she really has it in for me and is making my life miserable."

Her mother listened to the long list of complaints. "Latitia, have you turned the other cheek? Have you reached out in kindness to this girl? And why did you say, 'this *white* girl'? What's her skin color got to do with anything? You said she just moved here. Could she be acting mean because she's scared?"

"Well, I guess so . . . but that doesn't make it right!"

"No," her mother said slowly. "Of course not. But—"

"She hates me!"

"Do you hate her, Latitia?"

When no answer was forthcoming, her mother smiled and nodded her head. "Sounds like it's time for some peace cookies. What do you think?"

"What are peace cookies?"

"Well, Latitia, we make cookies, then we deliver them to this girl's house and make peace," her mother explained.

"No way! She hates me! She'll throw the cookies in the dirt!"

"Honey, if we go with loving hearts and offer the cookies in the right spirit, I promise you, she won't turn them down. Now, let's get busy."

God has given us all the ministry of reconciliation and the commandment to love one another—no matter what skin colors are involved. Look in your heart and then around your world. Is there someone in your neighborhood, church, or office for whom you need to bake a peace offering?

Steps of Faith

Dear God, help me to be a peacemaker between people of different races. Help me to see that reconciliation can begin with something as simple as a plate of cookies—offered in Your love.

The Name of God

*You shall not misuse the name of the LORD your God, for the
LORD will not hold anyone guiltless who misuses his name.*

EXODUS 20:7

*O*h, my Gaw-wd! You aren't serious! Oh-my-Gawd. She really
said that in front of all those people? Oh Gaw-wd! I would have
died!"

I glanced at the two raucous young women seated at the next
table then turned back to my friend Cheryl, expecting to share a
smirk. But Cheryl wasn't smirking. Cheryl wasn't even looking at
me. In fact, she looked like she was going to be sick!

"Cheryl, are you okay?" I asked, genuinely concerned.

Tears filled her eyes as she said gently, "I've been praying that
those girls will one day know the meaning of God's name. They just
don't understand."

Well, I was a Christian and knew the third commandment, but
wasn't Cheryl being just a little overdramatic? "Cheryl, I don't get it.
What are you talking about?"

Cheryl started with the third commandment, explaining the
meanings of the words *name* and *misuse.* In the Old Testament a
name is a designation of character. God has many names, but His
most sacred name is *Jehovah.* This name reveals God's plan of
redemption for His children, His covenantal promises (which He has
faithfully kept for thousands of years), and that He is a God of
loving, mutual relationships. Cheryl went on to say that to "misuse"
or "take in vain" the name of God is to speak it in an empty, insin-
cere, or frivolous way.

For days I pondered what Cheryl had said. Then one afternoon I
turned on my favorite radio talk show. Within 60 seconds the host
had misused God's name five times. I couldn't stand it anymore and
turned it off.

Have you become desensitized to the profaning of God's name?
Are you guilty of misusing it yourself? Confess your sin, and ask God
to give you a deeper understanding of the holiness of His name.

Steps of Faith

*Almighty and Eternal God, I praise You for Your majesty and glory,
Your power and Your love. Your name is so precious to me. Don't
allow my heart to harden against its misuse, but give me grace to
pray for those who don't understand its awesome essence.*

Taking Inventory

*Reflect on what I am saying, for the Lord will
give you insight into all this.*

2 TIMOTHY 2:7

*M*aybe it was the "seven-year itch." Whatever it was, Bob and I knew we needed help—not high-priced counseling, but some guidance. Serious problems lay ahead if we didn't do something soon.

That spring our church sponsored a weekend marriage encounter. Our friends, Tom and Jeannie, asked us to go. Bob and I decided to attend, but we were skeptical. What could we learn?

A lot. First, we took a personality inventory, something neither Bob nor I had ever done before. What an eye-opener! I'd always known Bob and I were opposites. He's a one-man party; I'm a one-woman organizational system. He's extroverted; I'm reserved. He's spontaneous; I'm consistent. We realized that nine years ago those differences attracted us to each other. Now our marriage was suffering because of our lack of appreciation and understanding of each other's strengths and weaknesses.

As the facilitator discussed personality types, I could see that Bob and I weren't the only ones elbowing each other. Tom and Jeannie actually laughed out loud when someone asked about a marriage made up of two dominant personalities. They knew all about life with two strong-willed people always trying to take charge.

By the end of the weekend, Bob and I had gained a profoundly deeper understanding of each other. We're now more sensitive to each other's weaknesses, and therefore know when to lower our expectations. Through our strengths, we see why we were attracted to each other all those years ago. And by God's grace, we are using them to "complete" each other—instead of competing with each other.

Have you and your husband ever taken a personality inventory? You can learn a lot about each other—and yourself. Ask God to show you how to affirm your husband's strengths and how you can best blend your strengths with his. Also, ask for patience in dealing with your husband's weaknesses—and that he will be more tolerant of yours.

Steps of Faith

Lord, Your insight and wisdom for the glitches in my relationships are priceless. Help me to understand the different temperaments around me and then to encourage those people in their unique strengths and abilities.

Bosom Buddies

Carry each other's burdens.

GALATIANS 6:2

*I*n 1983, when my grandmother had to have an emergency double mastectomy, I was distressed. When she died in 1988 from the remaining cancer, I grieved. Then in 1991, when my mother gently told me that the lump found in her breast was malignant and she was going to have a double radical mastectomy, I became anxious. At age 32 I began having annual mammograms. The next year, right before Christmas, my 23-year-old sister had a benign lump (fibroadenoma) removed from her right breast. And I began to have nightmares.

I knew I was high-risk. Along with my family history, I have a severe hormonal imbalance and have not been able to give birth. My diet has been a rather high intake of fat, caffeine, and sugar and a rather low intake of fiber.

Then at age 34 my worst nightmare came true. A routine mammogram. A lump in my left breast. A biopsy. Hours of prayer. A phone call. Breaking the news to my husband. Hugs and tears. A meeting with the surgeon. More prayer. Surgery. My left breast gone forever.

Before I left the hospital, my surgeon told me about a support group for women who have had breast cancer called Bosom Buddies. As loving as my husband was, I knew that I needed the company of women like myself so that the anger, fear, and despair would not overwhelm me.

I began attending the monthly meetings. I met courageous women who would talk frankly, even joke, about having one breast or no breasts. And as I learned to cope with my loss, I found courage to support other women. Some of them have become my closest friends.

You don't have to belong to an organized support group to be supportive, and you don't have to wait until you have cancer. Just pair off with a friend and hold each other accountable for regular mammograms and self-examinations. It's a great way to encourage a friend.

Steps of Faith

Most merciful God, I know You have carried me through many fiery trials. You have never forsaken me. However, You also know that there are times when I need human support and, more specifically, female support. Thank You for providing it through groups like Bosom Buddies.

WEDNESDAY

The Art of Hugging

*May the Lord make your love increase and overflow
for each other and for everyone else.*

1 THESSALONIANS 3:12

*P*olly watched people streaming from the silver Amtrak train. Her nine-year-old daughter had spent the summer on Cape Cod with her grandmother while Polly finished her master's degree in Boston.

"Mama, don't you recognize me?"

Polly turned to see a barely familiar young lady. "Why, Christy, you've grown three inches at least over the summer! And what have you done to your hair?"

The burnt-copper hair that was once quite smooth and flat now curled in all directions like so many corkscrews.

Christy laughed. "Don't worry, Mama. It's not permanent. Grandma used rags to make these curls and they'll wash right out! She said she used to do the same thing when you were a little girl. Don't you remember?"

Polly did indeed recall submitting to the hairstyling. It was the only time her mother ever touched her, which was why Polly endured the tortuous twisting and pulling of her locks night after night.

Deliberately, she pulled Christy into a satisfying hug. Years before, Polly had decided that affectionate hugging and kissing would be part of her own family's life, and she had set out to learn the art of hugging. She'd watched mothers and children in the park until she mastered the easy way they interacted. It had taken longer to learn how often to hug family members and when it was appropriate, but Polly had been determined. She had even prayed, asking God to heal her own wounded heart every time she reached out to hug someone.

Did you spend your childhood longing for more affection? It's not too late to learn the art of hugging. There are side hugs and full-on front hugs and bear hugs and little hugs which are more like squeezes, and well, you get the idea. . . .

Steps of Faith

Dear affectionate Heavenly Father, thank You for teaching me how to show love. Please heal those areas of my heart that were wounded because affection was not given freely when I was growing up. Help me to receive all You have for me.

Dear Mom

I thank my God every time I remember you.

PHILIPPIANS 1:3

$\mathcal{I}$ sat outside the dressing rooms and watched women with arms full of dresses and sweaters stream in and out. It was the annual Spring into Spring sale—an event Mom and I rarely miss.

"Lindsey!" Mom was leaning out of her dressing room. "How does this look?" she asked, smoothing the skirt of the elegant green dress.

I stood back to admire her. "It looks great, Mom. You'll be the belle of the ball."

She grinned. "I'll settle for your father's 'most glamorous girl.' I think this is a keeper. And it's 40 percent off!"

As I waited for her to buy the dress, I thought about how close we had become now that I was out on my own. We saw each other often, and we talked on the phone about everything. She listened to me, believed in me, and encouraged me.

"How about some lunch?" she asked. "I'm willing to go to El Mexicano just for you."

I laughed. "Willing? Ha! You love it as much as I do!"

At lunch, I told her about the Bible study group I had recently joined. "I'll always thank you and Dad for giving me a spiritual foundation and encouraging me in my Christian walk."

"And we're thankful for such a great daughter."

At home, hours later, I pulled out a pretty note card and wrote what was on my heart: "Dear Mom, Thank you for being such a special friend." I knew my note would bring tears to her eyes and a smile to her face. I knew she would call to say I had brightened her day. As she did mine.

Look for ways to strengthen your friendship with your mother, like helping her with yard work, running errands with her, or simply sending a note with a word of thanks.

Steps of Faith

Lord Jesus, You are the perfect Friend. Show me how to reach out to my mother and be the kind of friend she needs.

F
R
I
D
A
Y

Loving Preparation

*Listen . . . to your father's instruction and do not
forsake your mother's teaching.*

PROVERBS 1:8

*W*hen I look back on the 15 years Wayne and I were married, I realize how he allowed me to be a relatively carefree wife and mother. He paid all the bills, did all the yard work, took care of the cars, and fixed things I didn't even know needed fixing. In spite of all his good intentions, Wayne was setting me up for a devastating collision with reality.

But then Wayne had no idea he'd die before his 37th birthday.

At first I thought I would fall apart. How could I survive without the man who had done everything for me? But as God gave me the strength I cried out for, I began to tackle—one by one—all the little chores Wayne once did for me. And it was then that I was given fresh insight into my parents' love for me.

As a young girl, I couldn't understand why my "cruel" parents made all of us work out in the yard on Saturdays: mowing, raking, pruning, edging, and sweeping. Or why my father often asked me, instead of one of my brothers, to help him change the oil in the car or make other minor repairs. Or why my mother insisted I take the sewing class at school.

Little by little, all these things my parents had taught me were coming back, like atrophied muscles being flexed back into shape. However, the firmest foundation my parents laid in my life was my faith and knowledge of my Lord Jesus Christ.

Nothing could have prepared me for life as a widow—but in many ways, my parents had been preparing me almost all of my life.

Do you appreciate the time and effort your parents invested in you? Do they know how much you appreciate them? Consider writing a thank-you note to your parents. It doesn't have to be a long letter, but try to be specific. Tell them how their help has helped you. You honor your parents with your gratitude, and God as well.

Steps of Faith

Father, You chose two people to be my parents. In Your perfect wisdom You knew they would be the best parents for me. Thank You. Help me to be mindful that, as they enter their final years, my time with them is limited. Please give me at least one more opportunity to say thank you.

Thy Will Be Done

*Everyone who asks receives; he who seeks finds; and to him
who knocks, the door will be opened.*

LUKE 11:10

Sharon sat close beside her little daughter as she began her bed-time prayers. "God, please help Sandy not to be scared when he has to go the vet tomorrow," Julie prayed. "And help him get better soon. And please bless everybody in my class and look after them tonight when they're asleep . . . except Lisa, because she's mean. . . ."

"Julie," interrupted Sharon.

"Mom, she is mean. Today she tried to get Brittany and Susan not to like me. She gave them candy so they would play with her and not me. I don't want to pray for her."

"I can see why you don't want to pray for Lisa, and I think God does, too," said Sharon. "But you can't just pray for the things you want, or the people you like. God wants us to pray for the things He wants. And He loves Lisa just as much as He loves you."

"That's not fair," said Julie. "If He loves me, then why does He let Lisa act mean to me?"

"Well, as I recall," said Sharon, "you were pretty mean to Chris yesterday when you thought I wasn't looking. If you want God to punish Lisa, He'll have to punish you, too. He doesn't stop loving people because they sin. And you know, it sounds like Lisa needs more prayer than your friends do. Maybe Lisa has trouble making friends and that's why she doesn't have any."

"She doesn't have any friends because she's so mean," said Julie.

"Then we need to pray for her especially, and to pray for you, so you don't feel like being mean to get back at her," said Sharon. "That's what prayer is for. So God can give us the help we need to do the things He wants us to do."

Children find it just as difficult to put their faith into action as adults do at times. Encourage them to pray with perseverance when they face trials and to have hope that their prayer will make a difference.

Steps of Faith

Father, as I pray daily for my children's protection, I also pray for opportunities to teach them how to pray according to Your will. Give them the desire to please You in every way, Lord.

M
O
N
D
A
Y

The Watermelon

Honor your father and your mother, as the LORD
your God has commanded you, so that you may live
long and that it may go well with you.

DEUTERONOMY 5:16

*M*y family was vacationing at the beach. My mother and I were buying groceries and I wanted a watermelon. I think I was seven.

After numerous emotional appeals, I had failed to convince my mother of the necessity of the watermelon. Still, as she left the produce section, I had an idea.

I approached the watermelon display and found a big one. I hoisted it, struggled to get my balance, and staggered toward the cereal aisle, calling for my mother. Surely when she saw how much I wanted this watermelon, her heart would soften, and she would buy it for me.

When I found her, however, she was furious! She told me to return the watermelon immediately. Instead the heavy melon hit the floor with a split and then a splat.

I got my watermelon that day, along with a humiliating spanking in the grocery store. While I cried, I vowed that when I had children, I would give them everything they wanted. That was real love.

I've learned a lot since then. I love my children too much to allow them to become little tyrants. I would be denying them God's blessings. Unfortunately, that's what many parents are doing when they allow their children to continuously defy them. God promises a long, happy life to those who honor their parents. As a parent, I have an obligation to teach my children that truth—just as my mother continued to teach it to me long after the watermelon episode.

Children who are reared to respect their parents become a blessing to those parents and enjoy God's blessings as they mature into adulthood. Children who are not become a burden to their parents (and society) and bear the burden of God's judgment. Which would you call real love?

Steps of Faith

Father, I love my family and pray that Your blessings would always fall upon them. Grant me the strength and wisdom to command respect from my children. I know that defiance cannot be accepted in our family. It's certainly not accepted in Yours.

Shattering the Myth

Rise in the presence of the aged, show respect for the elderly and revere your God. I am the LORD.

LEVITICUS 19:32

*O*ur family had just finished watching a video, and now Claire, my 12-year-old, was helping me in the kitchen. We laughed as we recalled some of the funnier scenes, but one aspect of the movie wasn't funny to me. It had hit a nerve.

The relationship between the wife and her mother-in-law was the classic Hollywood stereotype—and it depicted my own relationship with Tom's mother. From our wedding day, Lillian had been a meddling menace who hadn't been able to find anything right with me. As I watched the two characters clawing each other in the movie, anger and bitterness burned in my belly.

It continued to burn so strongly after the movie that I broke a cardinal rule of family relationships. As we loaded the dishwasher, I lowered my voice and with a smirk told Claire that she had finally gotten to see "the real Lillian."

I remember Claire seeming confused, giggling nervously, and then looking past my shoulder in horror. Tom was standing in the doorway. When I turned to look at him, I saw his angry, hurt eyes. He stormed past us and went outside.

I felt sick. In one moment I had damaged the trust I had built between my husband, my daughter, and myself. Worst of all, as much as I had tried to teach my children to respect the elderly, I had shown blatant disrespect behind the back of a beloved mother and grandmother.

That was the last time that happened.

Do your actions and words perpetuate the mother-in-law myth in your home? If they do, your behavior is telling your children that respect for the elderly is not necessary. If you struggle with resentment toward one of your in-laws, confess it and ask for forgiveness. Pray for reconciliation and healing of the pain.

Steps of Faith

Lord of love, thank You for my husband's mother. Even though we may not agree on everything, help me to love her and to always show respect to her, even when she isn't around.

WEDNESDAY

115

A Haughty Spirit

*Confess your sins to each other and pray for each other
so that you may be healed. The prayer of a righteous
[woman] is powerful and effective.*

JAMES 5:16

They called me the "prayer warrior" at my church. I loved to pray. I had "a direct line to God," they used to say.

That's right, *"used* to say." I was at the pinnacle of my walk with God. My life was absorbed with Jesus. I was in constant communion with Him. But I tolerated unconfessed sin in my life, and it gave birth to other sins and almost destroyed my ministry.

My sin was pride. It crept in the day Judy told our Bible study group how God had miraculously healed her husband's tumor. I had been out of town the week the tumor was discovered and then disappeared, so I hadn't prayed about it. Instead of rejoicing with Judy and praising God, I felt resentment.

That was a critical moment. Instead of confessing and repenting of the pride, I nursed it. Little by little, I began to pray less. Quickly, my prayer life lost its power and effectiveness. Eventually, I wasn't praying at all.

I was fooling everyone—except God. One week in my Bible study we were sharing what God was teaching us that week. My heart ached as each woman shared with genuine joy and excitement. When it was my turn to speak, I couldn't. The jig was up.

I confessed my pride and self-centeredness. The tears came as I shared how my fellowship with the Lord had been soured by my sin. I missed Him. And for the first time in years, I asked other people to pray for me.

Do you wonder why God doesn't seem to answer your prayers? Psalm 66:18 says, "If I had cherished sin in my heart, the Lord would not have listened." Only you know what that sin could be. Confess it. Repent of it. Keep a pure heart before the Lord. When you do, His Word promises that your prayers will be powerful and effective.

Steps of Faith

My Lord, thank You for the joy prayer brings to my life. How I look forward to that special time with You. Protect me from those "little" sins that rob me of hours of sweet fellowship with You.

The Greatest Teacher

I tell you, her many sins have been forgiven—for she loved
much. But he who has been forgiven little loves little.

LUKE 7:47

There were three things I'd never do: have an abortion, commit adultery, or abandon my family. I remember listing these to a friend when I was 20 years old, still in college, and convinced I had all the answers.

Then I fell in love with Barry. Even though I was a virgin (and proud of it!) and active in my church, Barry's influence was greater. When I told him I was pregnant, he told me to get an abortion. A month after I did, he dumped me.

I married Jon on the rebound. I felt safe, and I never told Jon about the abortion. In fact I let him believe I was still a virgin. Naturally the deception, along with the unresolved guilt and grief, festered in my marriage. After my third child was born, the depression was overwhelming.

I convinced Jon that a job would help me get focused. That was where I met Gary. The first time I saw him there was a physical attraction between us. In a few short months we were having an affair. Soon I was at the bottom. God woke me up and I started a journey home. Even though I had grown up in the church, I had never made Jesus the Lord of my life. The sins of my past and present reflected that.

It took God's grace and mercy to heal me and our marriage. Jon and I spent much time in Christian counseling.

That was 18 years ago. God has allowed Jon and me to share our story in many places and see God's redemptive work being done in the lives of others.

I'm so thankful that God doesn't use only "perfect" people.

Have you ever been tempted to believe that the sin in your past has destroyed your usefulness to God? Not so. The issue is not the severity of your sin. The issue is humility—an understanding of who you are and what you're capable of apart from Christ—and failure is our greatest teacher.

Steps of Faith

Most merciful God, only You would structure life in a way that allows
people with the most failures opportunities to transform them into the
most beautiful triumphs. Thank You for all the little miracles You've
blessed me with. Show me how I can use them to bless others.

117

Now and Then

Give everyone what you owe him:
If you owe taxes, pay taxes.

ROMANS 13:7

*D*eath and taxes. The joke is you can't avoid them. Ah, but you can prepare for them—making them much more comfortable experiences.

Having made my preparations for death years ago, when Jesus Christ became my Lord and Savior, I had only taxes to worry about. And I had been woefully neglectful in that department. It's embarrassing to admit that I was 42 before I realized April fifteenth came every year.

As a single mother who worked out of her home, I knew that I needed to get my finances in order. I bought a book about women's finances and software for personal and business expenses. If that sounds expensive, I'll tell you that the secret to my success was neither. All I really needed ten dollars' worth of accordion files and notebooks. And the rest was history.

I had one file and notebook apiece for personal and business use. In the personal notebook I recorded monthly projections for household expenses, and then broke it down into four weeks. I recorded almost all of my expenses at first, so I could make more accurate projections later. I used my business notebook to record mileage, office supplies, and business transactions. The notebooks went with me everywhere.

But it was those files that kept my accountant from going insane. I kept all my receipts: gasoline, medical, office supplies, etc. There was no more guessing because I had documented evidence.

The miracle is that eventually, with the help of a nifty tax software program, I stopped needing an accountant!

Come on, death! Come on, taxes! I'm ready for both of you!

How prepared are you for death and taxes? Concerning taxes, you don't need an elaborate organizational system. A notebook and a shoe box will suffice and make facing the tax man much less excruciating. What about death? Is Jesus Christ your Lord and Savior? If you were to die tonight, do you know for sure you'll spend eternity with Him in heaven?

Steps of Faith

Father, thank You for destroying the sting of death by the resurrection of Your Son, Jesus. I trust in the power of His blood to wash away my sins and clothe me in His righteousness.

A Little Preparation

*This is the day the LORD has made;
let us rejoice and be glad in it.*

PSALM 118:24

Yelling, crying, slamming doors, blaring television, splitting nerves, and screeching tires pretty much described our Sunday mornings a few years ago. By the time we got to church, we were all so stressed that it's amazing we were able to concentrate on anything.

Then, after a typical Sunday morning, our Sunday school teacher, Lee, and his wife, Katy, shared how they got themselves and *six children* to church on time every week. They begin Saturday evening. The children pick out what they want to wear, and if it's dirty or needs mending, it's taken care of that night. Bibles and Sunday school materials are laid out on the dining room table. No one stays up late. In the morning praise music is played—no television. Lee makes sure the boys get ready while Katy dresses the girls. Breakfast is quick and simple. And if Katy is *really* organized, dinner is in the oven or Crock-Pot when they leave.

Once in the car Lee opens a prayer. Each child thanks God for something and prays for someone in the church. They close by reciting Psalm 118:24, "This is the day the LORD has made; let us rejoice and be glad in it."

As I listened to Lee and Katy, I thought, *There's no way Sherman and I could ever be that organized.* But the following Saturday evening I began to get things in order for Sunday, and I had to admit, it was a vast improvement over most Sundays.

Sherman and I still aren't as organized as Lee and Katy, but our Sunday mornings have come a long way. All it has taken is a little preparation.

Are your Sunday mornings exhausting and stressful? Try preparing for Sunday morning on Saturday evening, even if it's just laying out what your family will wear to church. A little preparation on Saturday can make a big difference in your worship experience on Sunday.

Steps of Faith

Holy Lord, when I think about all the preparations the Jewish women made before Sabbath, it reminds me that there's much I can do to prepare for my day of worship. Give me the discipline, Lord, to think ahead and plan for this glorious day that is set aside to honor You.

M
O
N
D
A
Y

119

The Knife

You will forget the shame of your youth.

ISAIAH 54:4

*A*n old movie, my latest cross-stitch project, and a quiet house. What more could I ask for on a Sunday afternoon?

But funny things can happen in the quiet. Without warning, a memory, buried in a secret place, shot into my mind. And I could feel that knife—the one I'd ignored for years—begin to twist in me once more.

It was so clear. There he was, a guy named Mike. We were high-school seniors. He was looking at me, no, glaring at me. He'd never looked at me like that before. Then he said to his companion, loud enough for me and everyone around to hear, that I was the ugliest girl in the school.

The worst part was that he hadn't been the only one saying that lately. Ever since I'd asked the baseball player to the Sadie Hawkins party, I'd been getting anonymous phone calls saying I was so ugly that no one wanted to be seen with me. In fact, everyone hated me. I believed him.

That was 20 years ago. The knife had been there that long.

When John came home, he found me curled up in a ball in the dark, weeping in anguish. The knife was still turning.

John rushed to me but I pushed him away. He had also played baseball in high school. I accused him of thinking I was ugly and being ashamed of me. He didn't love me. He was incapable of love. How stupid I'd been to marry one of those "dumb jocks."

But in spite of what my emotions were telling me, John was living proof of the truth. He held me tightly and spoke tender words of love until I finally collapsed against his chest, sobbing.

That night the knife was finally removed, and I began my journey back into the truth.

Do your emotions ever distort reality? Feelings aren't facts. Truth is all that matters. Jesus is the truth (John 14:6), and He wants you to know nothing but truth. Only when your emotions are rooted in Him can you know real peace and joy.

Steps of Faith

Author of truth, my emotions sometimes warp my perspective. Show me the truth, even when I don't want to see it. Jesus is the truth, and I should never be afraid of Him.

Christ at the Counter

*He who has the Son has life; he who does not have
the Son of God does not have life.*

1 JOHN 5:12

It had been a miserable Easter vacation. As I walked through the airport, my heart was heavy at the devastation in my daughter's life. Her husband of one year had left her to live with another man, and she was almost immobilized by shock and sorrow. Because she was an air-traffic controller, she was now terribly worried about her ability to stay focused.

I stopped to buy souvenirs for my grandchildren back home. While the credit card processed, the smiling clerk asked how I liked her home state.

"It's beautiful," I replied, "but I say that about nearly every place I visit."

"Yes," she nodded, "God has made a beautiful world for us to enjoy. So much variety. What did you see on your vacation?"

Immediately the tears welled up. The grief was raw and close to the surface. "It wasn't a vacation. Just a serious family problem, and my daughter is having an extremely hard time. I hate to leave her," I stammered.

"Oh, but God is good. He will work on your daughter's behalf."

"I know," I nodded in agreement, "but the pain is very great."

She slid a pen and piece of paper across the counter. "Will you write down your daughter's name? I'm a Christian and I'd like to pray for her. And for you, too."

So I did. As I signed my receipt, she patted my hand. Then she reached across the counter, cupped my face in her hands, looked at me tenderly, and said with quiet authority, "God is in control. He will work everything out for good."

"I know," I whispered back through tears that now flowed freely. From that counter I took away more than my small purchase. I took away a touch of Christ's resurrection power—the power of God's love to reach out to a stranger and touch a hurting heart.

When you let Jesus Christ replace your life with His resurrection life the Holy Spirit will use you to touch others in ways you could never imagine. And in ways you—and they—will never forget.

Steps of Faith

*Almighty God, keep me always alert for ways You want to work
through me in someone else's life. Be glorified in me.*

The Wake-Up Call

I belong to my lover, and his desire is for me.

SONG OF SONGS 7:10

*O*ur sex life seemed doomed. Seth was always eager for sex first thing in the morning. Ugh! That was the last thing I was interested in—until later at night. But by 10 P.M., Seth was out like a light. The only response I would get then was an irritated groan, followed by snoring.

Therefore, as a young bride, I came to the conclusion that Seth didn't like for me to initiate sex.

Then one night in my frustration I prayed as I climbed into bed next to my snoring husband. "God, I want him so much. Show me what to do." I drifted off to sleep. At about 12:30 A.M. our phone rang. It was a wrong number. As I hung up the phone, I gazed at the beautiful man lying next to me. Assuming he was asleep, I lightly kissed his face and then his ear lobe. To my delight I felt his hand slide around my waist and draw me closer to him. Then . . . well, let's just say God answered my prayer!

The next morning we were still glowing. Before he climbed out of bed, he held me close and whispered, "You know, I like it when you get things started like you did last night."

That woke me up all right. "You do? Then how come you've turned me down so many times before?"

Seth thought about it for a moment and said, "I guess it was because I was so tired. But last night I'd had some sleep." Then he playfully leered at me and tucked the covers back over my shoulders.

Since then I've been more confident about initiating sex. I know Seth desires me and that he enjoys my assertiveness. Most of all, I know the optimum time for both of us.

Do you ever initiate affection or sex with your husband? Most men admit that they like for their wives to do this. If you haven't had the most encouraging results, the problem may be timing. Ask God to bless your sexual relationship with your husband. It was His wedding gift, and He wants both of you to enjoy it to the fullest.

Steps of Faith

Giver of all good things, sex is difficult for me to openly discuss with my husband. I know he wants me to be more assertive some-times. Lord, I love him and I don't want to disappoint him. Give me wisdom to do what's right.

Here I Am Again

I have the desire to do what is good,
but I cannot carry it out.

ROMANS 7:18

*H*ere I am again, Lord. I can hardly believe it, but then again, maybe I was foolish to believe I could really change things in our marriage. I thought this time would be different.

"The scary thing is, I had no intention of starting an argument with Paul. I sincerely wanted to apologize for what I had done. But it came out all wrong and he didn't understand. So I tried to explain, and the more I talked, the angrier he got. And within a few minutes we were screaming insults at each other all over again, only worse this time. And now he's gone, and he probably won't be back all day.

"I was so looking forward to this weekend so that we could spend some time together doing things we enjoy. Another weekend wasted.

"Why is it so easy to think clearly and reasonably when we're apart? When I'm alone, it's perfectly obvious to me why we fight and how it begins—the critical remarks, the little barbs, my lack of consideration for Paul's feelings. But as soon as we're together again, it's just a matter of time before we're arguing. I'm completely powerless against it.

"I don't know what the use is of asking for forgiveness again, even though I know it's the right thing to do. You know it's going to happen again, Lord, so why even try? I can't change, no matter what I pray or what I do. I can't even allow the Holy Spirit to change me because I'm too concerned with how He should be changing Paul. Help me, God, please. Give me hope that there's still a chance. I'm exhausted, but I know in my heart that if You can overcome death, You can help me find a way to overcome sin."

How many chances can God give us to weed sin out of our lives before He gives up on us? As many as it takes. As long as we still have the desire to change, and the will to repent and try again, He has the power to help.

Steps of Faith

God, I seem to be stuck in a destructive pattern that I'm unable to break. I know Your desire is for me to be controlled by the Holy Spirit, not my bad habits. I need help. Please show me how to go about dealing with this problem.

Golfing Guys

*She watches over the affairs of her household
and does not eat the bread of idleness.*

PROVERBS 31:27

"*H*oney, I'm playing nine holes this afternoon with the guys. I'll be home at six."

Okay, no problem, Nancy thought as she erased the message. She had encouraged her husband to do something he enjoyed—apart from her and the family.

She had a number of friends she cherished spending time alone with. But this was the second time this week John was golfing. Even though he came home at a reasonable hour, their evenings were consumed with family activities, and household repairs piled up quickly.

"Honey, could we spend Saturday morning giving the house a face-lift?" she asked that evening. "The boys can help you outside while I clean inside."

"I promised the guys I'd golf. I'm the fourth man. They're depending on me."

"Yes, but—"

"Remember, this was your idea," he quickly answered.

Taking a deep breath, Nancy asked calmly, but resolutely. "When *can* you help me?"

"All right. Let's see. I can be home by one. Where's the list?" he asked grudgingly. She handed him a masculine-looking note card with a picture of a refined golfer on the outside. He opened it and read: "1) fix dripping faucet, 2) sweep garage, 3) mow lawn, 4) warm the bed (*my* side)."

Warm the bed? John smiled. "No problem, honey! By the way, Sunday is all yours!"

It can be hard to allow our husbands to spend time on hobbies or pursue athletic or musical interests. It's all part of balance, and balance comes with communication. Talk. Share your expectations in creative, encouraging ways.

Steps of Faith

Dear God, help me to allow my husband time from home without resentment. Give me the wisdom to express my needs, concerns, and desires in a manner that expresses the feminine qualities You've given me. Teach me to trust You to fulfill my needs as well.

Positive Spin

*Everything that was written in the past was written
to teach us, so that through endurance and the encouragement
of the Scriptures we might have hope.*

ROMANS 15:4

*B*ecause of a serious illness, my oldest child missed a lot of school: half of the third grade and many weeks of the fourth. Coupled with a first child's tendency toward perfectionism, this caused Merry a great deal of stress whenever tests rolled around. There were gaps in her learning to be sure, but she was an avid reader and a good student.

I longed for a way to bolster her confidence and help her see how much she really knew. But most of the time, the evening prior to an exam brought tears and numerous outbursts of, "I can't do it! I can't remember anything I read! I hate myself!"

I needed help. I thought of Joan, an elementary school teacher who had temporarily retired to be home with preschool children. She did some private tutoring, and her specialty was organization.

The first thing Joan did was have Merry write Philippians 4:13 on the inside cover of each notebook. That way, every time Merry began to study a subject, she read: "I can do everything through [Jesus Christ] who gives me strength." In just a couple of sessions, Merry was aware of the negative cues she was feeding herself. "I can't" was replaced with "This is easy" or "This is fun."

Joan also got Merry organized. She taught her to leave everything in a file at home except for the work of the last two weeks, instead of carrying all the papers for the whole year in her notebook. Now doing homework and studying for tests aren't so confusing and overwhelming.

And best of all, Merry's confidence continues to be reinforced by improving grades.

How many of us are so preoccupied with teaching our children the value of success that we neglect teaching them the value of confidence? School work struggles are a great opportunity to encourage our children to lean on God.

Steps of Faith

Father in heaven, thank You for being my strength. Help me to offer my children a "positive spin" to those experiences where they fear failure.

125

Tear Down the Walls

*For he himself is our peace, who has made the two one
and has destroyed the barrier, the dividing wall of hostility.*

EPHESIANS 2:14

*M*aybe 50 years ago—but in the nineties? I couldn't believe my eyes when I read the newspaper article. According to the story, a young Caucasian woman had recently given birth at a local hospital. When taken to her room, she discovered that the nurse assigned to her was African-American. The young woman demanded that another nurse—"a white nurse"—be assigned to her. She would not allow the African-American nurse to touch her or her baby.

I wanted to run to my African-American friends and neighbors and yell, "She's an exception! I'm not like that! No one I know thinks like that! The way she treated that nurse was vile and hateful! She's ignorant. Please forgive her."

But I said nothing to my African-American friends. I couldn't work up the nerve. Was it shame? Maybe. Was it fear? Possibly. The issue of race stirs up anger and hostility on both sides, if allowed, and the consequences are unpleasant.

I came to the conclusion that it was shame and fear, combined mostly with grief—the grief of what their ancestors endured at the hands of my ancestors. It's overwhelming when I dwell on it, and I don't think I could talk to any of my African-American friends about it without weeping.

I would change history if I could, but I can't. Our task now is to tear down the walls of shame, fear, anger, bitterness, and grief in the power of Christ. He is our only hope for peace and reconciliation.

Are you allowing God to work in your heart on the issue of racism? It comes in many forms and virtually no culture has been completely spared. Almost all of us have felt its sting to one degree or another, so most of us can understand the pain and humiliation that it causes. Let the healing begin with you.

Steps of Faith

*Almighty God, there are many things I don't understand about life,
but I trust You to redeem the pain of the past and present for a better
future for all people. In the meantime speak to the hearts of Your
children, no matter what color they are. Give us all the strength to
tear down the walls.*

Careless Curses

I tell you that men will have to give account
on the day of judgment for every careless word they have
spoken. For by your words you will be acquitted, and by your
words you will be condemned.

MATTHEW 12:36,37

James and I met at a private Christian college our freshman year. He was my first boyfriend and my first love. After a few months we were already talking about our future together. How my heart pounded every time he told me what a great pastor's wife I would make!

Then we had our first "real" fight. I don't remember what it was about, but we were both very upset. Before I knew it, foul language began to pour out of James' mouth—words I'd never heard him use. Pouncing on the opportunity, I said, "That's just wonderful language for a future pastor! What would Dr. Wallis think if he could hear you?"

James's face went white with rage. And in a low, measured voice, he cursed me in God's name and told me I could rot.

I ran into the bathroom and vomited.

A couple of days later James called to apologize and ask my forgiveness. I forgave him, but I told him I couldn't see him anymore. Two months later he dropped out of school. I never saw him again.

Over time God has used that experience with James to teach me the awesome holiness, love, and power associated with His name. It is a name to be cherished and celebrated, praised and pondered.

I've also learned what profanity reveals about a person's heart, no matter how godly he or she may act. That person is to be pitied.

Dr. Kent Hughes writes in his book, *Disciplines of Grace:* "To damn someone in God's name is a monstrous misuse of God's name. The tongue that descends to such abuse houses a hideous mouth and soul." Anyone who carelessly or calculatingly profanes God's name is in serious spiritual trouble. If someone you love is guilty of this practice, don't lose hope (2 Peter 3:9). Seek wisdom and hope through God's Word and prayer.

Steps of Faith

Holy Father, I shudder to think what happens in the spiritual realm when anyone uses Your name as part of a curse. Tragically, it's becoming more common for people to use such language. Have mercy on us, Lord. Give us, the church, strength and wisdom to change this trend.

Behind Enemy Lines

*All these people were still living by faith when they died.
They did not receive the things promised; they only
saw them . . . from a distance. And they admitted
that they were aliens and strangers on earth.*

HEBREWS 11:13

*G*od's not worried about you being *happy,* darlin'," my mother's friend, Sally, used to quip in her perky Southern accent. "He knows you've got all of eternity to be happy with Him when you get to heaven. Right now, He's got a job for you to do while you're on earth, and He's gonna give you all that you need to do it right."

For years I didn't understand what Sally was talking about. God wasn't worried about my happiness? Didn't Jesus tell us that He came so that we would live life "to the full" (John 10:10)? So, I reasoned, if I experience failure, sickness, rejection, or disappointment, God must be punishing me.

Then I grew up. I have had my share of failure, sickness, rejection, and disappointment. The world is a cruel place. As often as I was tempted to give up on God, He did not give up on me.

Over the years Sally's words echoed in my heart. They meant dying to self, trusting God in all my circumstances, and learning to delight in His will for my life and for the whole world. Like the countless saints before me and those to follow, I am a citizen from another world, with a small but significant part in the vast, eternal plan of God.

I am on a lifelong mission behind enemy lines. What soldier expects a carefree, blissful life in the midst of war?

Sally was right. God's not primarily concerned about my happiness . . . because He knows that peace and the fullness of His joy abounds in the woman who views life from eternity's perspective—and praises God for it every day.

Have you ever glimpsed the eternal purpose and value of your life? When you do, you will see that what heaven holds for you is infinitely more exciting than anything with which the world tries to tempt you. And always remember: There's a reason why God commands you to "put on the full armor of God" (see Ephesians 6:10-18).

Steps of Faith

Eternal Lord, I praise You for Your mercy, love, and guidance in my life. I praise You for allowing me the privilege of serving You with my life. I praise You for equipping me with the power, tools, and weaponry necessary to complete Your eternal purpose through my life.

Today Is the Present

*Encourage one another daily, as long as
it is called Today, so that none of you may be
hardened by sin's deceitfulness.*

HEBREWS 3:13

$\mathcal{T}$raffic at the four-way stop was moving slowly. As I crept, car by car, to the distant grocery store, all I could think about was everything I had to do when I got home. And to really stress myself out, I began planning the following day and then the weekend. Pretty soon my thoughts were flying months into the future.

I've been that way as long as I can remember—always looking forward to or dreading something. So, I'm a future-oriented person. Big deal. I have to be as a wife and mother of four.

Right then the words on the Cornerstone Church marquee jumped out at me: "Today is God's gift to you. It's called 'the present.'" *Whoa, Lord. Is this for me? It sure feels like it. Okay, Lord, what am I supposed to learn from this?*

Thoughts and images began to flood my mind. Impatience. Lack of contentment. Seeing only the negative of the present, always anticipating a positive, perfect future. *I can't wait till I have this baby, then I'll feel better. . . . Maybe Ashley will learn to feed herself early. . . . Six more months until Johnnie starts the first grade. . . . In three years Lauren will be able to drive herself. . . . Then she'll graduate, and I'll have one less child to worry about. . . .*

Sitting in traffic I began to realize why my life lacked joy. My focus was so intense on the future that I had been neglecting the daily "present" of my marriage, my family, and my Lord. "That's going to change right now, today, this minute, pronto!" I said out loud. "Tonight I'm giving my family a surprise party. And my present will be my ever-present presence!"

Are you so future oriented that you lose the joys of the "present"? Or are you so focused on the past that you miss God's gift of today? Joy escapes those who tend to look forward and back, instead of up and around. Ask God to help you see the joys in each day He "presents" to you!

Steps of Faith

Eternal God, thank You for the gift of the present. I want to discover each and every jewel hidden in my days. Help me to savor my time with my family and friends, enjoying who and where they are today. Tomorrow they will be different, never to be the same again.

129

That Time

*Better to live on a corner of the roof than share a house
with a quarrelsome wife.*

PROVERBS 21:9

*S*pring was in the air that sunny Sunday morning. Before Roger
and I left for church, I stood outside deeply inhaling the fresh, warm
air. *Aahhh. Life is good.* But something happened between the trips to
and from church. I became irritable and sulky. And poor Roger
couldn't say or do anything right. In fact he no longer even *looked*
right. *Why did I even marry this guy?* I wondered as I silently stared
out my window.

At home, as I set the table, I could feel my nerves splintering. When
I told Roger that dinner was ready, he called back from the family
room, "Just bring it in here. The Braves are playing the Pirates and—"

"What?" I screeched. "We can't *ever* have a decent Sunday dinner!
You *always* have to eat in front of that stupid television! You *never*—"

"Okay, okay!" Roger stammered as he jumped up. "Don't get
upset."

Later, as I was cleaning the kitchen, I got mad at the sink stopper
and threw it on the floor, screaming. I ran to the bedroom, slammed
the door, and fell on the bed.

What is wrong with me? Am I going crazy? I wondered.

Then it hit me. I counted the days. PMS. It wasn't exactly cause
for celebration, but at least the emotional roller coaster made sense.

A few minutes later there was a light tap at the door. Roger sat
down on the bed beside me and began stroking my hair. "I've been
praying for you," he said. "All I can figure is that it must be close to
'that time.'"

As he put his arms around me and gently kissed my forehead, I
could no longer fight the tears. *Now I remember why I married this guy.*

Premenstrual syndrome (PMS) affects more than half of all
women. If you suffer with PMS, education is the first step. Ask your
doctor to recommend books for you and your husband. Your mate's
sympathy and patience will increase as his knowledge of PMS
increases.

Steps of Faith

*Dear God, there are those times of the month when I need You more
than others—simply because it is "that time of the month." I hate
the way I look and feel and how I make others feel, especially my
precious family. Immerse me in Your soothing grace.*

"Nothing, Really"

One man pretends to be rich, yet has nothing;
another pretends to be poor, yet has great wealth.

PROVERBS 13:7

By the time my sister Deborah entered middle school, she knew she was going to be a lawyer. Deborah's kind of ambition always eluded me because my only ambition was to be a godly wife and mother.

By the time Deborah and I were in our late thirties, she was winning cases, being promoted in the firm, and making all kinds of money. Her beautiful husband, children, home, clothes, and car completed the picture of a woman who seemed to have it all. On the other hand, I was rearing five children and helping my husband in his part-time ministry. All my dreams of cooking, sewing, and gardening had come true because we rarely ate out, I made most of our clothes, and my vegetable garden reduced our grocery bill. But I wasn't complaining. In fact, I was very happy.

Then one day I overheard my 13-year-old daughter, Rebecca, answer a friend's question about what I did. "Nothing, really," Rebecca said. "She's just a mom. She doesn't even earn any money. Not like my Aunt Deborah. She's so cool!"

I was crushed. Did Rebecca actually think that I did nothing? Did she admire Deborah more than me? Was I really that insignificant?

Fortunately God quickly brought me back to the truth. Rebecca was too young to appreciate the significance of being "just a mom." Like Deborah's calling to let God use her in the legal system, I had felt God's call to be a stay-at-home mother. Both of us were happy with—and challenged by—our choices.

Rebecca walked up as I pondered all of this. "What are you thinking about, Mom?"

"Nothing, really," I said with a smile. Then I gave her a big hug.

Many stay-at-home moms struggle with feelings of insignificance because they don't make money. If you do, you must keep in mind the priceless investment you're making in your family. Every sacrifice will yield dividends of love, security, and stability for your children.

Steps of Faith

Father, I'm so grateful that my worth isn't based upon the amount of money I make. May my standard always be Yours, not the world's.

131

Closet Clearance

"And why do you worry about clothes?"
MATTHEW 6:28

I went through this every spring. I had a closet jammed with clothes and nothing to wear. Why did I always make the same mistakes? I had skirts that didn't fit, tops that went with nothing, and a few dresses that were suited to no occasion in particular. This time I took out the clothes I did like. What did my favorite clothes have in common?

The most obvious thing was color. The clothes that I liked were pretty, basic colors or classic prints with simple, clean lines. They fit well, emphasizing what I liked about my figure and gliding over what I did not.

My favorite clothes were also versatile. The different pieces could be mixed and matched, and they still looked good. They could be updated with new accessories. Only a few were limited to specific occasions. And though I had bought some on sale, all were good quality. I realized that one well-made skirt that could make up five outfits was worth far more than five "value" skirts purchased on clearance.

I made a list of questions I would take along the next time I considered buying a garment: Is it a good buy, or merely cheap? What else do I have to buy to make it wearable? Does it fit well? And, most important, do I like it? Because if I didn't, it would just hang in my closet and gather dust.

From then on, I've bought far fewer clothes, but I wear all of them. My closet is clear and so is my conscience.

Does God really care about what you wear? Yes, because even what you wear reflects Him and His provision for you. *Decent, modest, durable,* and *not excessively extravagant* are qualities that please Him and can be applied to your wardrobe. So are *creativity, beauty,* and *variety.* Remember, color and texture were His ideas. Dowdy is not. However, the primary thing to remember when buying or making clothes is this: Don't dress to attract attention to your body. Dress to reflect what He has done in your soul and spirit.

Steps of Faith

Father, when I shop for clothes, please give me wisdom about what to choose and how much to spend. Help me find items that will reflect the inner beauty You have created in me.

Private Solo

Is anyone happy? Let him sing songs of praise.

JAMES 5:13

*S*inging—I was always singing. It was the balm Jesus had given me to heal a lot of wounds from my abusive childhood. I sang in our small church choir. One day the director of the choir gave me a tape and some sheet music. "Look this over. I think we'll do this in a couple of weeks, and I want you to be ready."

When I got home and listened, I was thrilled to find the tape was primarily for a solo, with the choir coming in only on the chorus. I had never sung a solo before, but here was my big break. I practiced for hours in the bathroom, using my toothbrush as my microphone. I pictured a standing ovation, recording contracts around the corner, visits to other churches, and eventually world tours. This song was just the beginning.

After rehearsal the next week, I told Richard, the director, that the song was "tight" (music lingo for perfect).

"Great. Now when the rest of the choir learns the chorus and June learns the solo, we'll be ready to go," he said.

"June is singing the solo?" I asked faintly.

"Of course. She's the only one who has a solo voice among the altos," he replied.

I was an alto, so what did that tell me? I was devastated. As I drove home crying, I felt His still, small voice ask, "Will you sing for just Me?"

"Yes, Jesus, I will." I sang "Trusting Jesus" for my audience of one. He loved my singing, but more than that, I knew He loved me.

If our self-esteem is based on our performance, we will forever be trying to earn God's favor. There comes a time when we must recognize that His love is not earnable—it just is.

Steps of Faith

Dear Jesus, I want to do something big for You. I don't know if it's so I'll somehow feel I'm worthy of Your love, or if I just want to show my gratefulness for what You've already done for me. Show me my heart and let my self-esteem be rooted in my value to You alone.

Awakenings

Those who sow in tears will reap with songs of joy.

PSALM 126:5

*T*oday was the first day that my first thoughts upon waking were something other than "Robert is dead." I had forgotten to close the blinds completely the night before. When I woke, the sight of the sunlight streaming into the room was so lovely that I rose to look out of the window and admire the beauty of the morning. Only then did I remember my new companion—grief.

At first I panicked. Was I forgetting Robert? Was he already receding into the haze of the past? A flood of memories brought a fresh wave of pain and a sharp, emphatic "no." But this morning was different.

The initial shock of Robert's death (he was only 55) had too soon given way to agonizing pain; each waking moment brought tides of realization that he was permanently and finally removed from my life. Then there was nothing but consuming anger—anger toward Robert for dying, and anger toward God for taking him from me and from his children and grandchildren.

Grief is still my companion and will be for some time to come. In a sense, I, too, have died and have been buried. But God, in His mercy, is breaking through to show me that with each passing day, I am still becoming a new creation. He has not removed my pain. But neither will He allow it to swallow up joy, hope, and love. In the end, He will prove a more faithful companion than grief.

Those who are in the process of grief may go through a time of questioning their faith in God—to them He seems an indifferent bystander to their suffering. At this time, what they need most from their friends is prayer, understanding, patience, and a willingness to listen.

Steps of Faith

Merciful Father, human beings chose to sin and therefore to die. You did not choose it for us. But in Your infinite love You have given us eternal life. Help me to celebrate and rejoice in that eternal life every day so that when I come face-to-face with death, I will not lose my hope.

Goodbye, Security

Therefore do not worry about tomorrow,
for tomorrow will worry about itself.

MATTHEW 6:34

$\mathcal{I}$'m sorry, but I have to let you go," the crusty old city editor said. "You can clear out your desk today and collect your paycheck on your way out." Stunned, I turned away quickly, hoping to escape his office before tears came.

I quickly packed notebooks and file folders into a box and headed out the door. My heart ached. My head throbbed. My stomach knotted. I felt miserable. All I wanted to do was go home and have a good cry and feel sorry for myself.

Outside, walking toward my car, I started to pray: "Dear God, what am I going to do? What if I can't find another job? How will I pay my rent? Why did this happen? Please help me!"

Without warning, a tiny kitten darted under my feet. I tripped and fell, the contents of the box spilling onto the pavement. I didn't know whether to laugh or cry. The mischievous kitten licked my hand. He wore no collar and looked hungry. Impulsively, I tossed the gray ball of fur into the box.

"You made me smile, you little rascal!" I said. "Hey! That's what I'll call you—Rascal! You're welcome to come home with me, Rascal, but I can't promise much."

The kitten looked at me with complete trust.

Right then, I knew I would be okay if I trusted the Lord to provide for me the same way the kitten looked to me to provide for it. The Lord had begun to answer my prayers. He'd sent Rascal, and He'd reminded me to hold on to my sense of humor.

Now, if I hurried, I still had time to call about a few jobs.

If God feeds the birds and finds homes for lost kittens, why do we worry when circumstances, such as the loss of a job, change our lives? God has promised to always take care of us.

Steps of Faith

Dear God, thank You for taking care of me. Thank You for sending humor (and kittens!) at just the right time. Help me to trust You more every day.

A Second Wind

*Record my lament; list my tears on your scroll—
are they not in your record?*

PSALM 56:8

*R*ay's face glistened with sweat. He leaned against the frame of the front door, the thin T-shirt clinging to his portly frame.

"I think that's about got it," he said between heaving breaths.

"Why don't you sit down for a few minutes? You know what the doctor—"

"Won't you ever stop?" Ray interrupted. "Nag, nag, nag. I can take care of myself!"

"I'm sure you can. It's just unusual to see you work so hard around the house," I retorted.

"See ya." He slammed the door.

Twenty-two years of my life devoted to what . . . a fantasy that life would be fair, would be good, would be joyful? Ha! I thought being a Christian exempted you from this kind of pain. We were a Christian family. What happened?

Mundane living happened. Less and less communication happened. And finally divorce happened. I was perplexed and crushed. My dreams of a happy marriage and family just backed out the driveway in a U-Haul.

I crashed facedown onto the sofa. I began to cry. I cried so hard my chest hurt. I knew why. My heart was broken. Increasing my agony was knowing that I would have to talk to Ray again on the weekend to arrange for him to have the children. I was constantly going to see the object of my grief and disillusionment. *Will it ever end?* I wondered. Though this new place felt horribly unfamiliar, I somehow knew as long as I held onto the hand of my Savior, I'd be okay. He would not leave me alone in this wilderness of fear.

And He didn't.

Jesus never said it would be easy. He promised us He would walk beside us through the valleys, never leaving or forsaking us. With His help, we can overcome anything in this world, even the tragedy of a broken marriage.

Steps of Faith

Dear Jesus, life doesn't make sense to me right now. I don't know if it ever will again. Help me keep my eyes on You so I can finish this marathon of a race. Please give me a second wind. I need it.

Friendship's Sorrow

When you walk through the fire, you will not be burned; the
flames will not set you ablaze.

ISAIAH 43:2

I grew up hearing the popular rhyme, "Make new friends, but keep the old. Those are silver, these are gold." I learned through my school days that friendships come and go, like the seasons. As an adult, I discovered circles of friends. I no longer had one best friend, rather several in one group and more in another group. I moved across the country and found new friends slowly replacing those so far away.

However, nothing prepared me for the pain and anguish of losing a friendship when I was not ready to let go. Marie was a kindred spirit, the dearest, closest friend of my life for 12 years. Although I was married and raising a family and Marie was single, we found many things to share.

Then, quite unexpectedly, she began seeing a man who did not know the Lord. She seemed desperate for the relationship and would not listen to my warnings. In the end, she began living with this man and eventually became pregnant.

Marie pushed me away although I wanted to love her and to show compassion. Her own shame kept us from continuing the relationship. Not long ago, she moved a thousand miles away and never even said goodbye.

Confused, I pleaded with the Lord for some comfort, some sign of hope for my friend's restoration both to God and to me. He gently reminded me that Marie has made her choice for now.

The pain, even as I write this, is suffocating. Losing such a friendship would be unbearable except for the comfort the Lord brings.

Have you lost a special friend? Have you continued to pray? Consider writing her a letter, one that may never be mailed but that would allow you to pour your grief out on paper.

Steps of Faith

Dear God, please fill the empty places in my heart that my friend used to occupy. Help me to lean into Your arms and experience Your love and comfort in a new way.

My Barnabas

*When [Barnabas] arrived and saw the evidence
of the grace of God, he was glad and encouraged them all to
remain true to the Lord with all their hearts.*

ACTS 11:23

T
U
E
S
D
A
Y

*M*andisa and her family left Johannesburg during the height of the terrorism and violence that ravaged South Africa in the eighties. Mandisa's father, Aquinas, was a minister of a small church outside of the capital. After seeing churches burned to the ground, other ministers crucified, and one of his sons brutally executed, he, his wife, and their seven surviving children fled to the United States.

Mandisa, the oldest of the children, got a job answering telephones in the customer-service department of a large department store. Her cubicle was next to mine. I could hear her soothing voice as she politely dealt with irate customers. Just listening to her inspired me to treat each caller with the same gentleness.

Mandisa and I discovered we shared a common love for the Lord and our families. We soon became friends and prayer partners. And the more I learned of Mandisa's life in South Africa, the more amazed I was at her demeanor. She was an encourager, always looking for the best in people and in situations—and praising God every step of the way.

God used Mandisa to help me understand more about His love. Because of her unbridled trust in God, along with her bottomless reservoir of joy, I began to understand my own value in God's eyes. Mandisa isn't shy about walking arm in arm with me, or giving me a big hug when she senses I need it. And she never gives me a word of encouragement without pointing me to Jesus. She usually says, "Just remember you're the little lost and wounded lamb the Shepherd has found. He's so happy He has you back in His arms where you are safe from harm."

His name was Joseph, but the apostles called him Barnabas, meaning "son of encouragement." Barnabas had the gift of exhortation. He knew when an individual or a group of people needed to be encouraged—and hundreds came to Christ because of him. Are you a Barnabas?

Steps of Faith

Gracious Lord, You are the author of encouragement. Every time I give or receive it, I know it ultimately comes from You. You know just when it is needed the most. Bless You. And as I go through this life, help me to be a "daughter of encouragement" to hurting people around me.

Please Forgive Me

Above all, love each other deeply, because love
covers over a multitude of sins.

1 PETER 4:8

*H*orrified, I watched Marsha's face turn bright red before she exploded in my direction. "How dare you talk about my child like that?" she shrieked. Her rage produced a fury unlike anything I'd ever seen before. I was shocked, paralyzed. I couldn't think what to do or say as she screamed at me for several minutes. I glanced around the table; everyone was frozen.

We'd been playing Scrabble: Marsha and Pete, Lee and Warren, my husband and I. Our children were watching a video upstairs. What had I said to set her off? I remembered saying something about her son being a strong-willed child.

Her husband, Pete, was trying to calm her down, but I could see he was gathering their things to leave. I tried to approach Marsha, but she wouldn't let me near her.

In another few minutes, Pete had his little family out the door. We prayed for Marsha before Lee and Warren left. Everyone reassured me that my comment had been innocent and that she had overreacted.

"She'll call you tomorrow to apologize, you'll see," Lee encouraged.

But Marsha didn't call the next day or the next. *She's probably embarrassed,* I thought. A full week had gone by when the Lord impressed me to call her and ask her forgiveness.

Why, Lord? I argued. *She's the one who should call me.*

Still, I made the call. Marsha answered and in a few minutes, everything was right between us. She never did ask my forgiveness, but our friendship is more important than who was right or wrong.

When we make reconciliation more important than being right, we open the door for forgiveness and healing. Ask yourself what is more important, having the last word or saving the relationship. Then practice saying, "Please forgive me."

Steps of Faith

Dear Lord, thank You for showing us Your grace through forgiveness. Help me to humble myself and bring reconciliation about in a broken relationship. Thank You for reconciling us to the Father and to one another.

Little Things Count

Parents are the pride of their children.

PROVERBS 17:6

*M*aggie woke to the smell of something burning. She jumped out of bed, grabbed her robe, and ran downstairs to the kitchen. Her seven-year-old daughter, Ruth, was standing in the middle of the kitchen with oven mitts on. Some blackened toast popped out of the toaster, there was blackened bacon draining on a half-roll of paper towels, the dog was licking something that looked like raw egg off the floor, and there appeared to be jelly in Ruth's hair.

"Surprise, Mommy," yelled Ruth. "I knew you were tired so I made you breakfast!"

Maggie looked at her daughter. She looked at the kitchen and at the dirty dishes in the sink. It would take an hour to clean up the mess, and Maggie didn't have time to do that and get ready to leave on time. She didn't relish the prospect of facing this after she got home from work tonight.

Ruth handed her a cup of instant coffee—made with unground coffee beans. "We're out of sugar," she said.

Maggie made a decision that moment. "Did my big, grown-up girl really do all of this by herself? I'm so proud of you!" Maggie exclaimed as she hugged her daughter. "In fact, I think it's time you started to learn how to help me in the kitchen. Would you like to do that?"

"Can I really?" Ruth beamed.

"As soon as we get home tonight," Maggie promised. "Now let's eat fast and get ready for school."

Maggie sighed. She was already tired, but she was glad she hadn't fussed about the mess. She had done the right thing.

Nothing builds a child's self-esteem like doing something to please his or her parents. Even when you must give criticism, try to say something positive as well. Your child needs to know that he or she really does have your approval.

Steps of Faith

Dear Lord, You know that raising children isn't easy. I can't possibly do everything right all the time, but please, help me to teach my child that her worth is centered in Jesus. Help me to weigh words of criticism and correction carefully.

Exodus and Easter

Your statutes are my heritage forever;
they are the joy of my heart.

PSALM 119:111

*A*s Jewish believers in Jesus as our Messiah and Lord, my husband and I feel it's important to give our children an awareness of the heritage of our people. So, in addition to celebrating the resurrection of Jesus (or *Yeshua,* as He is called in Hebrew) on Easter Sunday, we celebrate Passover as well.

To most Jewish families, Passover is the biggest holiday of the year—it's the Christmas of the Jewish calendar. In the Old Testament, God commanded the Israelites to remember how He freed them from slavery and brought them out of Egypt by keeping the Passover for seven days.

The first day of Passover is a special Sabbath which we observe by having a *Seder,* or Passover dinner. It's a fun, festive meal with traditional holiday foods like lamb, matzo (bread made without yeast; during the seven days, no foods made with leaven are to be eaten) and haroset (a mixture of chopped fruit and nuts). Before and after the meal itself, we read the *Hagadah,* which tells the story of Moses leading the Israelites to freedom. Everyone gets to take part in the reading—the kids love it.

In our family, Jesus is the focal point of our Seder. In so many ways, He is symbolized in the story of the Passover. He is the one who set us free from the bondage of sin. Just as the Israelites marked their homes with the blood of a lamb, so God has "marked" us with the blood of Christ. And as we eat our Seder meal, we remember Jesus as He ate His last Seder with His disciples before He went to His death. We eat and drink in remembrance of our heritage and in remembrance of Him.

This year as you celebrate the resurrection of our Lord, remember to pray that our Jewish brothers and sisters will come to know Jesus as their Messiah. And, if you have the opportunity, try to attend a Messianic Seder. It's an experience you won't forget.

Steps of Faith

Father, I thank You that You have remained faithful to Your people over the centuries. Let me never take for granted Your long-suffering patience, Your grace, and Your willingness to die on the cross even while we were still sinners.

A Time to Mourn

Rejoice with those who rejoice; mourn with those who mourn.

ROMANS 12:15

*F*or Barbara, the news brought both tremendous relief and bitter disappointment. Her surgery had been successful; they had removed all traces of cancer. But she had had to undergo a hysterectomy. Now her hope of bearing a child was gone—forever.

Barbara accepted her situation with a readiness that secretly amazed her friends, cheerfully brushing off condolences with the assertion that she was happy just to be alive.

At home, her friend Joan came regularly to visit and help with meals and housework. As they sat in the garden in the cool of the day, Barbara explained her plan of action. "The first thing is to get through chemotherapy and recovery. And then I plan to plunge back into work with a vengeance."

Joan hesitated a moment before saying, "You have to give yourself some time to grieve, Barbara."

"Now you know I'm not about to sit around wallowing in self-pity. What good would that do? It won't change a thing."

"I don't mean that. You've experienced a deep loss. You can't avoid the pain by bypassing the whole thing. It will only delay the process."

Barbara was silent. Then, haltingly, she spoke. "I'm afraid if I start thinking about it and asking God, 'Why?' I'll fall to pieces. I'd rather just accept it and go on."

"I'm not suggesting that you focus on it or question God," said Joan. "Just allow yourself some time alone to cry and to pour out your heart to Him. Then He can give you acceptance and the ability to go on. God's grace is sufficient."

Grief is much more than a simple emotion or even an experience. It's a season of life. Nobody likes to talk about it or consider going through a time of grief, yet it's something we all will face. Understanding the phases of grief will help us draw more deeply on God's strength.

Steps of Faith

Father, I confess that I am afraid of grief—afraid of losing someone I love, my health, or my dreams. But when this season of my life comes, I will look to You for strength. Your grace will be sufficient.

Our Journey

Though he brings grief, he will show compassion,
so great is his unfailing love.

LAMENTATIONS 3:32

*H*ow I miss her weekend phone calls, her laughter, her touch, her genuine concern for my family. We shared the joys of watching our children grow as well as the sorrows of life-threatening visits to the hospital. She was always there to hold my hand and to touch my heart.

Carol had a long battle with cancer. She fought it with such grace, always believing she would be victorious. The last few weeks of her life she blessed all who came to visit with a smile. She had words of encouragement for her teenage boys and devoted husband. She seized the beauty of each moment.

Carol and I grew up together, and now we were spending the last days of her life together. *How could our lives have passed so quickly?* I thought. It was a sad time but a precious one, which I was privileged to be part of.

One warm July afternoon, I commented, "You smell like a beautiful rose." Carol loved tending her flower garden, filled with fragrance and color. She smiled gently at me, closed her eyes, and lapsed into a coma moments later. The next morning she slipped peacefully into the arms of our Savior.

Carol is in a beautiful place now. Those of us left behind have cherished memories we strive to keep alive. We are left with an emptiness that only God can heal, in time.

Do you miss someone you loved deeply? Has the Lord given you a memory, such as a beautiful rose, that will bring your loved one into a tender place in your heart today? God promises to bestow on us "the oil of gladness instead of mourning . . . a planting of the LORD for the display of his splendor" (Isaiah 61:3).

Steps of Faith

Father in heaven, thank You for providing me with a lovely way to remember my precious friend. Thank You, Lord, for giving us hope through the resurrection of Your Son, Jesus, in an inheritance that can never perish.

My Nanna

[She] who walks with the wise grows wise.

PROVERBS 13:20

For 45 years my grandmother ("Nanna") lived three blocks from the university from which she, my late grandfather, father, uncles, and aunt graduated. It had been my dream to continue the family legacy at that university and at the same time live for awhile in my father's hometown.

Right before my freshman year, I learned that I wouldn't be able to stay in the dorm like I'd planned. Nanna offered to let me stay with her; however, as much as I loved her, at 18 the thought of living with an elderly relative didn't thrill me. I'd been anticipating a social life filled with dates, parties, and nights on the town. When I mentioned this to my mother, she wisely told me that it would be just for the fall semester. By January, I would be living in the dorm with girls my own age. *Okay, I can handle that,* I thought.

Life with Nanna was a pleasant surprise. She loved having me with her, but went out of her way to stay out of my way. No curfews. No sermons. She'd just say, "I'll do the praying, and you enjoy your youth!"

In January there were still no dorm rooms available—but I wasn't disappointed. The party scene had gotten old fast, and now studies had top priority. And there was no place more peaceful than Nanna's. It was about that time I began to realize I'd never move into the dorm.

Six years later I had earned my bachelor's degree and was finishing up my master's in education. Nanna and I were still together, and I knew I was a better woman because of it. I couldn't imagine how I would have survived without her steadfast presence and wisdom. She had comforted me through a broken engagement and prayed for me through countless midterm and final exams. Sure, I had several friends my own age, but no one like my Nanna.

What kind of relationship do you have with your grandmothers or any other older woman? A relationship with an older woman can bring priceless blessings into your life. Her wisdom and experience are worth their weight in gold, just as your friendship will be to her.

Steps of Faith

Father of all, thank You for the older women in my life. I am a wiser woman because of every one of them. Bless each one in a special way today. Help me to heed their wise counsel and example and to be able to demonstrate it to those younger women who are watching me today.

Force of Habit

*Let us not be like others, who are asleep, but let us
be alert and self-controlled.*

1 THESSALONIANS 5:6

I don't know how it happened . . . well, that's not true.
Actually I know exactly how it happened. I was doing so well; it was
only 11:30 and I had already checked off half the things on my to-
do list.

Then I flipped on the TV to catch the noon news. Immediately
afterward was a promo for *The Proud and the Pathetic*. Now, I am not
by any means hooked on the soaps. I mean, the plots are so predictable; the dialogue is so ridiculous. If I watch them occasionally,
it's just for the laughs. But I remembered that today was the day that
Tiffany, who had had amnesia for two months, was supposed to find
out her true identity. That would be a hoot. As soon as I saw that
part, off would go the TV.

Well, you know the rest. Two soap operas, three talk shows, and
a large bag of potato chips later, there I was, still on the sofa. The
beds weren't made, the clothes weren't washed, and dinner was still
in the freezer. I felt disgusted with myself, and I had a feeling that
Jim would share my sentiment when he came home. I had wasted
another day.

What I hate most is the fact that I don't even enjoy watching TV.
After spending a day on all that trash, I feel so depressed. Then I feel
even more depressed about not getting anything done around the
house. I'm not a lazy person. I want to be available to minister God's
love. I've asked for God's forgiveness so many times, I don't feel I can
face Him anymore.

Sometimes the sheer force of habit is so powerful that we feel
helpless against it. That is never the case. If you've tried and failed
to break your habit through willpower, attack it directly. Start by
removing the temptation from your home.

Steps of Faith

*Lord, I've had to ask Your forgiveness for the habit of _____
so many times that I feel ashamed. But I refuse to give up. Please
forgive me once more, and help me to grow in strength so that I can
persevere in conquering my bad habit. Help me to put You first in
my life.*

Unmet Needs

*If you do not do what is right, sin is crouching at your door;
it desires to have you, but you must master it.*

GENESIS 4:7

You have the voice of an angel," he said in all sincerity.

"Oh, Elliot, you probably say that to every girl in the choir," I bubbled.

"Only those with wings," he laughed. "Say, you want to grab a cup of coffee between services?" he asked innocently.

"Sure," I said, mesmerized by his clear blue eyes.

Over the next several months we shared a lot of coffee between services. He listened to me and thought my opinions interesting and intelligent. I couldn't wait for choir rehearsals and Sundays.

There was only one thing wrong—we were both married. In my marriage I no longer felt Jim listened to me or thought my opinion was worth considering. To have someone fill this need felt like eating a banquet when I was used to bread crumbs.

Fortunately, a good friend in choir saw what was happening and warned me of the danger. She suggested I see a counselor. It was hard to go to the counselor because I knew she would tell me to give up the "banquet."

She did, and encouraged me to bring my husband into counseling and tell him what I needed from him. It was difficult, but two years later my marriage is once again on solid ground. My husband is aware of my feelings and works hard to be affectionate and attentive. And I concentrate on making my relationship with my husband the best it can be.

In our neediness sometimes we find ourselves doing things that feel good but aren't necessarily right. Are you careful to protect yourself with clear boundaries from impending danger?

Steps of Faith

Dear Provider, though intellectually I know that You will provide all my needs according to Your riches in glory, my flesh still craves immediate fulfillment. Thanks for sending a friend who gave me the word in season. It was only by Your grace that I didn't really blow it.

The Transition

*I said, "I have labored to no purpose; I have spent my strength
in vain and for nothing. Yet what is due me is in the LORD's
hand, and my reward is with my God."*

ISAIAH 49:4

*B*rian and I married at 18 and had to work to pay for college. We were so focused on earning our degrees that we spent every free moment between our jobs studying. Only God knows where we got the stamina.

We graduated together, and I immediately went to work while Brian faced several more years of medical school. My passion to succeed ran higher than ever in my new job. I worked overtime almost every day, but I loved every second of it. I had a purpose, an identity, and I was the one making the money.

Years later, after Brian had begun practicing medicine, we decided to start a family. By this time I had moved into management and was making a fabulous salary. The day I discovered I was pregnant I felt not joy but ambivalence. *What have I done?* I silently wondered.

After much prayer, Brian and I agreed that I would stay home with the baby for at least the first two years. But after the excitement of having a new baby had worn off and reality had set in, my home began to feel like my personal prison. I grieved over the loss of my career and identity.

Then the day my daughter, Katharine, smiled at me for the first time, my heart almost burst. She knew me. She needed me. She was a part of me. I knew I was where God wanted me to be for that time in my life. And three years and another baby later, I have grown to love my career at home. I have opportunities to use my abilities in ways I could never have imagined, so for this season of life I don't need professional prestige.

Transitioning from a full-time career outside the home to full-time motherhood in the home can be a difficult, even traumatic, watershed for some women. If you are facing this transition, ask God to grant you an extra measure of grace to embrace your new career as a full-time mother.

Steps of Faith

*Almighty Father, change has never come easy for me, especially
when I feel like the work I've done establishing myself in one situation will all be for nothing. Father, I trust that You will use that work
and give me faith to trust You with my future.*

My New Life

*Just as Christ was raised from the dead through the
glory of the Father, we too may live a new life.*

ROMANS 6:4

*W*hen I walked into the banquet room, everyone immediately fell silent. Other village people were permitted to come in to watch the festivities from a distance, but I was not welcome there. The host was one of the most prominent religious leaders in the city, and I—well, they all knew what I was.

But I knew He was my only chance. I might never get such a chance again, for everywhere He went, people thronged to Him. I was desperate.

When I saw Him, I could not hold back my tears. I fell at His feet and poured my jar of perfume on them. Some of my tears spilled on His feet. Having nothing else, I dried them with my hair. Anyone else would not have let me do such a thing, but I knew He would not despise me.

The host remarked that He must not really be a prophet, or He would have known what kind of woman I was. But He did know. And when He spoke to me, there was no condemnation in His voice. He looked into my eyes, not with a haughty stare of contempt, but with love. He knew all about me.

But what astonished me most was that He shamed Simon the Pharisee for being a discourteous host—He actually defended me in front of all those people! I will never forget His words to me that evening: "Your sins are forgiven." I can't explain what it meant. The people in the room continued to whisper about me. But I don't blame them. How could they understand? Such righteous people as they could have no idea how it felt to have the weight of sin lifted from their hearts.

The heart that loves the most is the heart that knows it is forgiven. Read Luke 7:36-50. As you do, try to put yourself in the place of Simon the Pharisee. Would you consider yourself to be like the man who had the greater debt or the small one?

Steps of Faith

*Gracious Father, I know that Your forgiveness covers all of my sins,
but it did not come cheap. I treasure the new life which Your resurrection power has enabled me to live.*

Don't You Know?

Do you not know? Have you not heard?
The LORD is the everlasting God, the Creator of the ends
of the earth. He will not grow tired or weary, and his under-
standing no one can fathom.

ISAIAH 40:28

Every summer my nephew, Andrew, spends about a month with my family out in the country. Andrew is an extremely bright boy whose parents don't attend church. However, he goes with us during his visits.

I try to take advantage of the summer break to encourage my children to continuing learning. They participate in the library's summer reading program, and I keep lots of arts and crafts supplies on hand for rainy days. Their "masterpieces" testify that creativity is alive and well.

Andrew jumps in and enjoys every moment with us, especially the trips to the natural history and space museums in the city. Andrew was ten when he first began to seriously question origins. The Sunday school class he and my son, Buddy, were in that summer studied Genesis and the creation of the universe. Andrew was full of questions. Several times, to my amusement, I overheard him asking Buddy about what they'd learned, and Buddy would answer impatiently, "Don't you know that God created the universe? . . . You've never heard that He did it in six days? . . . It's in the Bible."

Last summer, when Andrew was 14, he prayed to receive Christ. Later he told me that he wants to become a scientist, one who approaches science from a biblical perspective. He wants to spend his life studying God's creation and then teaching others about it.

When I asked him what had influenced this decision, he smiled at me and said, "Don't you know? It was every summer I spent here with you."

Have you ever considered how the time you spend with your children is encouraging their growth and influencing their futures? Especially the time spent teaching them about their Creator, who loves with infinite love. That is an investment that will yield returns "no one can fathom."

Steps of Faith

My Creator and Lord, there is so much to know, and I feel so limited. I confess, though, that many of those limits are self-imposed. Create in me, Lord, a thirst for knowledge and understanding of Your ways. And may that thirst be contagious to my children and others.

M
O
N
D
A
Y

149

The Family Priest

Fathers, do not exasperate your children; instead, bring them up in the training and instruction of the Lord.

EPHESIANS 6:4

*H*ank was a Christian. I was a Christian. We both professed to believe and obey the same Bible. And that Bible exhorts every husband to be the spiritual leader of the home. So when we got married, I just expected Hank to do his duty.

No such luck. The first time I brought my Bible to breakfast for our morning devotion, he said he didn't have time. (But he did manage to finish the sports section of the newspaper.) Later that evening he said he just wanted to relax and watch the news (and then a three-hour baseball game). Over time I discovered that just getting him out of bed on Sunday morning in time for the 11 A.M. service bordered on miraculous.

I noticed there were many of us "married-single" women sitting in the pews. Three of us were in my Sunday school class—the one for young "couples." Sara, Becky, and I were all married to Christian men who neglected their spiritual responsibilities to their families.

"Bruce can recite Ephesians 5:22 backwards in his sleep," Becky said, the sarcasm rising in her voice. "But he ignores the verses that follow. He doesn't realize that I'm supposed to 'submit to my husband as to the Lord' because God and I have entrusted my spiritual well-being to him. And the children are more confused than I am. They see their parents operating under two totally different sets of priorities. It's so frustrating!"

Becky's words haunted me for weeks. Hank and I don't have children, but we plan to. Things would have to change, but how?

Most Christian men want to be the spiritual leaders of their homes, but they have been inadequately prepared. Here's how you can help your husband. First, pray Colossians 1:9-11 for him every day. Second, ask your church to develop programs to train men to be spiritual leaders. Third, let your husband determine the time, place, and subject for family devotions. You can offer to find the resources that will make it easier for him.

Steps of Faith

Father, my husband is one of Your greatest gifts to me. Help me to help him be all that he is supposed to be. And when he seems to neglect his spiritual duties to our family, speak directly to his heart or use another man to encourage him. Help me to not nag him.

Facing It

Dear friends, do not be surprised at the
painful trial you are suffering.

1 PETER 4:12

*L*es walked into the kitchen mid-afternoon. He held a stack of files and his briefcase. Staring out the window, he said, "They just wouldn't listen, wouldn't even try to understand. I can't compromise what I know to be right. Peg, I quit."

"Honey, I'm so sorry," I sympathized. His pained expression was killing me. "Here, let me fix you something to eat. You'll feel better."

"No, I'm going to make a few phone calls and then take a nap." He went back toward our bedroom.

But I opened the fridge and saw the cheesecake. I needed some consolation. So I sat down and polished it off. One half of a cheesecake later, I felt somewhat better. Why? Eating was my way of dealing with my feelings about any problem. It seemed so dumb. I realized that I hated feeling anything unless it was pleasant. I was carrying around years of ungrieved pain that I would swallow back down with another piece of cheesecake, another bag of french fries, another doughnut. I felt hopelessly trapped in this cycle. Would it ever end?

Admitting my problem was half the battle. Fighting my pride was the other half. Mustering all the humility that was in me, I began going to a 12-step eating disorder meeting that met at a large church. I found I was not alone and that I needed God's help to teach me a new way of coping with my problems. There was hope for me yet.

Many addictions develop as ways of facing the suffering in our lives. Yet suffering is very much a part of God's plan for us. If we do everything in our power to deny our addictions, are we keeping ourselves from the necessary valleys He would have us walk through as we grow in Christ?

Steps of Faith

Dear Jesus, I've cried a lot over the last couple of years. But I've eaten a lot less, and I feel Your sweet presence like never before. I've gotten to know You a lot better since giving up my addiction. Thank You for helping me face it.

W
E
D
N
E
S
D
A
Y

A Mother's Sacrifice

When [Moses' mother] could hide him no longer,
she got a papyrus basket for him and coated it with tar
and pitch. Then she placed the child in it and put it among
the reeds along the bank of the Nile.

EXODUS 2:3

*E*very boy that is born you must throw into the Nile, but let every girl live." So decreed Pharaoh (Exodus 1:22), and thousands of Hebrew baby boys died and thousands of mothers screamed and fainted with grief. That was fine with Pharaoh. Not only was he making an extravagant offering to the crocodile gods of the Nile, but he was also breaking the spirit of these Hebrews. He believed this would teach them not to have any more babies—or believe in their impotent Hebrew God, a god of slaves.

But the Hebrews cried out to Jehovah God more than ever, and had more babies than ever. Jochabed and her husband, Amram, were among them, and God heard their cries. He gave them a "fine" son, and they were able to hide him for three months. Jochabed nursed him, sang him to sleep, felt his little fingers wrap around one of hers, and saw his first smile. She bonded completely with her tiny son.

Eventually they could hide Moses no longer. So Jochabed—not an Egyptian soldier—put her son in the Nile. Did she weep? Was she frightened? Did she pray for her little son? Probably. And God honored her faith. Pharaoh's daughter found Moses and kept him as her own. Moses' sister, Miriam, who had been watching in the reeds, offered to get a Hebrew wet nurse. "Yes, go," the princess said, and Miriam ran to Jochabed (Exodus 2:5-9).

Picture the joy of that moment. Tears of grief turned to tears of joy. Jochabed must have wondered if she was dreaming as she pulled Moses to her breast and her pounding heart.

Jochabed's courage and faith in God brought blessings and deliverance for herself and the whole nation of Israel. Imagine what God can do today through one Christian woman who protects her child from the evils of the world and sacrifices that child into God's almighty hands.

Steps of Faith

Jehovah God, motherhood has opened up a whole new realm of fears. How I worry about my children sometimes. Yet I know that no matter how powerful the world's influence is upon them, You are much more powerful. Thank You for Jochabed. Help me to learn from her.

An Honor to Honor

If a widow has children or grandchildren, these should learn first of all to put their religion into practice by caring for their own family and so repaying their parents and grandparents.

1 TIMOTHY 5:4

*B*efore November 10, 1976, I was living the American dream: I had a loving, successful husband, five beautiful children, and a home in the country surrounded by family members and lifelong friends. Then my second child, Scott, broke his neck and was paralyzed from the shoulders down. He needed help bathing and dressing, and I was often either wiping up urine and feces or being covered with them.

In 1987 Scott married and moved out. Only my youngest remained, and she was in college. I was free—at least for a while. Just a few months later, my mother had a severe stroke. She moved into our home, where I bathed her, helped her dress, and coped with her incontinence.

By the time she died in 1990, I was so exhausted and depressed it was a relief to see her go—at least for a while. Then the grief and guilt came crashing in. However, before I could let it overwhelm me, my mother-in-law, Sarah, began to get feeble. She now has a live-in companion during the week, but every weekend her four children, who all live in the area, rotate keeping her. She needs help bathing and dressing, and often she, too, is incontinent. We don't know how much longer she will live.

The last 20 years haven't exactly been carefree. Sometimes it seemed Satan was whispering, "God is punishing you," and often I believed the lie. But in 1991 God sent a friend who reminded me that I was honoring my mother and mother-in-law by doing what I could to repay them for all they had done for me. God would give me the strength I needed and turn the burden into joy.

She was right. God encouraged me through prayer until I can say that it has been an honor to honor my parents in this way.

Have you and your parents discussed how they want to be taken care of in their old age? Reassure them that, because they are your parents, they will never be a burden.

Steps of Faith

Dear Lord, as my parents age, help me to be mindful that as I've grown independent of them, they may yet grow dependent upon me. Give me grace and strength to honor them to their very last day.

Praying for the Band

*I tell you that if two of you on earth agree about anything
you ask for, it will be done for you by my Father in heaven.*

MATTHEW 18:19

*M*y husband and two of his friends have played together in a Christian band for several years. They are usually on the road three weekends of every month, along with the wives and sometimes the children.

Some people think it's an exciting and glamorous way to live. That's true about 5 percent of the time—the rest is hard work, endless rehearsals, boring travel, and a constant spiritual battle. However, our reward is seeing hundreds of kids come to Christ through the music and ministry of the band.

From the beginning, Nora, Sue, and I have prayed for the band and its audiences. It was clear Satan hated the band and its impact. It seemed at least one of the families was always under attack; sometimes all three were.

Last summer the guys were at the point of splitting up. There was stress, tension, and anger that wasn't being handled in a godly way. In desperation Nora, Sue, and I met one day for lunch and prayed for almost two hours. By the end of the week, everything was calm.

This opened our eyes to the power of our prayers when we stood together for our men and their ministry. We needed to do this regularly! But that was impossible. I work full-time, both Sue and Nora homeschool their children, and we live several miles from each other. We agreed to pray about it. Gently, God gave us the solution. Every Thursday at noon—whether at home or the office—we pray 30 minutes for the band's ministry, each band member, each family, and all of our engagements for the month.

What a difference prayer makes! Satan still hates us, but the Spirit of power that surrounds the band testifies of God's pleasure and protection that He has promised us in His Word.

It's said there's nothing more powerful than a wife's prayers for her husband. Do you pray regularly for your husband, his work, and his ministry? Get into the habit of praying for him at a certain time of day and then periodically remind him. He may start praying for you then, too!

Steps of Faith

*Faithful Father, thank You for my dear husband. Guard his heart
and mind, bless his health, and protect him from temptation. Draw
us closer to You and each other every day.*

Yours . . . Mine . . . Ours

Like arrows in the hands of a warrior are sons born in one's youth. Blessed is the man whose quiver is full of them.

PSALM 127:4,5

Linda never dreamed she'd raise children other than her own three. But then Linda never imagined that her first marriage would end and that she would later remarry—Greg, a man with two children of his own.

Linda and Greg spent hours talking and praying about this decision. They sought the counsel of their pastor, who gave some solid advice. He then warned them to expect a five- or six-year transition before they and the children would fully adapt to the new living arrangements.

Several months before the wedding, Greg and Linda decided to build a new home of their own. They let all five children take part in the planning, making it "their" house. It marked a new beginning for the seven of them, and gave them an opportunity to spend time together and get better acquainted.

After the wedding, disciplining a stepchild became inevitable. Greg and Linda tried to take it slowly at first, treating the stepchild the way a babysitter would, leaving the natural parents as final authorities. Instead of trying to step into the shoes of the children's absent biological parents, Greg and Linda eased into their roles by acting more like an uncle and aunt to their stepchildren.

They began celebrating birthdays and holidays one week early so the new family could spend the entire day together. Then the children could spend the "real" day with their other parents.

Greg and Linda's new family is still in transition, but they continue to trust God as He teaches them patience, love, and most of all, flexibility.

There are three ways to develop a healthy blended family. First, mutual acceptance is only possible when you get to know each other. Second, if possible, work with all parents involved to establish an authority system of consistent rules, limits, and freedoms. Finally, new vacation sites, family activities, and special events will establish your new family's identity.

Steps of Faith

Eternal Father of all, I thank You for the privilege of being a part of Your everlasting family. It is the most blended family in the universe! For our earthly families, blended or otherwise, I ask You to bless and protect them from the enemy's attempts to rip them asunder.

Caregiver

*Honor your father and your mother, so that you may live
long in the land the LORD your God is giving you.*

EXODUS 20:12

*A*t age 38 Momma suddenly found herself a widow with three children. She had no marketable skill, so she enrolled in beauty school and eventually opened shop in a little room at the side of our house. She worked hard and put all three of us through college.

Momma had always been a fiercely independent, strong-willed woman. And when she wasn't working, she sure knew how to have fun.

After I married, Momma was a pillar of strength for me while I was rearing my five children. We didn't have much money then. I can't count all the Sundays she fed us dinner and sent us home with leftovers that would feed an army.

I suppose I thought Momma was invincible. But in 1984, after her first stroke, and then a massive heart attack a year later, I was forced to confront her mortality and vulnerability. It made me sad.

At the time my "nest" was emptying. My husband and I had the means to take care of Momma and asked her to move in with us. She refused. Then in late 1987 she almost died in her bed after another stroke. This time we all agreed—it was time for her to move in with us.

Momma's condition continued to worsen. She could no longer fix herself a sandwich or get a glass of water because she couldn't remember how—as though portions of her memory tape had been erased.

I hurt for her and for myself. I was losing my mother.

Few of us have the foresight to anticipate or prepare for the adjustment of caring for our aging parents. Have you? During this transition, you will need to 1) give yourself permission to grieve over the loss in the life of your parent, 2) accept his or her level of ability, 3) love him or her in a healthy, balanced way. A sense of powerlessness may make you feel angry and frustrated, but you must remember that you cannot reverse the effects of old age. Your aging parent needs your smiles, hugs, and listening ears, along with your prayers and the comfort of God's Word (Isaiah 46:4).

Steps of Faith

Glorious Father, thank You for my parents. They have sacrificed so much for me. Give me the strength and grace to know how to best care for them when they can no longer care for themselves.

Pillar of Strength

If a widow has children or grandchildren,
these should learn first of all to put their religion into
practice by caring for their own family and so
repaying their parents and grandparents.

1 TIMOTHY 5:4

*M*y sadness for Momma eventually turned to depression and guilt. I was torn between my duties as a wife, mother, grandmother, and daughter. Now that the children were grown, I wanted to travel with my husband on business trips. But the few times I did, Momma would sob herself to sleep. The guilt was overwhelming.

Many mornings I awoke to find Momma lying in the hall or by her bed. She had fallen during the night on her way to the bathroom. When Momma reached the point that she could no longer bathe or care for herself without my help, my depression and guilt began turning into resentment and self-pity.

As much as I still loved my mother, I started asking God to take her. She was suffering. She was depressed. She couldn't even speak. All she could do was watch television. In some ways she was already dead. But I submitted myself to God's will, asking for the strength to care for Momma as long as He allowed her to live.

When Momma died in November 1990, I felt relief at first—for both of us. But a few days later, I was crushed. Doubts that I had not done enough for her tormented me.

Then came a tremendous sense of loss. Momma was dead. I would not see her again in this life. I was shocked at how much I wanted her back with me, no matter what her condition.

I thank God for all the years I had with Momma, even those last difficult ones. I see now that God was enabling me then to be the pillar of strength for Momma that she had always been for me. I owed Momma at least that.

Being a caregiver will test and mature your faith in God. If you foresee caregiving in the near future, consult your Christian bookstore for titles that will facilitate this transition in your life. Also seek counsel from those who have cared for aging parents. They will be a wealth of wisdom.

Steps of Faith

Lord of life, I want my love for my parents to be backed with actions—not just words (1 John 3:18). Help me to love them in practical, tangible ways, ways that demonstrate Your love, care, and appreciation for them, along with mine.

157

Mother-Not-to-Be

*Sing, O barren woman, you who never bore a child; burst into
song, shout for joy, you who were never in labor*

ISAIAH 54:1

*G*od knows who can handle children and who can't," my
sister-in-law clucked as I lay in the hospital bed. Were those
words supposed to reassure a 33-year-old woman after three miscarriages and a subsequent hysterectomy? Were they meant to express
compassion to the woman who never has had—and now never would
have—children?

I managed to maintain my composure, but after she left, I cried
out to God in confusion and despair. Questions which were not to
be answered tormented me. Was I really not "woman enough" for
motherhood? What about the 1.5 million women who abort their
babies every year? Or the mothers who bring an innocent life into a
godless environment of drugs and crime? Are they more qualified for
the job than I?

That was four years ago. As I've trusted God with my childlessness,
He's transformed that pain into a mysterious joy and peace—especially when I hold a baby. It's as though Jesus is hugging me, and I am
enveloped by His love, joy, and peace instead of jealousy or grief.

In the meantime being childless has allowed my husband and me
to travel on mission trips, visit prisons, host a Bible study, babysit,
or spend time helping a friend or neighbor in a crisis.

In other words, God has blessed us with a quiver full of "spiritual" children. And as I think about my sister-in-law's words, I praise
God for giving me what it takes to handle all *these* children!

Glib answers are never appropriate to questions of childlessness.
If you can have children, be sensitive to the loss your barren friend
has suffered. If you are barren, you must face this loss and allow
yourself to grieve for what will never be: feeling your child stir
within you, giving birth, witnessing the first steps, bandaging the
skinned knee, and so on. Name and mourn each loss. Then ask God
to help you accept your identity apart from being a mother. You have
no less value as a woman because you are childless.

Steps of Faith

*Dear Heavenly Father, thank You for Your promises that offer hope
for a future that may not include bearing and rearing children. I
trust in Your perfect wisdom to fulfill the desires of every earthly
daughter's heart.*

T
H
U
R
S
D
A
Y

Unplanned Joy

*For I know the plans I have for you . . . plans to prosper you
and not to harm you, plans to give you hope and a future.*

JEREMIAH 29:11

J'm what?" Even though I'd been feeling queasy and tired the
last several weeks, pregnancy was out of the question. We were too
careful. We didn't want any more children. The nurse must be mis-
taken. "Are you sure?" I asked, hoping she'd say, "Whoops!"

Instead she said, "Yes, I'm sure."

I started crying. I was angry. Just what did God think He was
doing, messing with my plans?

The nurse tried to console me, "Cindy, it's not the end of the
world. You can always do something about it."

I cringed. "You mean an abortion?"

"Just something to think about," she said.

I hung up the phone pondering her suggestion. I was startled to
find myself giving it consideration. It was certainly a solution to my
problem. I spent the morning wrestling with the Lord. Marshall had
just started his own company. We were living off savings and had no
insurance. Our two boys were a handful, and I was just beginning to
see some light at the end of the diaper tunnel.

I called my mom, looking for some consolation. Praise God she
was home. I jumped in the car and raced over to her house. As soon
as I walked in the door, I told her my news. She was thrilled. "But,
Mom, this wasn't planned," I cried.

She quickly responded, "Well neither were you!"

Some consolation.

Mary Kelley is now six and has brought immeasurable joy to our
family. I sometimes wonder what we might have missed had I gone
with my plan instead of God's.

Are you struggling with a difficult decision? Could it be that you
are considering a compromise of your faith in order to ease your circumstances? Being obedient is not always the easiest path to take,
but God promises that it always leads to blessing.

Steps of Faith

*Dear Lover of my soul, thank You for surprises. Thank You for my
mom. Bless her. Continue to give me the faith to rely upon Your protection and control, even when things seem out of control.*

F
R
I
D
A
Y

159

Perfect Hindsight

*My guilt has overwhelmed me like a burden too heavy
to bear . . . because of my sinful folly.*

PSALM 38:4,5

*H*istory could repeat itself—but it won't if I can help it. Just call it 20/20 hindsight.

Sixteen years ago my son, Carl, married Kelly, not the girl I would have chosen for him. She came from the "other" side of town. She didn't talk like us, cook like us, dress like us, pray like us, or vote like us. She just wasn't one of us.

I had my ways of making sure everyone else in the family knew how different Kelly was from us. For the first few years of their marriage, every time Carl and Kelly visited, I would "innocently" steer our conversations toward our differences. Within minutes Kelly was frantically trying to defend her views—in the middle of Sunday dinner!

Pretty soon Carl was visiting by himself, and that was fine with me. Even after their two children were born, I continued to make Kelly feel like an outcast instead of a member of the family.

Then in 1990 my husband died from a stroke. Six months later Carl was killed instantly in a car accident. Two years later Kelly remarried, and she and my grandchildren started their new life with another man in another state.

Today I am the outcast. Kelly wants nothing to do with me. But the thought of never seeing Carl's children again is almost unbearable. Every day I tearfully ask God to forgive me and allow me one more chance.

This may be it. In June my grandson is getting married. His fiancée reminds me a lot of Kelly. My advice to my daughter is to welcome that young woman into the family. God will fix in her what needs fixing. The family should accept her as she is.

The tension and strife between mothers-in-law and daughters-in-law stretch across millennia. The effects are destructive and painful for everyone involved. If you are having problems with an in-law, reach out to her with the love Christ has given you. You will never regret it.

Steps of Faith

Dear Father, You give Your love so freely. Right now I need an extra measure of that love. You know the situation between my in-law and myself. Please give me the faith to allow You to love her through me.

Cindi

Be still, and know that I am God.

PSALM 46:10

Cindi Behrmann is learning the meaning of Psalm 46:10—some might say the hard way. She wouldn't.

One day during college Cindy went blind in one eye and her left hand became totally paralyzed. She didn't have health insurance, so she didn't go to a doctor. Two weeks later, her vision and movement were restored as quickly as they had disappeared. A year later she began to experience numbness in her feet. This time, after months of medical diagnosis, nothing abnormal was discovered. In fact she was still jogging regularly. A few years later Cindi began to experience overwhelming fatigue, so severe that she could not sit up in bed. This time she was diagnosed with multiple sclerosis.

For a while Cindi continued to live normally. Her only physical struggle was with the relapses of the disease that occur with seasonal changes and cause intense fatigue.

When Cindi married Richard Behrmann and became pregnant, there was no danger of passing MS to her unborn child. The challenge would be to care for the child after it was born. During the pregnancy Cindi started using a wheelchair for shopping. After Michael was born, she discovered she could actually care for him better in the wheelchair. A couple of years later she had another son, Joseph.

Today with three boys, Cindi says her disability has taught her to "mother with her head." She says God has blessed her with a supportive family and friends. "If God told me I could trade one of them for my former athletic body, I would say, 'Thank you, but I'll keep the MS and deal with it.'"

Multiple sclerosis, which is more common in women than in men, is a medical mystery. Researchers don't know what causes it or how to cure it. MS causes scarring of the protective sheath of the spinal cord, thus impairing motor ability. Thousands of people struggle with the debilitating effects of MS and other diseases, but those like Cindi, who trust God with their weaknesses, will always be given the strength to cope.

M
O
N
D
A
Y

Steps of Faith

Dear Master Creator, I cannot comprehend what life with a debilitating disease would be like. Help me to be sensitive to the needs of those who "deal with it," so that I will see the person instead of the disease.

A Wife's Prayers

May the favor of the LORD our God rest upon us;
establish the work of our hands for us—
yes, establish the work of our hands.

PSALM 90:17

T
U
E
S
D
A
Y

*W*hen Scott and I married, he was a CPA working for a small firm in our hometown. There wasn't much of a future there, so on April 15, Scott gave a six-week notice. *Certainly he will find a job in that time,* we thought. He was unemployed for six months.

At the time we were struggling in our marriage and in our respective walks with God. Praying for each other wasn't a part of our daily routine.

Finally Scott was hired as an assistant controller at a hospital in a metropolitan area, 600 miles from home. Two weeks into the job, the hospital's ambulances were repossessed. A few weeks later the garbage pickup was terminated, and there was a widely publicized federal investigation into the hospital's failure to comply with health standards. Then paychecks started bouncing. Scott and 60 other employees were laid off.

Three months later Scott was hired by a bank as an auditor. Scott knew it wasn't a good match, but at least it was a job. (It still never occurred to me to pray for him.) He gave it his best, but after 18 months he was asked to resign. Thus we entered one of the longest, darkest phases of our marriage—nine months of unemployment.

God used those terrible months to get us in spiritual shape. A lot of ugly stuff surfaced and we worked to skim it off. We started regularly praying together and for each other.

When God did provide a job, He also provided the perfect verse for me to pray for Scott: Psalm 90:17. I pray it every morning.

Two and a half years later, Scott continues to flourish in a job that challenges and stretches him. He has regained his confidence and ambition. He's ready to conquer the world.

Ask God to give you a special verse to pray for your husband's career. There's nothing more powerful than praying God's Word back to Him. And there's no more effective way for a wife to minister to her husband.

Steps of Faith

Dear God, thank You for my husband and what You are doing in his life. Thank You also for using my prayers to strengthen and encourage him. Help me, Father, to be sensitive to the professional burden he carries. I want to help him be the best he can be.

Prodigal Daughter

"So there is hope for your future," declares the LORD.
"Your children will return to their own land."

JEREMIAH 31:17

My husband and I lost a 20-year-old daughter several years ago. Ashley didn't die, though sometimes we mourned her as though she had. Everything we believed in, everything we fought and prayed for, everything we tried to teach our children, Ashley rejected.

In college she became a convert to humanistic and evolutionary theories. "Individual rights for everyone" became her rallying cry. She completely rejected our values.

She wrote letters to our local newspaper warning of the dangers of "the ignorant and malicious religious right," specifically maligning traditional Christianity. Once we saw her on television marching with the local gay and lesbian rights group.

For four years I had virtually no contact with Ashley. They were difficult years. I still loved her. And I missed her. It seems I prayed for her constantly. I knew the truth was buried in her heart somewhere, but it was up to God to help her find it again. That was my only peace.

Then out of the blue Ashley called. She abruptly requested a meeting with me at her apartment. When I first saw her I couldn't resist hugging her. Then I looked into her eyes. I saw a glimmer of something familiar and soft. What was going on?

Four hours later I knew it all. As I stepped out of her apartment, joy and peace overflowed my heart. God had not allowed me to give up on her. He had brought my Ashley home.

There's something uniquely effective about a mother's prayers for her children, especially her prodigal children. Ruth Bell Graham, wife of evangelist Billy Graham, knows firsthand the heartbreak of loving prodigals. Her book, *Prodigals and Those Who Love Them*, is full of advice, comfort, and inspiration for anyone praying for a prodigal.

Steps of Faith

Lord, as I work about the house, You know my thoughts are else-where—with those of my family whose lives also need Your cleansing and Your touch. Please, Lord, sweep through their lives with convicting power, then tenderly apply the balm of Your love to their bruised and broken hearts and emotions as You have to mine.

Praying to Pray

*If from there you seek the LORD your God, you will find him if
you look for him with all your heart and with all your soul.*

DEUTERONOMY 4:29

*F*or so long I felt like a spiritual failure. Every time someone
described the glorious quiet time he or she had with the Lord every
morning, I was consumed with frustration and envy.

You see, I am a stay-at-home mother raising and homeschooling
four children ages 12, 10, 5, and 4. I get an average of five and a half
hours of sleep a night. I'm lucky if I get to shower three days in a
row. My legs get shaved about twice a month. With my life in a constant state of motion and crisis and chaos seemingly daily occur-
rences, "quiet time" is not in my vocabulary.

Then one day while sitting in the car I heard on the radio a short
quote from a Charles Spurgeon sermon: "I believe that when we cannot
pray, it is the time that we pray more than ever. And if you answer, 'But
how can that be?' I would say, pray to pray. Pray for prayer. . . ."

It hit me like a lightning bolt. Right there in my minivan I prayed
to pray. I promised God I would offer no more excuses.

Slowly I began to practice the reality that God is always ready to
listen to me wherever I am, whatever I'm doing. The more I prayed
to pray, the more opportunities I discovered to pray: while folding
the laundry or washing the dishes, for example. And I've invested in
some praise tapes and keep them playing in the background.

The most exciting answer to my prayer is that I have incorpo-
rated prayer and Bible study into the children's lessons. Now all of
us are having a regular quiet time—in the middle of the day!

God and His peace have replaced crisis and chaos. And I've
determined that even though my body may be in constant motion,
my heart is learning how to be still before the Lord.

What priority does prayer have in your life? God knows how
hectic your life is. That's why He wants you to spend time with Him,
praying and meditating on His Word. He can give you quiet and rest,
even in the middle of crisis and chaos.

Steps of Faith

*Blessed Lord, thank You for the privilege of prayer. Forgive me for
my self-centeredness and shortsightedness when it comes to setting
aside time with You. It is obviously Your will, and so I should trust
that You will find a way. Make me aware of every opportunity to fellowship with You.*

Passing the Torch

Continue in what you have learned and have become convinced of, because you know those from whom you learned it.

2 TIMOTHY 3:14

During our most recent visit to my hometown, I noticed something was different, but I couldn't quite put my finger on it.

We visited my husband's grandmother, who is in her late eighties. We had been hearing for months that she was not doing well. It was sad to see how much strength and cognizance she had lost.

I also paid a visit to the pastor of our former church. He's been pastoring there for decades. During our visit it seemed to me he had aged overnight. I had to remind myself that 15 years had passed since I had been actively involved in the church. He had been in his forties then. He was the same fearless, godly man, only a more subdued and grayer man in his sixties.

But the final blow came during church that Sunday. The pastor announced that Mabel Lewis had died early that morning. Mabel had taught two generations of seventh-grade girls' Sunday school. I had been fortunate enough to be in her class years ago.

I had always loved and admired Mabel, but from afar. We were not close. Yet tears I couldn't control began streaming down my face. I slipped out of the pew and hurried to the bathroom, where I cried and cried.

After asking God to show me what was wrong, I realized that during this trip my eyes had been opened to the progress of time. All those people—the courageous Christian leaders, who wore the crowns of wisdom, who would always be there, who seemed immortal—were really mortal. And even more frightening was the realization that I, and my generation, had to be ready to step into their shoes one day, a day that suddenly seemed to be fast approaching.

Have you experienced the realization that one day people will be looking to you for leadership and wisdom? If you are in your thirties, forties, or fifties, pray that God will enable you to be a strong leader for future generations. If you are older, pray for those who will follow in your footsteps.

Steps of Faith

God of the ages, I thank You for the example of the countless saints who have marched through time under Your banner. May our present leaders be inspired by them and be just as fearless and dedicated.

Blueprint for Hope

*Sons are a heritage from the LORD, children are
a reward from him.*

PSALM 127:3

Seven years ago Tom Richards and I were raising our children and were happily married—to other people. We belonged to the same church, but because he and his wife, Sara, were several years older, we didn't know each other very well. However, in the same year Sara died of breast cancer, my husband, Jay, died in a boating accident.

Some friends introduced us, and before we knew it, Tom and I were in love. In the summer of 1993 we were married.

Shortly after my three boys and I moved into Tom's house, I became worried that it wasn't going to work out. "Sara" was everywhere, and I sensed tension, even resentment, from Tom's older sons that another woman was running their mother's house.

When I suggested to Tom that we find or build another house, one for the *whole* family, he smiled sheepishly and pulled out some house plans he'd been working on. I jumped up and gave him a hug.

All the boys agreed that it was a good idea. My three would have one big room with two bunk beds and their own bathroom. For Tom's older, college-aged sons, we designed a bonus room over the garage with a private staircase and bathroom. The fourth bedroom would be the office/computer/sewing room. And of course, Tom and I were especially interested in the master bedroom and bath. We knew I would feel much more comfortable.

Since we moved in, there's been an easing of the tension between his boys and me, and I've been able to relax and enjoy our home. Things aren't perfect, but we finally live in "our" house.

Blending a family means a new identity for each person involved, either as a stepparent, stepchild, stepbrother or -sister. It's a stressful adjustment that can take five or six years—and a lot of love, patience, and prayer—before everyone adapts. Living in a home that's neither "yours" nor "mine" but "ours" can lay the foundation for a healthy blended family.

Steps of Faith

Everlasting Father, I thank You for the wisdom You promise to those who ask for it (James 1:5). It is especially needed in handling all the variables in a blended family. Lord, bless these families with peace and joy.

THREADS OF SUMMER

Restoring

Restoring

Red traffic lights, five full grocery carts in the check-out line, a sign reading, "Take a number please." Any of these can trigger a response that is less than desirable.

During a typical last-minute trip to the grocery store, I was taught a valuable lesson. I whipped my cart in behind a man unloading his groceries under the sign that clearly read, "1–10 items, cash only." The man noticed me visually counting the items in his cart, and he sheepishly said, "My wife said they will let you through with just a few items over the limit."

I smiled and responded, "Sir, I live over the limit." While I impatiently waited, I realized how true that statement was for most of us. We do live over the limits. We frequently overcommit and find it necessary to work late or plead for mercy on deadlines.

Summer can be a time of adding to an already over-the-limit schedule, or we can choose to find time for rest, relaxation, and restoration with our family and friends.

Our bodies and souls cannot live a healthy life if we are always over the limit, so find time this summer season to relax and discover how rewarding it can be to step out of the fast lane.

Quiet your heart and ask the Lord to give you perspective. Talk to Him, read His Word, and He will restore you.

An "A" for Mom

Apply your heart to instruction
and your ears to words of knowledge.

PROVERBS 23:12

*M*om and I walked into the classroom, our huge World Lit anthologies under our arms, and sat down. I could hardly keep from beaming as I introduced her to my friend Regina.

Dr. Barnett came in, his battered briefcase in his hand. He smiled and nodded at Mom and me. He had taken a special interest in us ever since he found out Mom was a student, too. We were his first mother/daughter student duo.

I was a freshman when Mom decided to pursue her long-buried dream to go to college. I was so proud and excited for her! Dad, my sister, Donna, and I encouraged her as she began the application process.

She had a few obstacles to overcome, including getting her transcripts from her high school (which was now closed) and taking the SAT. When her SAT scores came in, we couldn't believe it: my mother, who'd been out of school for 30 years, scored higher than several of my friends in high school!

And now it was summer quarter, and we were classmates. Mom took excellent notes, which I borrowed after missing two classes to go to Florida. (My priorities were in the right place!) We studied together for the difficult tests Dr. Barnett liked to give, and she always scored a few points higher than I did. At quarter's end, I had a B and Mom had an A.

I still love to tease her about that!

Learning at every stage of life is important, but you don't have to get a formal education. You can take noncredit courses or correspondence courses. Sign up for classes at a craft store. Research a favorite subject at the library or start a Bible study. If we aren't learning, we aren't using our minds the way God intended.

Steps of Faith

Father, You know everything, and You've given me the ability to
learn what You already know. Help me to always seek to discover
more about You and Your creation.

Sales and Sense

Teach me knowledge and good judgment,
for I believe in your commands.

PSALM 119:66

*A*ngie looked at all the stuff in Vicki's yard and sighed. "Do you think anyone will come? We worked so hard getting this yard sale together!"

"I think so," Vicki said. "It's still early."

Angie glanced down at the box full of health magazines. "Those sure caused me a lot of headaches."

"Why?"

"I subscribed to those magazines because I wanted the latest information on nutrition," Angie said, arranging some dishes. "But every few months some new study would contradict what another one had said. One month, coffee's deadly, the next it isn't. Now they're saying that salt isn't really that bad for you. It's so confusing! Maybe I should just feed my kids burgers and fries and forget it."

"I went through something similar when I was pregnant with Amber," Vicki said, stacking some old books on the table. "I read everything I could about parenting. Some of it was pretty bizarre! The more I read, the more intimidated I became. I began praying that I'd learn what God wanted me to learn. I bought a few Christian parenting books and magazines. Then I realized that parenting is often just using common sense and relying on the Lord. Now I do what makes sense to me and what I believe will work with Amber."

"Maybe I should pray, too, and just concentrate on the basics of nutrition like the food pyramid—and forget all this other stuff from left field," Vicki said. "My mother always says, 'Everything in moderation.'"

"Good advice, I guess. Look! Our first customers!"

With all the information at our fingertips, it's easy to get bogged down in it and lose perspective. Pray for discernment and trust the Lord to make clear what you should believe. Read your Bible, and seek out information from Christian sources to balance what you get from secular ones. And don't forget a valuable, God-given tool: common sense.

Steps of Faith

Lord, so much of the information I'm exposed to is false and contra-
dictory to Your Word. Please don't let me get caught up in it, but
instead, help me to look to You as the final authority on everything.

Living Promise

The promise is for you and your children.

ACTS 2:39

The sweet sounds of children's voices drifted across the park to the bench where Jodi and Marie were taking a break from their mid-morning walk. The neighbors were also good friends; their babies were just a few weeks apart in age.

As they listened to the youngsters singing the contemporary tune at the corner church's Vacation Bible school, each woman gently rocked her baby in a stroller. For Jodi, the voices reminded her of growing up in this neighborhood. She and her siblings always looked forward to the fun events planned at the church each summer, a break from the usual "make-your-own-fun" days they had at home.

"I used to hate going to Sunday school," Marie confided to Jodi. "Why would a kid want to go to Vacation Bible school in the summer?"

"Great snacks!" Jodi blurted out, then laughed. "We loved it! I learned a lot of Bible stories, but what I remember most is how special those teachers made us feel. I really knew Jesus loved me because they loved me. I can't wait for Brandon to go!" She lifted her wriggling six-month-old son from the stroller and hummed the song along with the Bible school children.

She turned to Marie. "It's important that we remind these little guys often how special they are—that God created them and they are one of a kind."

Marie was thoughtful for a moment and then lifted little Jordan into her arms. "Hey there, special boy! You want to go to Vacation Bible school with Brandon?"

Jodi smiled. "You're special, too, Marie. A special mom and a special friend!"

Are you reminding your children or grandchildren or nieces and nephews how very special they are? Growing up, children need to hear often that they are loved, cherished, and precious in God's sight.

Steps of Faith

Dearest Father, thank You for making us in Your image. Each of us is distinctive, an exclusive creation designed by You, the same God who created all of the universe. Truly awesome!

Leaving

Therefore shall a man leave his father and his mother.
GENESIS 2:24 KJV

*L*et's talk about what leaving our parents means for us today. . . ."
As the speaker began, Barry and I sat motionless. This marriage seminar had been mildly interesting so far, but now the speaker was
addressing "the subject"—the one Barry and I had argued over more
than once during our six-month engagement.

The seminar leader's wife shared what the early days of their marriage were like. "George and I were still in school, and we lived in
the apartment over his parent's garage. We saved money, and his parents loved having us nearby. The problem was that George had very
strong emotional ties to his parents, and we were all just too close.
Many evenings George would stop to see his parents before coming
upstairs. He would fix himself a plate of leftovers and tell them
about his day. By the time he came up to our apartment my novice
meals had no appeal, and he didn't want to rehearse the events of his
day again. It seems like a small thing, but for a new, insecure bride,
this was fodder for big-time resentment.

"At that point in our lives our primary need was to establish a
strong bond with each other and proper boundaries with our parents. It was never a matter of physical distance. In our case, the
leaving needed to be emotional.

"I'm happy to report that we solved that problem and avoided a hazardous situation. After George understood my growing irritation, he
called a family council. His mom and dad agreed that we should all set
some boundaries. George had the most difficult adjustment, but his conscious choice to put me before his parents saved us much future pain."

Barry and I looked at each other silently. Then Barry looked away.

Just as the umbilical cord must be cut at birth, there must be a
severance from parents that establishes an independent family unit
if a couple is to enjoy God's design for their marriage. If that was
never done and has caused problems, a Christian counselor can help
you get back on track.

Steps of Faith

*Heavenly Father, Your plan for marriage is so beautiful. When my
children are ready to leave, give me the strength and wisdom to set
them free. I pray that I would never stand in the way of their happiness.*

And Cleaving

Therefore shall a man . . . cleave unto his wife.

GENESIS 2:24 KJV

*T*hese people don't realize their formula doesn't fit every situation," Barry said, chuckling nervously as he handed me a cup of punch during the break at the marriage enrichment seminar.

The couple we were chatting with were startled. "But it's not just a formula," Angie said quietly. "George is talking about the God-given foundation for a good marriage. Evan and I know from our own experience the importance of leaving and cleaving." Angie grinned at Evan, who took up the story.

"Shortly before our wedding I was accepted by the fire department in my hometown and had to start the training course. They allowed me three days off for the wedding, so we spent our honeymoon in the city where Angie lived. Before we came home, we stopped by Angie's house to say goodbye. Big mistake. When we left, she started crying and didn't stop for two hours. I was sure her mom or dad had said something about me. And I was angry. My resentment grew every time Angie talked to her mom.

"On our first anniversary I mentioned those tears again. Angie was astounded. It had had nothing to do with me. Her tears had been triggered by the fact that during those three days her younger brother had moved into 'her' room, lock, stock, and barrel. She felt like she had been erased from her family."

Angie continued. "You have to separate from your parents emotionally to form a new family unit, and you have to stick to your spouse like glue. This doesn't mean that you stop loving your parents or reject their opinions. But you do have to work out a reasonable level of interaction with the in-laws that's comfortable for you both. The best time to do this is before you get married. We're proof of that."

My heart stopped. That was my answer. Right then I knew Barry and I would be having a serious discussion later that night.

Cleaving means there is nothing more important in the world than your spouse—even children. By God's design, anything or anyone allowed to come between a husband and wife will cause painful problems.

Steps of Faith

Father, thank You for my husband. Forgive me for the times I neglect him by putting other things—even seemingly good things—before him. Protect our union from outside harm and renew our oneness in You.

Healing the Scars

*Flee sexual immorality. All other sins a man
commits are outside his body, but he who sins sexually
sins against his own body.*

1 CORINTHIANS 6:18

*T*his time I wouldn't repeat my mistakes. I was married to Greg, the most wonderful man in the world. He was ambitious, strong, and independent, and he was a Christian. How could I help but be happy?

During our first year, I had been so excited about my new home and a move to another city that I had ignored some problems that had begun to emerge as our life together stabilized. I had received Christ as my Savior just six months before Greg and I married. As a baby believer, I loved Jesus and I loved my husband, but I had dragged a truckload of unresolved garbage from my past into the marriage. Even though Greg knew about my promiscuous behavior before and after my first marriage, I felt as if I were trash. Greg should have—and could have—married a "nice" girl. I deserved only the kind of man I had been married to before, one who verbally and sometimes physically abused me.

And what if my friends from our new church learn about my past? They will reject me. I would if I were them.

With thoughts like these loose in my mind, Satan began to torment me mercilessly. I was sure this marriage would never work. Eventually Greg realized what was happening and took us both to the counselor at our church. Over time and through much specific prayer, the Holy Spirit freed me from the sins of my past. Greg and I have never been more in love.

If he can, Satan will use sexual sin or sexual trauma from your past to sabotage your marriage. The best time to deal with such matters is before you marry, as marriage itself will not heal your scars. But whenever the need arises you can count on Christ for healing. You and your marriage will be strengthened as you accept the forgiveness Christ offers for every sin of your past and learn how to accept His love.

Steps of Faith

Almighty God, sometimes I expect from my marriage what is only possible from You. Keep my expectations realistic and my relationship with my husband honest and loving. May I always trust You with all my heart.

One Flesh

They will become be one flesh.

GENESIS 2:24

*H*ow about us going camping at Hard Labor Creek next weekend?" my husband, Larry, asked as we drove home from church.

I turned to him quickly and cried, "What did you say?" My sudden reaction to his question startled him, and he almost ran off the road. "I can't believe this! I was just thinking the exact same thing!"

Larry smiled and shook his head gently. "Like I've been telling you for the last nine years: We're one . . . honey bun." We laughed for a moment, then Larry got serious. "It's like God says, 'We're one.' And it gets better every day." Larry looked deeply into my eyes and smiled. He could still make my heart flutter.

Throughout the week I thought about that conversation. It seemed the longer we were married, the more we caught each other thinking about the same things. It was as though we literally had the same mind—but not all the time. Larry, with all his strengths and weaknesses, was still Larry. And likewise for me. But there was an undeniable, increasing synchronism of our minds and spirits.

There is also our physical relationship, which is more than sex. Take nonsexual touching. If Larry puts his arm around me, or I put my hand on his shoulder, it's not just contact—it's a melding of two objects that are perfectly fit for each other. It feels different from touching anyone else—even my children. It's because I'm not one with any of them, just Larry.

Believe it or not, five years ago Larry and I almost abandoned our marriage. Instead we gave it to God and agreed to live it according to His plan. It's taken lots of love, patience, and prayer, but God has been faithful.

A church in Liberia, Africa, gives a special gift to newly married couples to remind them of their vows. It is a carving of two heads connected by a wooden chain, all carved from the same piece of wood. Illustrated is the truth that the two become one, but still remain two distinct individuals.

Steps of Faith

Lord Jesus, all praise and glory go to You for Your wonderful design for marriage. I want to experience all the joy possible with my husband. Give me the wisdom to abide in Your Word and Your will.

Guarding the Heart

Above all else, guard your heart,
for it is the wellspring of life.

PROVERBS 4:23

$\mathcal{B}$en, his wife, Kathy, and their three children moved into our subdivision about six years ago and joined our church. Soon my husband, Edwin, and I became great friends with them. We played games, watched movies, talked politics, and became so close and were so compatible that we began talking about investing in retirement property together. With seven children between the two couples, we even joked about our "tribe."

Over time, Ben and I, who were both extroverts and somewhat musically talented, started singing together. Occasionally we sang at a funeral or wedding. As far as I knew, we had the complete support of our respective spouses. Then one Sunday Kathy and I were talking to a woman who had recently joined our church. "You and Ben were so wonderful this morning," she gushed. "You sounded like you practice day and night, and you're so easy together on the stage. I could hardly believe it when I found out you aren't married to each other."

I immediately felt Kathy stiffen. All at once I perceived that what Ben and I enjoyed so much was in some way painful for her. That afternoon the four of us talked. Given the opportunity Kathy and my sweet Edwin admitted some ambivalent feelings about our singing. Kathy cried when she whispered that she thought Ben sometimes resented her for having no musical ability. Her wildest fear was that Ben wanted to leave her for me.

Ben's eyes filled with tears as he took Kathy into his arms, and it was as though a knife seared my own heart. Had Ben and I, in our collaboration, truly avoided all appearance of evil? Had we been completely innocent?

Your spousal allegiance, loyalty, and love must be reserved for your mate. All other friendships and working relationships must be completely circumspect and guarded from every appearance of evil. Count on God rather than another man to fill any unmet emotional needs you may have.

Steps of Faith

"Create in me a pure heart, O God, and renew a steadfast spirit within me. Do not cast me from your presence or take your Holy Spirit from me. Restore to me the joy of your salvation and grant me a willing spirit, to sustain me" (Psalm 51:10-12).

Our Faithful God

"Return, faithless people," declares the LORD,
"for I am your husband."

JEREMIAH 3:14

*J*n ordaining marriage between men and women, God has revealed much of His character and nature. God is our creator, the author and sustainer of life, and our heavenly Father. But His love, protection, and faithfulness are most clearly seen through the covenants He made with His people, beginning with Abraham and continuing with the church, the bride of Jesus Christ. God's love for us is so great that He gave His only Son, Jesus Christ, who through His death redeemed the church from the power of sin.

Marriage between two people is also a covenant relationship, though on a human scale. Today many marriage vows might well read, "I promise to love, honor, and cherish you so long as I feel inclined to do so." But that is not the quality of commitment God expects His people to make to each other. Marriage is modeled after God's covenant with His people, and it is not to be entered into lightly.

God intended a husband and wife to delight in each other, and to have intimate fellowship on a physical, emotional, and spiritual level. He expects each partner to be utterly committed to the welfare of the other. This is the quality of love that Jesus has for the church. So great is His love for His church, His bride, that He gave up His very life for her. Many marriages could be saved—and the partners would be happy—if the husband and wife would have a Christlike attitude, putting the interests of the other—and the children—before their own. There is no room for self-centeredness in marriage.

The family is the incubator for faith. It is the matrix for teaching children such concepts as trust, honor, duty, integrity, and love. It is the environment where the fruit of the Spirit can flourish and values and virtues can take root and grow. Recommit your marriage to the Lord. Purpose to subordinate your personal desires for the greater good of the family.

Steps of Faith

Father, I thank You that You have established Your covenant with Your people for all eternity and that I am included in it. Make my heart faithful to reject all that does not honor You in my marriage.

W
E
D
N
E
S
D
A
Y

The Balancing Act

You, O LORD, have helped me and comforted me.

PSALM 86:17

*S*ummer vacation had not been such a big deal for us—until last year. Now the boys were old enough to enjoy the outdoor activities that Jeff and I had always dreamed of doing with them. But there was one problem: I had to work.

How it killed me to drop the boys off at the day-care center on those summer mornings when their friends would be spending the day with their moms doing fun things. Going to the pool, picking berries, and picnicking at the park with their mom weren't part of Adrian's and Cameron's summer days—and wouldn't be part of their boyhood memories.

I knew if I didn't change my schedule during the summer, I would live to regret it.

I prayed that God would show me what to do. I had to work. I had already cut my work week to three days, but the days off often filled up with doctor's appointments, housework, and errands. And sometimes I had to travel. I tried to make time for them when I was home, but I knew it could be better.

Then my neighbor Nancy pointed out that, as a geologist, I already had a strong science background. I could easily get my certification to teach. Then I'd be working the same schedule as my children.

So that's what I'm doing. I started teaching in the fall of 1997. It meant a big cut in pay, but being there to enjoy my sons' summer days makes it all worthwhile.

If you're a working mom, how are you balancing your job and your children's summer vacation? It's usually a time of added stress. Balancing this demand in your life could mean some sacrifices or a job change. If you sense that God wants you to make some changes, ask Him to show you what to do. He wants what's best for you and your children.

Steps of Faith

Holy Father, I want to make this summer vacation a special one for my children. Show me how to make memories with them that they will always treasure. Help me to balance all the demands on my time and energy, giving top priority to You.

Cleaning House

Turn my eyes away from worthless things.

PSALM 119:37

*A*fter hours of helping with the baking, cleaning, and shopping, Brad and I ducked out of the house before the guests arrived. My 25-year-old sister, Allison, had spent the summer with us and had become very involved with the singles group at our church. She asked us if she could host a party at our place. We were delighted.

But our delight turned sour when we returned late that night. To my horror every video that we owned had been laid on the sideboard in the dining room. Several thoughts went through my mind. First, we have a VCR in our bedroom, and all those videos had been pulled out. Second, it was obvious the movies had been watched in our bedroom—on our bed. But worst, and most convicting, were the movies themselves. I had no idea we owned so many R-rated movies.

Brad and I were stricken with guilt and shame. Both of us are in church leadership. Our hypocrisy was inexcusable.

The next night Brad and I shared our feelings about the videos. I knew in my heart what we should do, but I wondered if Brad would be willing to do it. Then I heard him say, without a trace of hesitation, that we had to throw away the R-rated movies. He went to the pantry, got some plastic shopping bags, and we began filling them. Brad dumped the bags in the garbage can outside.

I confess that I tallied the value of the videos, and it made me sick. But obedience usually comes at a price, and we've never regretted what we did. We know our home is now honoring to Christ. And the next group that rifles through our video collection will find nothing but wholesome entertainment.

How would you feel if a group from your church examined your video collection, reading material, or music library? Would any of it cause you embarrassment and shame? If so, throw it out. Keeping your mind pure before the Lord is much easier when your home is pure before Him.

Steps of Faith

Holy Lord, shine Your light in my life. Show me those things I set before my eyes that are harmful to my spirit. Give me the strength to do what's necessary to keep my mind pure before You.

F
R
I
D
A
Y

Not by Choice

Dear friends, do not be surprised at the painful trial
you are suffering, as though something strange
were happening to you.

1 PETER 4:12

*M*ichele glanced through the prayer list, her eyes stopping at the request written in bold type: TAMMY'S BABY IN CRITICAL CONDITION. Tammy's newborn son had been delivered by C-section and rushed to a distant hospital.

A strong, piercing pain struck Michele's heart. Heavily burdened, she knelt by her bedside. The familiar ache inside brought tears to Michele's eyes as she began to pray, "God, comfort Tammy . . ."

Two years earlier, Michele's daughter had died of cancer. The long fight with childhood leukemia had meant many hospital stays and many ups and downs on an emotional roller coaster of pain and hope. Again and again during the three years of her daughter's illness, Michele had been comforted by other parents who had been through the same pain. Since then, the Lord had prompted her to pray for numerous other mothers with children in crisis situations. Some had miscarried; others had lost children in accidents or after long illnesses.

In each instance, as Michele reached out to comfort these other mothers in a tender way, she discovered God had given her a supernatural gift to bear another mother's pain and burden.

Michele was grateful for this gift, for it filled her with a passion to minister God's love to the hurting women around her.

Only God's love can bring healing to the wounded hearts of mothers who have lost children. The sorrow they experience needs the gentle touch of one who understands. Reach out with great sensitivity to such hurting parents. Just your effort ministers to their pain.

Steps of Faith

Dear Lord Jesus, help me to always remember to have my arms
open to those who are feeling empty. Let the love of Your Spirit flow
forth to fill them with the comfort and compassion You freely pro-
vide through others.

Hard Words, Software

You shall not steal.

EXODUS 20:15

"Yeah, this software is great. It's really helped us get our finances in order," my sister said.

"Sounds perfect for us," I replied. "Where'd you get it, and how much did it cost?"

Gail laughed. "Don't worry about that! I'll just put a copy of it on a disk. It'll save you some time and money."

"No thanks, Gail," I said, looking her squarely in the eye, "That's stealing, and I don't want any part of it."

Gail laughed again, this time a little nervously. "Come on, Paula. What's the big deal? Do you think that software conglomerate is going to miss your thirty bucks?"

"That's not the point at all. What you're suggesting is immoral. Ultimately, it's stealing from that company. I wouldn't be able to sleep at night."

Gail wasn't convinced. "Look, any chance I have to save some money, I do it. I don't see anything wrong with it. You just need to chill out and not be so judgmental."

"Gail, what if everyone began pirating all the software on the market? And then everyone began to do the same with videos, music, books, and magazines? The price of those products would go sky-high, leaving honest people to pay the difference. In fact, that's what's already happening. That $30 piece of software might've cost $20-25 if the company didn't have to factor in the price of pirating."

I wish I could say I convinced Gail of this sin, but I didn't. Sometimes she still brings it up. That's okay. It only confirms to me that I hit a nerve that day and my prayers for her are working.

"You shall not steal." It's a command of God that should permeate every aspect of your life. Does it? Don't let the crumbling morals of our culture deceive you into rationalizing stealing or any other sin. It will destroy your witness and your relationship with God.

Steps of Faith

Father, thank You for the command not to steal. In our society today it would be so easy to justify it. I pray that You would reverse this trend by the power of Your Holy Spirit. Open eyes to the truth of the sin.

Gearing Up

You also must be ready.

MATTHEW 24:44

*M*y sister-in-law Pam is a wife, mother of two, full-time teacher, and part-time college student. And she is one of the most organized people I know. She has to be—especially when August rolls around.

Pam starts gearing up for the coming school year shortly after summer vacation begins. In her children's school district the next year's school supplies lists are distributed with the final report cards in June. By that time Pam has already bought some of the anticipated items, if she's found them on sale. She'll purchase the rest of the items over the summer.

The same goes for school clothes. Sometime in June or July she takes a day or two alone with each child. The stores aren't jammed with other back-to-school shoppers, plus the children enjoy the individual attention.

Their school district also allows parents and students to visit the classroom to which they are assigned. The children like knowing where their classrooms are and what they will look like. They can even meet their future teachers. Pam says it seems to soothe any anxiety they might have about all the changes.

When August arrives, the children begin easing into a "school mentality." Pam asks the children to think about what they'd like in their lunches or for their after-school snacks. Bedtime is more strictly observed. Pam wakes them up earlier as well.

The last week of summer vacation is quiet and noneventful. No activities are scheduled, and the family spends as much time together at home as possible. Pam believes this is the most critical week of the entire year. It's a time of rest and readiness that they won't be able to enjoy again until next August.

In Matthew 24:44 Jesus admonished His disciples to be ready for His return, even though they wouldn't know the hour of His coming. It's also a lesson to be prepared for the big changes and events we have marked on our calendars! Being prepared is part of being a "faithful and wise servant" (v. 45).

Steps of Faith

Heavenly Father, keep me clearly focused on getting my family ready for another school year—physically, emotionally, and spiritually. I want to do what I can to make the transition as smooth as possible, for all of us.

Nobody's a Nobody

*His divine power has given us everything we need for life
and godliness through our knowledge of him.*

2 PETER 1:3

$\mathcal{M}$y childhood was anything but happy. My parents suffered
from depression and were divorced by the time I was four. Neither
one seemed to want me. Sometimes my mother would simply leave
me in the parking lot of my father's apartment complex without noti-
fying him. One winter day when I was nine, I spent eight hours outside waiting for him to come home. When he saw me, he looked
angry and disappointed.

Both parents remarried more than once. I was nothing but a bad
memory of one of their many mistakes. I spent years trying to win
their love, but it only invited harsh criticism. One of the most devastating remarks came when I was 12. My period had just started,
and I told Mom that I couldn't wait to get married and have a baby.
Her reply was, "You can forget about that, girl. No one's going to
marry a nobody like you."

By high school, I was quiet, shy, melancholy, and always telling
myself and others how inept I was. I had a few friends, but I was
afraid to show them the real me. It would only invite more pain.
Besides, I was "nobody." In my eyes I had no worth, nothing to contribute, and nothing to look forward to.

When I was a junior, Laurie Colstock, one of my school friends,
invited me to church. I loved it there. The people there didn't criticize me; instead they talked about love. This would be my refuge.

Because of the verbal and emotional abuse I'd suffered, I would
spend years in that church before I was able to truly accept Jesus'
love and His sacrifice for me on the cross. And then I had to face the
issue of forgiving my parents. They stole years of joy from me, but
God wants me to love and forgive them. And He has given me the
power to do just that.

Has anyone ever robbed you of your self-esteem with harsh, critical
words? No matter what anyone says, in Christ you're not only some-
body, you're worth the life of the sinless Creator of the universe.

Steps of Faith

*Lord Jesus, thank You for seeing every individual as a priceless gift
from Your Father. Help me to see others with Your eyes so that I
speak only words of truth, healing, and edification—always in love.*

W
E
D
N
E
S
D
A
Y

183

Robbing God

You are under a curse—the whole nation of you—because you are robbing me. Bring the whole tithe into the storehouse.

MALACHI 3:9,10

Tithing was an issue my husband, Frank, didn't want to discuss. Even though he'd been a Christian for several years, he wasn't convinced that not tithing was stealing from God. After many arguments, I determined to pray that God would give him wisdom.

Finally, after several months, Frank told me that we were going to start tithing. God had answered my prayers. The following Sunday Frank wrote our first tithe check. On the way to church I casually unfolded it. I was in for a surprise.

"Frank, this isn't the right amount," I said quickly. "This is 10 percent of the net, not the gross."

"So? It's still tithing. It's 10 percent of what I have left to spend."

"Right, after the federal government, state government, your pension, and the health insurance company take what they need. And that adds up to much more than 10 percent!"

"Calm down, Jackie. The fact is we can't possibly afford to tithe the gross."

"Then we must be spending too much on other things. Like cable—we don't need 200 stations. And eating out—if we limited it to once a week, we would make up the tithe difference right there."

It took some time and prayer before Frank was willing to make the sacrifices and "bring the whole tithe into the storehouse," but when he did, it was with joy. And I know that brought great joy to God as well.

The latest statistics show that only 4 percent of evangelical Christians tithe 10 percent or more of their income. Imagine if that number were 100 percent! Many government social programs would no longer be necessary because the church would be able to do its work. Are you tithing?

Steps of Faith

Dear Lord, I know that even if I tithe there are other ways I steal from You. Often I withhold love, forgiveness, compassion, or time. Give me a heart that rejoices over giving everything thing I have to offer.

A Holy Example

Make every effort to live in peace with all men and to be holy;
without holiness no one will see the Lord.

HEBREWS 12:14

*F*ive years ago my friend Sharon married Keith, who has joint custody of three children. Sharon knew when she married Keith that she'd probably never have children of her own. God had called her to create a godly refuge of love, peace, and stability for Keith's children.

It wasn't the children who tested Sharon's faith as much as Meg, their mother, did. It had been a bitter divorce, and Meg was a constant looming presence—a vengeful woman who had a score to settle.

Unfortunately, it was usually Sharon who had to deal with Meg when she picked up the children. Often Meg would try to instigate an argument with Sharon, in front of the children. But Sharon always prayed beforehand and refused to let Meg get to her. Besides, Sharon wanted to set an example of love and holiness for the children.

One afternoon Meg showed up unexpectedly and accused Sharon of abusing the children. Sharon lost it. She began screaming at Meg, eventually ordering her out of the house. The glass in the door cracked when she slammed it behind her.

For days Sharon was tormented with guilt. She had failed God and the children. As she prayed, however, she sensed God telling her to apologize to Meg. That was out of the question—at first.

Eventually Sharon called Meg and apologized to her. And to her shock Meg apologized to her! It was the first time Meg had spoken politely to her in five years.

Today Sharon and Meg aren't exactly friends, but at least they're beginning to live in peace. And when one person is sowing seeds of holiness in her life, peace is usually the fruit.

Do you have a passion for holiness? Are you so absorbed with Jesus that you live to please the Father and no one else (John 5:19)? Such a life is possible when yielded to the work of the Holy Spirit. The more of your life you give to Him, the more you want to give to Him.

F
R
I
D
A
Y

Steps of Faith

Holy God, only by the power of Your Spirit can I glorify You.
Cleanse my heart, Lord. Shine the light of truth in my heart. Give
me a passion for holiness that points others to You.

185

Word for Word

The sluggard craves and gets nothing, but the desires
of the diligent are fully satisfied.

PROVERBS 13:4

*I*t was the first week of my job as a proofreader for a publishing company. Frankly, I thought proofreading was beneath me. For years I'd been a newspaper reporter in another city. Proofreading was so . . . elementary.

My editor, Myra, had given me a project to proofread with the admonition to read it "word-for-word." Yeah, sure. I glanced over it and decided to get some coffee. When I returned to my cubicle, I noticed the polish had chipped on a fingernail, so I pulled out a bottle of polish to make the necessary repair. Then I decided to call my husband, my mother, and an airline to check on a fare. Forty-five minutes had passed and I still hadn't proofread anything.

Then the phone rang. "How's it going with the Kenyon job?" Myra asked. Her tone told me she expected me to be finished soon.

"Great," I lied. "Want to make sure I don't miss anything."

After we hung up, I raced though the copy. No problem. I made a couple of marks to make it look like I'd seriously contemplated the material. Then I marched to Myra's office and turned it in with a flourish. When she picked it up, she asked, "Did you read it word-for-word?"

"Sure," I said. Myra found five misspellings and two punctuation errors in the first three paragraphs.

I was lucky. Myra gave me a second chance. During the years I was to work under Myra, I learned a lot about what it takes to be a good editor, employee, and Christian. My laziness and pride were quickly replaced with diligence and loyalty to my employer.

In a recent survey American workers admitted to spending more than 20 percent of their time on the clock totally goofing off. That factors into a four-day workweek across the nation. Employee theft also comes in the form of turning in shoddy work; using a company phone for personal calls; using company funds for personal purchases and questionable "business" expenses; and pilfering stamps, envelopes, other office products, and copy- and fax-machine usage. Are you guilty of employee theft?

Steps of Faith

Heavenly Father, if I have been guilty of employee theft, please reveal
it to me. Give me the courage and faith I need to make restitution.
Then protect me from any temptation to commit that sin again.

Abortion

*If we confess our sins, he is faithful and just
and will forgive us our sins and purify us
from all unrighteousness.*

1 JOHN 1:9

It was shaping up to be a normal night at the hospital. The work was steady, but the halls were quiet. About 1:30 A.M. room 241 buzzed. Patti Wells was in the last stages of uterine cancer. She probably wanted some more pain medication.

As I padded down the hall, something told me to pray before going in the room. When I entered, I saw what was left of Patti. Death is ugly. It shows no mercy. After making her as comfortable as possible, I began to leave when she asked weakly, "Do you think abortion is murder?"

I stopped in my tracks and turned to face her. I was about to tell her she shouldn't be thinking about such unpleasant things when I saw the tears in her eyes. She was troubled.

"Yes, Patti, I do. I believe life is sacred. That's why I'm a nurse."

"Do you believe in God?" she whispered.

When I said yes, she asked, "Do you believe He's using this cancer to punish me? I had an abortion fifteen years ago."

I told Patti I didn't know why she was dying of cancer. But one thing we could count on was God's love and forgiveness, if we trust His work on the cross for us.

As we talked, it became clear Patti was afraid of dying. She asked me to read from the Bible, so I turned to Psalm 23. When I finished verse 4, Patti asked how she could know Jesus was with her.

"All you have to do is confess your need for a Savior. Invite Jesus Christ into your heart and trust Him at His Word. He loves you so much that He paid the price for your sins, no matter what you've done."

Patti received Christ that night and experienced His comforting presence as she walked through the valley of death three days later.

Abortion carries profound emotional, physical, and spiritual consequences—but it's not unforgiveable. If you know someone who's struggling with a past abortion, tell her there's forgiveness and restoration in Christ.

Steps of Faith

My Lord and Savior, thank You for paying the price for all the sins of the world, including abortion. Have mercy on those who have had abortions, and help me to be compassionate as well.

M
O
N
D
A
Y

187

Looking for Love

If an enemy were insulting me, I could endure it. . . .
But it is you . . . my companion, my close friend.

PSALM 55:12,13

T
U
E
S
D
A
Y

I experienced the usual amount of rejection as a young girl. Having freckles, braces, glasses, and pimples offered ample ammunition for all the bullies. Over the years it made me cautious and shy. Then in high school, when I revealed a crush on a boy, he and his friends humiliated me with jeers for a month. I had never experienced such cruelty. Was I really so awful? That possibility slowly became my biggest fear.

By the time I entered college, fear of rejection plagued me. Some guys took advantage of that fear by exchanging the attention I desired for sex. But I never felt loved. Finally, during my junior year, I attempted suicide.

A year later Christ became my Lord and Savior. Time in His Word and in prayer comforted and strengthened me. I'd finally found unconditional love.

Then I met Terry. He was everything I wanted in a man. We'd been dating off and on about three months when I wrote a poem declaring my love in a birthday card I'd designed. Terry politely accepted it. A year after we married I had the poem framed and gave it to Terry as a birthday present. As I reminisced about the first time I had given it to him, Terry lightheartedly admitted that initially he hadn't taken the poem seriously: I wasn't "exactly his dream girl."

All the fear and past rejection came crashing in. This wasn't an immature adolescent—this was my husband speaking my worst fears into existence. I was devastated.

As bad as both Terry and I felt that night, we agree it was a turning point in our marriage. Neither of us was aware of the unresolved pain I was carrying. Some time with our church counselor helped me to understand my identity in Christ and to begin healing.

Do you live in fear of rejection? Keep in mind that no fear comes from God, and His love will drive away all fears, including any fear of rejection (1 John 4:18).

Steps of Faith

Dear Father, all I have to do is look at the cross whenever I begin to wonder if anyone loves me. It is the symbol of unconditional love (1 John 3:16). Help me to remember the power of that love the next time Satan tries to deceive me with hollow fears.

A Gentle Answer

*A gentle answer turns away wrath, but a
harsh word stirs up anger.*

PROVERBS 15:1

*M*y objective as a parent has always been to make sure my four children grew into responsible and mature adults. However, as time passed, I became more controlling and intense with them. It seemed they could never meet my standards—and I was not one to hide my disappointment. I would end up screaming at one or all of them every day. And they would scream back. We were miserable.

My husband, Carl, and I began seeing a Christian family counselor. We learned how our approach to parenting was actually detrimental. The counselor worked with both of us to become parents that model and encourage the behavior we want to see in our children. (Instant conviction. I knew I had to stop screaming at them.) We began to pray for help.

It didn't happen overnight—but it did happen. Imagine Carl Jr.'s shock when he brought home a report card full of C's and D's. I looked at it, took a deep breath, and then gently said, "Sweetheart, I know you must be disappointed with these grades. But I know you can do better. How about you and I start spending 15 minutes each night going over your schoolwork? I bet by the next report card, you'll have B's and C's. And then we can talk about getting that new computer game you want."

He was stunned. And on his next report card he had four B's, three C's, one A(!)—and a new computer game.

Carl Jr. is just one example of how changing my harsh words into gentle ones began to affect each child in a positive way. And now the only screaming I do in our house is when I play with the kids!

How do you speak to your children—with kindness? Harshness? The words of a parent wield great power in a child's life. Use your words to convey your love and respect for your children. By doing so, you will show your children how to become capable and competent people.

Steps of Faith

Heavenly Father, You know how much I love my children and want the very best for them. Give me parental wisdom in disciplining, teaching, modeling, and participating in their lives. Most of all, give me gentle, kind, and loving words to convey my deep love for them.

Ultimate Justice

Do not take revenge, my friends, but leave room
for God's wrath. . . . Do not be overcome by evil, but
overcome evil with good.

ROMANS 12:19,21

*I*n our city of 50,000 we hear news reports of murders in the inner city—domestic homicides, drug- or gang-related shootings, robberies, and assaults of elderly people in their homes. But all that takes place *there*. We feel safe in our nice neighborhoods, churches, schools, and families.

But not anymore. Two years ago our neighbor's 17-year-old son shot and killed his father. This year a babysitter we knew killed the child she was sitting for by shaking it violently. And an older man in our church killed his wife and shot himself after losing his job. Suddenly murder hit very close to home.

As our church family reeled, our pastor called us to action. He traced these tragedies to a tolerance for violence and evil that has taken over our media and desensitized us and our children. Drugs are rampant. Families are unstable. Teenage pregnancies are astronomical. Guns of every sort are readily accessible. The legal system seems unable to punish the guilty and protect the innocent. Yet everyone who is murdered is an individual. The victims are not just nameless, faceless people. They have families and friends who stagger with the loss of their loved one in such a brutal way. The damage to society is incalculable and must be reversed. Our pastor challenged our congregation to get involved to stop the violence.

This year we've become partners with a church in the inner city. Leaders from both congregations maintain an active dialogue. Folks from our church work in some of their outreach programs. Our youth groups meet together once a month. And the pastoral staffs have set up a hotline for people who feel pushed to the brink. These are small steps, but in both churches, people feel like we're making a difference.

Does your church teach and talk about the sanctity of human life? Do you have an outreach program that actively addresses the problems mentioned in the above story? If not, do some research and then volunteer.

Steps of Faith

Lord God, draw me so close to You that I feel revulsion when I see
human life cheapened in the media. Help me take a stand against
programs and games that promote violence.

THURSDAY

Jehovah-Shalom

So Gideon built an altar to the LORD there
and called it The LORD is Peace.

JUDGES 6:24

A Bible study with an Israeli Christian friend has helped me understand that many words in the Bible are best understood in the original Greek or Hebrew. One such word is *peace*. Essentially it means "agreement, tranquility, lack of civil unrest." That's a good summary of what most English speakers mean by peace. We equate peace with the absence of war; we think that when all fighting, disruption, and strife is gone, peace is what is left.

The understanding of peace, in both ancient and modern Hebrew, is quite different. The Hebrew word *shalom* is formed from the same root as the words for *perfection, wholeness, completion,* and even *payment*. *Shalom* implies fullness rather than simply a lack of conflict. It emphasizes a state of rightness and perfection over that of unity and agreement.

The Hebrew language recognizes the importance of peace, or *shalom,* to the human mind and spirit. In English we say "hello" or "goodbye" to announce our comings and goings; Hebrew speakers say simply, *"Shalom."* We greet one another by asking, "How are you?" Hebrew speakers ask, *"Ma shlomech?"* which literally means, "What is the state of your peace?"

Throughout both the Old and New Testaments, it is clear that the peace that God brings does indeed necessitate the end of war and strife. But that is only the beginning of peace. Our God desires for us to know wholeness. He wants us to know *shalom*. It is what He desires for those who hurt, who grieve, who mourn, and who hunger.

From the beginning to the end, He is *Jehovah-Shalom*.

Only the peace of God—the peace that passes all understanding and fills our hearts—is sufficient to bring emotional healing, resolve our conflicts, and salve our hurts. This peace is the result of a personal relationship with His Son, Jesus. If you do not have peace *with* God or have the peace *of* God in your life, ask your pastor or a Christian friend to help you understand how you can obtain it. It's a free gift that will change your life.

Steps of Faith

Dear Father, You are the God of Peace. Though I may experience
conflict, disharmony, and disruption in my life, nothing can take
away the wholeness You have brought about within my heart and
spirit.

My Heart's Song

May my supplication come before you . . .
May my lips overflow with praise.

PSALM 119:170,171

*O*ne night Joel walked in the door and announced that he'd been laid off. I instantly knew our lives would never be the same.

I was right. First, my quiet time with the Lord became more intense; not only due to Joel's unemployment but because he had the radio or television blaring in almost every room. I could hardly hear myself think! I held off complaining and instead used my (not-so) quiet time to write out prayers for all of us: for Joel, guidance, courage, wisdom, and, of course, a job; for me, hope, and the ability to give Joel smiles, hugs, and encouragement, even when I didn't feel like it; for the children, peace and protection.

As I wrote out these prayers, the Holy Spirit revealed to me all I needed to praise God for as well: our family's health, Joel's optimism about finding a job, the money in our savings account, and a supportive church family. And an amazing thing happened: I began to see more of the good in our situation than the bad. And when that happened, all the other petitions fell into place. Except the job.

Then six months (and two notebooks of prayers and praises) later Joel finally got a job—500 miles away. As we scrambled to make all the arrangements, I continued to record my prayers and praises. It kept me focused and positive. But when we climbed in the car and waved our final farewells to neighbors and friends, I could feel my heart breaking.

I allowed myself a good cry for the first hour or so. (My family knows I'm sentimental.) Then I reached for my notebooks and began reading all the prayers that God had faithfully answered over the last six months . . . and all of those praises. It made my heart sing. I knew we were in God's loving, mighty hands—and I quickly wrote out my heart's latest song.

Do you ever write out your prayers and praises? It has a stabilizing, tranquilizing effect. If you've never done anything like that, today write a simple letter to God about your feelings, thoughts, concerns, even your tough questions. God wants you to share them. He can handle them.

Steps of Faith

"May my cry come before you, O LORD; give me understanding according to your word. May my supplication come before you; deliver me according to your promise. May my lips overflow with praise, for you teach me your decrees. May my tongue sing of your word" (Psalm 119:169-172).

For Sanity's Sake

The troubles of my heart have multiplied;
free me from my anguish.

PSALM 25:17

*I*t saved my sanity. Crisis upon crisis had overwhelmed me. It was my one grip on reality. And it was what led me back to God.

A friend at work suggested I take time on my lunch hour to journal some of my feelings—not for posterity's sake, but for sanity's sake. There were so many emotions erupting in me, so many conflicts and problems. Writing them down could help me identify them and sort them out.

As I did, a pattern began to emerge. Emptiness, isolation, and anger in my marriage; disappointment, fear, and anger with my children; bitterness, envy, and anger with a sister-in-law; betrayal, abandonment, and anger with God.

It was clear. Anger was destroying my life and some of the most important relationships in my life. When I began writing why I was angry at each of these people, I started to realize why they could (and should) be angry at me. There were a lot of tears during this time, but they were the evidence of healing; it hurt, but I knew I was making progress. And as I read and reread the words of my heart, I could feel my emotions clearing, stabilizing, and strengthening.

Finally I had to address my relationship with God. I realized I was the one who had abandoned and betrayed Him. For the first time I understood the analogy of the lost sheep. I had wandered off; I was helpless and scared. All I could think to do was write the Lord's Prayer in my journal and hope that He would hear me and come get me.

He did, and I've continued to chronicle my journey with Him. But now it's more for posterity's sake—my sanity is just fine, thank you.

A counselor once said: "If everyone journaled regularly and deeply, there would be less traffic to psychotherapists." When you experience a trial, do you ignore it or magnify it? Neither approach is healthy. But if you keep a journal, you are more likely to see the problem for what it is and respond appropriately.

M
O
N
D
A
Y

Steps of Faith

Dear Shepherd of my soul, the next time I experience a trial, give me the discipline and wisdom to write it all out, think about it, and pray about it. Bless my own words in a way that they will bless me back. And thank You for always being so close.

A Victorious Cycle

*We set our hearts at rest in his presence whenever
our hearts condemn us. For God is greater than
our hearts, and he knows everything.*

1 JOHN 3:19,20

*T*his year's women's retreat was . . . different. I wasn't prepared for the way it was going to affect me that weekend, but I praise God for the way it has changed my life as a wife and mother.

The speaker was a Christian counselor who addressed emotional and spiritual health. She opened with a prayer asking God to reveal in each woman's heart any anger or unforgiveness she might be harboring toward another person . . . or herself.

I felt a stab in my heart. She had hit a nerve.

When the speaker began discussing anger at oneself, my stomach and throat began to tighten. And when she pointed out that this anger not only affects our relationship with God but also with our children, I was overwhelmed with grief for all the times I had lost my temper or spanked my children for minor offenses. I realized that for years I'd been feeling guilty for withholding love from them and, when I didn't know how to compensate for that denial of love, I became even more angry at myself. It was a vicious cycle.

Before long, several of us were weeping. Bewildered, the counselor (who is not a mother) stopped and asked for some feedback. Different mothers tearfully expressed their feelings of inadequacy, fear, frustration, and guilt. And as we hugged and consoled each other, healing and hope flooded the room.

Studies show that most mothers suffer some degree of remorse and self-doubt. Do you? If so, consider: an accountability relationship with a friend or spouse; the power of Scripture to give you peace and guidance; planning what to say to your child before he or she makes you angry (be specific); a delayed reaction; giving your child permission not to be perfect (major on the majors); learning each child's unique learning style and personality, then adjusting your behavior accordingly; keeping consistent rules and expectations; and taking breaks from your children.

Steps of Faith

Dear Father, I had no idea how tough motherhood could be—but I'm so thankful for my precious children. Help me to be a godly mother, who can live at peace with You, my children, and myself.

A Model Figure

Is not . . . the body
more important than clothes?

MATTHEW 6:25

*J*ackie has a job that some women would consider the ultimate glamorous profession—she's a fashion model. She looks the way you would expect a model to look; she's almost six feet tall, very photogenic, with striking facial features and gorgeous auburn hair. There's just one difference between Jackie and most other models. Jackie weighs 230 pounds. She models clothes for women who wear size 16 or larger.

"I suffered so much all through high school and college," Jackie says, "trying to achieve the 'ideal' look, which was thin and lanky. And then, when I began to seek out modeling jobs, I realized that I couldn't maintain the desirable figure unless I consistently starved myself. So that's what I did.

"I finally woke up to reality when I knew that I didn't want to sacrifice my health, let alone my life, to the fashion industry. I learned to eat a healthy diet, stay physically fit, and to like my body the way it was. With the help of God, I finally learned once and for all to separate my identity and sense of well-being from my appearance. It's sad, but so many of those 'perfect' models can't do that. Believe me, they're not any happier than anyone else because of their looks. They're just under more pressure.

"Getting the opportunity to model for large-size clothing shops and catalogues has really been a healing experience for me. It's enabled me to have a career in clothing and design, which I love. But it also allows me to prove to women that *every* body type can be beautiful and feminine and fashionable."

It's a peculiar trait of human history that the standards by which a culture measures beauty tend to change over different periods. But our bodies, unlike architecture, music, and art, should not be judged by these standards; they serve other purposes. God never intended the female body to be an expression of the aesthetic values of a society.

Steps of Faith

Father, I thank You that You did not create my body to be merely a decorative object or a hanger for clothes; You had much nobler purposes in mind. I want my appearance to be pleasing, but I pray that You would protect me from developing a distorted, untruthful image of how my body ought to look.

195

Body Image

*The Lord Jesus Christ, who, by the power that enables
him to bring everything under his control, will transform our
lowly bodies so that they will be like his glorious body.*

PHILIPPIANS 3:20,21

T
H
U
R
S
D
A
Y

*T*hroughout my college years, I had anorexia nervosa. At five feet seven inches I should have weighed a healthy 130-140 pounds. I weighed 112 pounds, and I thought I was fat. I actually wore a girdle sometimes. I was obsessed with my appearance and terrified of food. However, I knew I had to eat something, so my daily intake of food was limited to one lean hamburger patty and a diet soft drink. Period.

After graduating and getting a job, falling in love and getting married, my life stabilized. I gained more weight until I hovered in the 130-140 pound range. Then with the birth of my first child and the stress of all the changes taking place in my life and my marriage, what should have been a temporary weight gain seemed to have become permanent. I had ballooned to 182 pounds.

I felt hideous, even though, depending on what I wore, I carried the weight rather well. But I couldn't see it at the time. I was still under the control of the god of physical perfection.

When I finally got some counseling, I began to see that my obsession with my appearance was simply an avoidance of peering into the trouble in the deep recesses of my soul. Whether I weighed 112, 135, or 182, there was pain I needed to confront. And when I began to realize my worth as a daughter of the Creator of the universe, the god of physical perfection was forever banished from my soul.

One-tenth of all young women struggle with some sort of eating disorder. Older women who are happiest with their weight are ten pounds underweight, and those who are at their ideal weight wish they weighed eight pounds less. Do you struggle with your body image? If so, list five positive features about your physical appearance. Next determine what you want to change, why, and if it is reasonable. Then make a plan to make it a reality. God has already given you the power to do it.

Steps of Faith

Almighty Father, even though I know this body is just a temporary shell, I often get swept into the world's perspective of what is beautiful and worthwhile. I want to honor this body You've given me, not worship it. And I look forward to the glorious body that awaits me in heaven.

The Refrigerator

Be devoted to one another in brotherly love.
Honor one another above yourselves.

ROMANS 12:10

*E*ver since I started working at XYZ Printshop, along with most of the other employees I have kept my lunch in the old refrigerator in the back corner of the warehouse. Even though the refrigerator is practically an antique, it is always clean. I figured the janitorial service must be taking care of it.

Then one Saturday morning I went into the office to catch up on my proofreading. The only other car in the parking lot was the late-model luxury car that belongs to Calvin Sanders, the vice president. Everyone loves Calvin. He is the kind of man who makes time to chat with the employees. However, when I stopped by his office to say hello, he was nowhere around.

Before I settled at my desk, I decided to get a soda. Since I keep a stockpile of diet soft drinks in the refrigerator, I made my way back to the warehouse. To my shock, there was Calvin on his knees, wearing blue jeans and a T-shirt, surrounded by plastic containers, cans of soda, and cartons of juice, wiping down the door and shelves of the refrigerator.

Calvin was startled at first, but then smiled and gave me a cheery "Good morning!" I asked him why *he* was cleaning the refrigerator. He chuckled and told me that every two or three months he takes a Saturday to clean and check it out. Noting the astonishment on my face, Calvin went on to say that this had been his parents' refrigerator, it held much sentiment for him, and he wanted to make sure it was taken care of. Then he added, "You guys work hard enough. You don't need to worry about keeping this old refrigerator clean. And besides, I enjoy doing it."

No one is above kindness. Jesus said, "Whoever wants to become great among you must be your servant" (Matthew 20:26). If God has placed you in a position of leadership or high esteem, ask yourself what kind of example you are setting for the people who look up to you.

Steps of Faith

Father, I confess that at times I have avoided a menial task because I thought it was beneath me. Please forgive me. Jesus washed the feet of His disciples; I can surely clean a refrigerator, empty trash cans, or wash some dishes. Show me how I can serve others with acts of kindness.

197

Plant, Water, Reap

I tell you, open your eyes and look at the fields!
They are ripe for harvest.

JOHN 4:35

I walked slowly out of church that Sunday, eyes fixed to the ground, stomach hurting. A guest speaker had preached about sharing Christ with others. He made it sound so effortless. He told one story after another about the Lord leading him to people who couldn't wait to receive Jesus as their Savior. Whether it was a person next to him on an airplane, in the grocery store, or at a baseball game—all he had to do was say "Jesus" and it seemed that person would enthusiastically drop whatever he or she was doing and pray the Sinner's Prayer.

Then toward the end of his sermon he hinted that anyone not enjoying that level of evangelistic success probably wasn't right with the Lord. There must be unconfessed sin in that life.

That's when I got sick. I love telling others about Jesus, but I have seen only a handful accept Him as Savior. That I didn't have a bunch of "soul notches" on my belt had never bothered me before; I had always sensed that God was blessing my work for the kingdom.

But suddenly I wasn't so sure.

The next Sunday our pastor told us that several members had spoken to him about the previous week's speaker. He had a few comments. "If you approach evangelism expecting everyone to respond positively, and they don't, you think there's something wrong with you. Satan will use that feeling to discourage you.

"The truth is, friends, evangelism is a process of planting, watering, and reaping. Some of us are planters, some are waterers, and some are reapers. We can't all be reapers all the time."

Are you one of those people who loves to share your faith with others but doesn't ever seem to see the fruit of your labor? Maybe you're a planter or a waterer instead of a reaper. And you may have a different role with different people. Ask God to give you insight and wisdom with each person with whom you share your faith.

Steps of Faith

Dear Heavenly Father, I praise You for Your faithfulness. I know You are with me whenever I speak the name of Your Son, Jesus Christ, to others. Give me courage and wisdom, Lord, as I obey Your command to share the Good News with those around me.

The Perfectionist

*For it is by grace you have been saved,
through faith—and this is not from yourselves,
it is the gift of God—not by works.*

EPHESIANS 2:8,9

*H*ello. My name is Anita, and I'm a perfectionist." It was a momentous event. I had just surrendered what had been my security for most of my life. I was exposed, and I was going to be held accountable.

At first glance we didn't look like a group of perfectionists. Some had every hair in place and perfectly starched clothes, but I wasn't that kind of perfectionist. Along with several others, I was a "pocket perfectionist."

My "pockets" were sewing, cooking, and dieting. I would set impossible goals for my age or level of ability. "I'm going to sew all of my summer clothes with designer patterns." "This Christmas I'll bake gourmet goodies for all of our friends." "I'm going to get into my size seven jeans again, the ones I wore in college."

When the clothes, gourmet goodies, or body didn't come out picture-perfect, I gave up. I felt like a failure.

Some of the exercises we did in our group were listing the benefits of making mistakes, naming our strengths, and discussing why it's impossible for us to be perfect. The one that really opened my eyes was writing out what I was currently putting off because of fear of failure. Then I had to write down a date that I would attempt it.

I began to understand my problem and saw a comparison between it and God's plan for salvation. I know I can't earn salvation through works. Yet without realizing it, I'd been striving for human acceptance. But no one expects perfection, not even God. I need to do the best I can do. Excellence is now the goal, not perfection.

Perfectionism is legalism, and it can creep into the life of the most dedicated Christian. Are you striving for perfection instead of excellence? Find a healthy balance. Do what you do best, know when to stop, affirm your efforts, and most of all, forgive your imperfections. God already has.

Steps of Faith

Glorious Father, Your love and acceptance of me as Your daughter is the greatest and most mysterious aspect of my life. And though I tend to be very critical of myself, give me the patience and wisdom to know that, through Christ, perfection has already been achieved.

M
O
N
D
A
Y

Smartly Dressed

She sees that her trading is profitable.

PROVERBS 31:18

"Maureen, I'm so frustrated. I spent the entire day shopping for clothes and I came home with absolutely nothing." After a long and fruitless day at the mall, Sally just wanted to collapse in an easy chair and talk on the phone to her friend.

"Why? Didn't you see anything you liked?" asked Maureen.

"It wasn't that. I just couldn't decide on anything. Clothes and shoes are so expensive. I need things for work, for church, and for Ellen's wedding. I thought with $200, I could easily get everything I needed, but that's hardly enough to buy one outfit."

"Really? Two hundred dollars would get me at least five outfits," Maureen said, laughing.

"Oh, sure," said Sally. "You don't fool me. You always look great. You must spend a lot on clothes."

"But I don't. First of all, I don't buy anything at the mall unless it's on sale. I mostly shop at outlet stores and those warehouse places. You get the same clothes as in department stores for less money. The main thing to remember, though, is that accessories go a long way. Start with just one thing: a well-made dress in a neutral color. I like black. If I wear it with a jacket and scarf, it's perfect for work or for church. If I want to wear it to dinner, I add my silver jewelry and take off the jacket. And if I wear it with pearls and dressy heels, it's fine for all but the most formal occasions. Your money will go a lot further if you buy fewer 'outfits' and more hosiery, shoes, and costume jewelry. I know mine does."

"I should have taken you with me today," said Sally. "Hey, are you doing anything next Saturday?"

Plan your wardrobe. Watch for sales. Buy classic, good-quality clothing that does not go out of style. Accessorize to suit your personal taste. And for even more fun, ask a friend whose taste you trust to join you in a shopping trip.

Steps of Faith

Father, thank You for providing me with money for new clothes every now and then. Please give me the wisdom not to waste money on clothes I do not wear, and the creativity to put together an attractive wardrobe without spending more than I should.

Patience for Peter

Be completely humble and gentle; be patient.
EPHESIANS 4:2

Greta, her husband gone on a week-long business trip, had been invited to dinner by her friend Pam. Pam had five children, one of whom, Peter, had Down's syndrome. Greta had no children. She was grateful for the invitation, but having experienced "family" dinners with her other friends, she resigned herself to an evening of chaos and noise.

The dinner was a new experience for Greta. As the evening progressed, she noticed several things. First of all, everyone, even the smallest child, was polite to everyone else. When someone asked for the butter or the salt to be passed, he sat patiently and waited; there was no grabbing, no raising of voices, no protests of "I asked for it first!" Not once did Pam or Jeff have to break up any quarrels or remind the children of their manners. When someone spoke, everyone else listened quietly without interrupting. Greta enjoyed the time with the family immensely.

As Greta helped Pam dry the dishes after dinner, she remarked, "I have to say, Pam, I've never seen such well-behaved kids. I'm in awe."

"Thanks, but I can't take all of the credit," Pam said. "It has a lot to do with Peter. He requires continuous patience. He can't keep up with the rest of the kids. It takes him twice as long to say a sentence. He can't run as fast or ride a bike yet. The kids have developed so much patience with him that they've fallen into the habit of being patient with each other all the time. It's amazing how just a little patience and courtesy can affect the atmosphere of the whole household."

Courteous behavior is mostly a matter of patience. We need patience over the long term to endure life's trials and hardships, but we need short-term patience in our day-to-day relationships if we are truly committed to loving our neighbors as we love ourselves.

Steps of Faith

Dear Father, when I consider the example set for us by Your Son, I understand that patience grows from love. I see that treating others with love and respect means exercising patience. I confess that I have often been impatient. Remind me throughout the day to use patience in my speech, actions, and even in my thoughts as I interact with other people.

China and Beyond

Is [the fasting I have chosen] not to share your food with the
hungry and to provide the poor wanderer with shelter—
when you see the naked, to clothe him, and not to turn away
from your own flesh and blood?

ISAIAH 58:7

*B*eing an American missionary to China has allowed me the privilege of living in two very different cultures. There are several events and people that led me to answer the call to the mission field, but none more powerful than the story of Lottie Moon.

I never knew who Lottie Moon was until I was 16, when a missionary from China spoke to our church. She, too, had been inspired by the sacrifice of Lottie Moon for the Chinese people.

Lottie was called to China in 1873 as a church planter. In 1911, after Lottie's almost 40 years with the Chinese people, a smallpox epidemic and severe drought struck. Lottie told the churches back home about the countless starving and homeless people and begged them to share their wealth and abundance with the less fortunate. They responded, meagerly. When she asked for more support, there was no reply.

Soon Lottie's own bank account and food supply were depleted, and she was starving along with the others. When she became critically ill, arrangements were made for her to return home by boat in the company of a nurse. But it was too late. Lottie died on Christmas Eve, 1912, aboard ship at a Japanese port.

The following year the women of Lottie's home church established a Christmas offering in her name to help provide for the needs on the mission field around the world.

How are you affected by stories about people like Lottie Moon and their sacrifice for others? Are you moved to discover whether you should go across the globe as a missionary or give a sacrificial offering to someone else's work? Either way you are participating in the Great Commission.

Steps of Faith

Almighty Father, I am in awe of Your grace, which empowers ordinary people like myself to do extraordinary things for You. I yield my life to You, Father, with the prayer that it will fulfill all of Your expectations.

The Intruder

The LORD . . . sustains the fatherless and the widow.

PSALM 146:9

*W*idowhood. Few words evoke more unhappy thoughts and images; few young wives care to contemplate this most unwelcome intrusion. But as death will always intrude upon life, so widowhood will always intrude upon marriage—for one spouse or the other. In my case, I was the one chosen to endure a season of widowhood. My husband died three years ago.

Though I can't say that grief is a thing of the past for me, I have discovered that life really does go on, and time really does ease the pain of separation.

It hasn't been easy. After the first few months I thought I saw the light at the end of the tunnel, but it was really the freight train of depression coming straight at me! I had to realize that my husband was not going to come back—ever. I was overcome with a sense of purposelessness and apathy. I couldn't sleep. During the day I didn't know what to do with myself.

One day I could stand it no longer. I called a close friend and told her I no longer wanted to live. She helped me enormously by listening—listening for hours as I sorted out my jumbled feelings. Then she began to encourage me to do things. She knew I didn't feel like going to the garden club, but she would pick me up anyway. She called every morning to make sure I had gotten up and had a plan for that day. If I didn't, she'd come over and we'd make one. Eventually I began to find my own way again.

And I know that God has been at my side every moment.

Seldom is anyone really prepared for widowhood. Women who have lost husbands carry a heavy burden; they need their friends to keep calling, to keep encouraging them, to keep praying—especially after the first few months.

Steps of Faith

Father, I don't want to think about having to survive the death of my husband, but I know that at some point it may happen. Make me especially sensitive to women in my church and neighborhood who are going through this. Use me to help keep them connected to others in our community.

Boxes and Bags

It is required that those who have been given
a trust must prove faithful.

1 CORINTHIANS 4:2

*A*fter years of getting frazzled about Christmas shopping, I finally found a system that not only maintains my sanity during the holiday season, it actually makes it fun.

In a corner of my basement I have a series of cardboard boxes and paper bags marked with the names of my husband, children, stepchildren, grandchildren, nieces, nephews, neighbors, friends, and one marked "Emergency." Throughout the year, whether I'm at a garage sale or an exclusive department store, I keep my eye out for things any of my loved ones might enjoy or need.

There are many advantages to this system, the obvious one being that I accomplish most of my Christmas shopping in advance. Another is that it makes me a patient shopper—there's no desperate impulse buying. I methodically make my rounds at the department stores. If I spot a sweater or blouse for someone, I'll watch it for weeks until it hits the clearance rack. Then I swoop in.

My favorite advantage is in shopping for my husband, who is impossible to buy for. One Saturday afternoon in April, in a moment of weakness, Harvey displayed a vague interest in some landscaping software we saw at the local nursery. I went back the next day and found out it would go on sale in July. Three months later I bought it at half price. And you should have seen Harvey's face when he unwrapped it on Christmas morning—I thought he was going to cry.

Ron Blue writes in his book, *Master Your Money,* "The longer the term of perspective, the better is the decision making." That's why beginning Christmas shopping before the season rush can prevent costly mistakes. Think of at least one person you will buy a Christmas gift for this month. Ask God to help you find the right gift at a price within your budget.

Steps of Faith

Lord, I want to handle money in a way that is pleasing to You. Often my perspective is not long-term, but immediate. Grant me the discipline to begin my Christmas shopping earlier. Maybe then I'll be able to relax more in the true spirit of Christmas and celebrate Your wondrous birth.

For Less Stress

An anxious heart weighs a man down,
but a kind word cheers him up.

PROVERBS 12:25

*M*aryanne slid gratefully into the steaming bathtub. She closed her eyes and consciously tried to relax. She imagined the foamy bubbles assaulting her taut nerves on all sides and pushing back the enemy—stress.

All day, she had juggled errands, phone calls, and appointments. She'd moved piles of paper at the office and, later, piles of laundry at home. She'd driven miles around town delivering kids to school, soccer, music lessons. Rushing home to prepare dinner, Maryanne was caught in a traffic jam and arrived late to find Mark and the kids eating take-out pizza.

On another day, she might have laughed and joined them at the table. But today, she felt she couldn't cope. She needed relief—fast! She remembered the Snickers bar she had left over from lunch. She had relished her treat while the tub was filling. Now, soaking in the bubble bath, she chuckled at herself. *No wonder they call chocolate "comfort food." Maybe I should repackage the Snickers bars and call them "Maryanne's Stress Reliever No. 1."*

As she added more hot water, Maryanne found herself mentally listing other ways to relieve stress: soft music, candlelight, curling up in front of the fire with a good book, eating popcorn in front of an old movie, making love, giving or receiving a back rub or foot massage, laughing until her sides hurt, spending quiet time with the Lord, taking a walk, and regular exercise. Over time Maryanne found that daily quiet time as well as exercise actually prevented stress!

Make a list of activities that cause you stress and consider how those could be changed or eliminated. Perhaps certain people push your buttons. Can you lessen daily contact with them? Take some time today to relax and relieve stress in your own life.

Steps of Faith

Dear Lord, You have told me not to worry or be anxious, and yet my life seems filled with stress. Help me to find ways to relax and to trust You more with my concerns.

No Longer Needed

*A man who strays from the path of understanding comes
to rest in the company of the dead.*

PROVERBS 21:16

*P*eople are often surprised to discover I'm married. This is probably because I'm seldom seen in public with my husband, Ed. We did manage to sit next to each other at our youngest daughter's wedding eight years ago. I have photographs to prove it. And I think we were spotted together at Uncle Morris's funeral, but no one was taking pictures that day.

Let me tell you a little about Ed. He's a good man and a dedicated employee. He doesn't beat or cheat on me, but Ed's been an absentee husband and father for years. He works a lot of overtime at the plant, sometimes double shifts. It took me years to realize that this was his way of saying, "I love you."

I tried to convince Ed that money wasn't as important as his time, his input, and his companionship. I finally gave up. The children and I adapted to a life with a husband and father who was either sleeping or working when we needed him. After awhile, no one needed Ed.

It hasn't always been that way. We used to go to church every Sunday—together, in the same car. Imagine that. Ed was raised in the church, but I'd often wondered if he knew what walking with Christ was all about. Between the children's activities and his increasing work schedule, we seldom had a chance to discuss the bills, the kids, or sex, much less spiritual matters.

Ed just faded out. And each family member, in the darkness of his or her private pain, gradually blocked Ed out of his or her heart and life.

Poor Ed. He's about to retire, and he doesn't know he's lost his family.

Are you married to an Ed? If you have an absentee spouse, pray for him every day (Colossians 1:9-13). Each morning before he leaves, ask him how you can pray for him. Involve yourself in his life. Also try to carve out a consistent time each week for a date with just you or the entire family.

Steps of Faith

Omnipresent Father, there is no one who spends more time with me than You. What a comfort that is. Guard my heart from hardening against my husband. He gets so busy and seems to forget the rest of us. Open his eyes to the potential damage before it's too late.

A Faithful Heart

The Lord has rewarded me according to my righteousness,
according to the cleanness of my hands in his sight.

PSALM 18:24

*B*renda prayed with the boys before tucking them in. "Help me to be good while Daddy is gone," Devon asked. "Me, too!" echoed Daniel. She hugged them tightly and kissed them both good night.

Later she prayed, "Father, please help me, too. Marty and I both believe this assignment in Japan is right for his career, and I understand why I can't go. But three months is such a long separation. I miss him so much, Lord!"

As Brenda crawled into bed, she recalled what had happened that afternoon. The new furniture for the boys' room had been delivered, and Jeff, her neighbor, had come to help her rearrange the room. As they were moving around the close quarters she had accidentally brushed against his arm. Brenda was startled by the feeling that came over her. It was her husband's touch she longed for. She wondered how other women managed separations. None of her friends talked about this aspect of their marriages.

Before she went to sleep Brenda made plans to resist temptation. First she would send lots of cards and letters as well as keep a journal for Marty to read when he got home. Second, she planned many special activities with the boys. And finally, she purposed to read God's Word faithfully and make her devotional life a priority.

The next day Brenda called a trusted friend and asked her to hold her accountable. That friend became her daily prayer partner and even took the boys for a long weekend three weeks after Marty finally arrived home.

If your husband goes on frequent or extended trips, the separation may be a strain. Yet God's command is that we remain faithful and pure in both mind and body. God loves you so much that He will give you the strength you need if you commit to obedience in this area. Ask Him.

Steps of Faith

Dear Heavenly Father, only You can help me remain faithful during this season of my life. Give me wisdom in handling these very real tensions every day.

Wapello or Bust

May God be gracious to us and bless us
and make his face shine upon us.

PSALM 67:1

Y ou can't be serious," my husband, Kirk, moaned. "Who ever heard of going to Wapello, Iowa, for a family vacation? Do you realize that's got to be more than a thousand miles—one way?"

"Eleven hundred, according to my calculations," I chirped. "I've already mapped it out for us. See?" I proudly handed him maps with our route to Wapello designated with a black marker.

"Hon-e-ey," he said, shifting to a borderline whine. "How . . . why . . . Wapello, Iowa?"

"Well . . . you know that map of the United States hanging in the boys' room? I decided to close my eyes and walk across the room with my finger pointed toward the map. Wherever my finger hit first was our vacation destination! The kids loved it!"

Okay, it wasn't the most sensible way to plan a vacation, but it turned out to be a smash hit. Kirk has always enjoyed learning the history of the Mississippi River. So we drove to Memphis, crossed the Mississippi, and drove north along the river through Arkansas, Missouri, and into Iowa. We got to Wapello around noon, ate lunch, had someone take our picture in front of the "Welcome to Wapello" sign, and headed out of town.

On our return trip, after crossing the Mississippi into Illinois, our alternator died. I could tell Kirk was concerned. For two hours the children and I prayed someone would help us before it got dark. Then, right at dusk, a farmer and his wife came to our rescue. They even fed us supper.

Years later, our children still talk about that trip and all the states they got to drive through. However, what they most remember is how God provided for and protected us when we were far from home.

Next vacation, map out your route so you can determine if there are any other places your family may want to visit along the way. And always keep in mind that no matter how far you are from home, it's not too far from God.

Steps of Faith

Dear Father, family vacations are exciting and exhausting, fun, and frantic. Planning always helps, but sometimes I don't know where to begin. Give me wisdom this summer as I try to put it all together. Protect me from stress, and allow me to just enjoy the time with my family.

Two Sisters

Leave your gift there in front of the altar. First go and be reconciled to your [sister]; then come and offer your gift.

MATTHEW 5:24

$\mathcal{F}$or 37 years, my sister, Alma, and I lived in the same small town, belonged to the same church, sang in the same church choir, and didn't speak one word to each other.

It all began in 1952 when our husbands decided to start a dry-cleaning business together. Alma's husband, Henry, and my husband, Gene, both invested $2,300, bought the necessary equipment, and leased a building adjacent to the courthouse. It was sure to be a success.

After two years of booming business, we discovered that Gene had a gambling problem and had embezzled thousands of dollars to pay his gambling debts. There was a terrible scandal and the business went bankrupt. Henry and Alma lost all of their savings.

Henry and Alma were so angry at Gene that Henry forbade Alma to speak to me. At first Alma and I tried to meet secretly, but over time, roots of bitterness strangled our relationship.

By 1991 both Henry and Gene were dead, but Alma and I were still not speaking. One day in August I found a small note taped to my front door. It was from Alma's daughter, Ruth. All it said was, "Momma has cancer. St. Joseph's. Room 216. Six weeks."

When I read those words all the anger, bitterness, and pride melted away. Love and concern for Alma overwhelmed me, along with a strange new peace. I was at her bedside 15 minutes later, holding her hand, as the two of us wept over the squandered years.

And 54 bittersweet days later, when Alma went home to be with the Lord, I understood why God wants all His daughters to be reconciled to one another. Sisters are precious. Peace is priceless.

Is there someone in your life to whom you need to be reconciled? Are unconfessed anger, bitterness, and pride standing in your way? If so, ask God to forgive you and heal you. When His peace fills your heart, God will be able to show you how you can be reconciled to that brother or sister.

Steps of Faith

Prince of Peace, how Your heart must grieve when Your children are estranged by sin. Please grant me the faith and wisdom I need to reconcile myself to anyone I may have injured. When I consider what You paid to reconcile us to You, any cost I may bear is minuscule.

FRIDAY

209

Play Mate

Enjoy life with your wife, whom you love.

ECCLESIASTES 9:9

Not only is my husband my best friend, he's my favorite playmate. But it took us several years to get to this point.

When Randy and I were first married, we often disagreed about what to do with our spare time. Randy is a sports fanatic, so naturally he wanted to watch football, baseball, basketball, golf, or whatever else was in town or on the tube. On the other hand, I wanted to go for a drive, have a picnic in the park, watch an old movie, or just talk about our future.

During that time, arguing was about all we did do together.

Over the years, as we've matured and gotten to know more about each other, we've learned to compromise and develop common interests. For instance, I decided to learn more about football and baseball. The more I learn, the more I appreciate what is happening in the game. And to make it interesting, sometimes we'll cheer for opposing teams—and the next morning the loser has to serve coffee to the winner in bed.

Randy's compromise was to go for a drive once in a while and be more willing to discuss the future. In fact we usually end up talking about our goals and dreams while on those drives. I love it because I have an attentive husband and no outside distractions. Some of our best discussions have taken place in our car.

A couple of years ago I was shocked to discover that my husband *loves* cooking shows. Since I enjoy cooking, we often tape our favorite chef and try some new dishes or a variation on old favorites. We have great fun shopping for all the ingredients, creating our culinary masterpieces, and even cleaning up the mess we make.

Not only is my husband my playmate, he's my soul mate. Randy and I share a deep and abiding faith in Jesus Christ, and that above all of our other interests is what keeps our love (and the fun!) alive.

Do you and your spouse set aside time to play? Do you have any common hobbies or interests you can explore together? If not, make an effort to discover a diversion the two of you can enjoy exclusively. And be willing to compromise.

Steps of Faith

Father of mercy and grace, thank You for my precious husband. He is so dear to me. Help me to enjoy what he enjoys. I want him to have more fun with me than with any other person. I want our friendship to grow.

W
E
E
K
E
N
D

The Look

The Lord turned and looked straight at Peter. Then Peter remembered the word the Lord had spoken to him. . . . And he went outside and wept bitterly.

*F*ew stories in the Bible give me goose bumps like the account of Peter's denial of Jesus. All four gospels report the event, but Luke's gospel is the only account which includes "the look."

I know "the look." I was raised with it. It is silent, yet speaks volumes. My father was a master of "the look." This meant he seldom had to yell or spank. "The look" was enough.

Once when I was about six years old, I became angry at my friend, Betsy. I stood in my driveway calling her every name I could think of. "Big baby" and "ugly dummy" were about the extent of my verbal arsenal, and they just didn't seem effective. Then I remembered a name, one I certainly had not heard in my house, and lobbed it. It must have been a good one, because Betsy screamed and ran inside to tell her mother.

I did an about-face and marched triumphantly toward my house. Unfortunately, I had not seen my father cleaning out his car. He had heard every word. When my eyes met his, my heart broke. He was giving me "the look." I burst into tears, ran into the house and down the hall into my room, where I cried for two hours.

Imagine Peter's reaction to Jesus' look. He must have been overwhelmed by the conviction of his sin, the denial of his Lord and friend. All he could do was flee the scene of the crime and mourn his mistake. But beyond that, maybe there was a newfound awareness of Jesus' meekness; that Jesus, who had the power to instantly annihilate Peter, simply looked at him. Was it a look of disappointment? Anger? Pain? Love? Concern? Maybe a combination of all those. That's what I always saw in my father's eyes, and it was enough.

As you read this account of Peter's denial, try to imagine the scene from both perspectives, Jesus' and Peter's. When have you denied your Lord by your words and actions? Can you imagine Jesus looking at you just as He looked at Peter all those centuries ago?

Steps of Faith

Most merciful Father, I am amazed at how You convict and discipline me through silence. Help me to be more aware of how my behavior hurts You and the world around me.

211

Cowboy Buddies

Children's children are a crown to the aged, and parents are the pride of their children.

PROVERBS 17:6

*M*y father and I were not close while I was growing up. In fact it would be safe to say that we were strangers living in the same house.

After high school, I went off to college, met my future husband, married, and had three babies. Dad was always somewhere in the background. And as I think back, if my husband had not taken a job that brought us to Dallas, I'm afraid I would have let Dad stay in the background. What a loss that would have been in my life.

For 25 years Dad has been a loyal Dallas Cowboys fan. Naturally he was thrilled to hear that we were moving to the home of the "greatest football team on earth." Dad began visiting us every football season and would treat us to a Cowboys game. Dad and I always sat next to each other, discussing plays and players. Eventually I, too, became a Cowboys fan.

The Cowboys became our common ground, and in it a special friendship began to take root. Dad and I began discussing other aspects of our lives, including our faith in God and love for prayer. We discovered we had much in common, things I thought I had developed independently.

Then one unforgettable night, everyone had gone to bed except Dad and me. We were sitting by the fireplace talking about, you guessed it, the Cowboys. At one point Dad paused, looked at me thoughtfully, and said, "You know, honey, we really are a lot alike. I wish I'd known that when you were little. I'm afraid we lost a lot of years."

All I could do was nod in agreement. I was too choked up to say a word. I was so thankful for the years God had saved for us to be friends.

If you and your father are not friends, you may be missing out on a precious relationship, one that can help you understand more about who you are. If possible, make a special effort to cultivate a friendship with him. You'll always be Daddy's girl, but now you can also be his friend.

Steps of Faith

Dear Father God, thank You for my special friendship with my father. Even though I regret that it took us years to discover each other as friends, I trust that Your timing is perfect. Bless my father, God, and our relationship during these remaining years we have together.

T
U
E
S
D
A
Y

Life at the Wheel

*Jesus did many other things as well. If every one of them were
written down, I suppose that even the whole world would not
have room for the books that would be written.*

JOHN 21:25

*W*ith four athletic teenagers, I have spent literally hundreds of
hours driving thousands of miles, toting them to and from their
respective activities. One day all four had games at about the same
time. I put more than 100 miles on my car that afternoon.

I confess that at times I felt resentful. As I drove, I would mentally check off a list of chores and errands that I could have been
doing. I also resented my sacrifice of much-needed time for *me*, and
no one seemed to appreciate it. Instead I was sitting in traffic or
racing down the expressway with a car full of teenagers who were
either rowdy or pouty.

And when I didn't feel resentful, I felt guilty! Even though I was
constantly busy, nothing ever seemed to get accomplished. I felt like
a failure as a wife and mother.

Finally I turned to God's Word for direction. I realized that Jesus
was probably the busiest person who ever lived; but His busyness
was rooted in purpose. He used every opportunity to achieve His
objectives.

God helped me see the value of the hours spent with my children
in the car. I was investing my time into their precious lives. What an
opportunity to encourage them or learn more about their friends,
hopes, and problems. Sure, sometimes they wouldn't talk, but I
learned to be patient and not force conversation. Sometimes they
wouldn't stop talking!

What I once considered the "curse of carpooling" is now a priceless
blessing in my life. I cherish that time and wouldn't sacrifice one minute.

Jesus was an expert time manager. Consider His strategy: He surrendered His will to God, knew His purpose, got the necessary rest,
had His priorities straight, and wisely invested His time. When
busyness is subject to God's will, it will not overwhelm.

WEDNESDAY

Steps of Faith

*Oh Father of the ages, though You are not bound by the constraints
of time, I know You can help me manage my time better. Please ease
my frustrations with Your wisdom. Open my heart to Your will. I
want to follow the example of my Lord, who accomplished so much
in so little time.*

When Play Isn't Fun

*We who are strong ought to bear with the failings of the weak
and not to please ourselves.*

ROMANS 15:1

*C*hildren can be cruel. As a Bible teacher once quipped: "If you need evidence for the depravity of man, observe the behavior of children."

There was a girl in my sixth-grade class who was the stereotypical bookworm. Stephanie was overweight and wore big, black-rimmed glasses. She was shy and awkward, but she came across as cold and aloof.

No one realized how badly Stephanie wanted to play. But physical activity was torture for her. No PE team wanted her, and whichever one got stuck with her usually protested to the teacher—to no avail.

One day we were playing kickball. Stephanie was playing her usual position: 100 feet beyond right field. (That way she couldn't mess up the game.) But someone kicked the ball over the head of the right fielder, and to everyone's horror, especially Stephanie's, the ball headed right for her. Her team moaned. The other cheered.

Stephanie tried her best to get the ball, but every time she reached for it, she accidentally kicked it farther away. Her team screamed at her and called her cruel names. They couldn't see the tears of frustration in Stephanie's eyes. Something in Stephanie was dying.

As an adult, after two divorces and years of therapy, Stephanie still struggles with her insecurities. But she has finally discovered the unconditional love of Jesus Christ, which is resurrecting her love for fun and fellowship with others.

Think back to your school days. Were you ever taunted or belittled? Did you ever experience the humiliation of being chosen last to play a team sport? Take time to observe how your children play. Correct any cruel behavior and model Christlike behavior. As a parent you can teach your children to play and have fun in ways that foster a spirit of caring and community instead of cruelty.

Steps of Faith

Dear Lord, thank You for loving us so much that You were willing to dwell here with us. I know I can't shield my children from the cruelty of the world, but enable me to teach them how to have fun, and at the same time, be patient "with the failings of the weak."

Father Pain

Though my father and mother forsake me,
the LORD will receive me.

PSALM 27:10

I had just walked into the party when I spotted him across the room. Duty dictated I must be polite and speak—after all, he was my father. And who knows, maybe this time would be different.

So I took a deep breath and moved in his direction. "Hello, Daddy," I said, giving him a perfunctory kiss on the cheek. He stepped back and said in a loud voice, "Tell me, which one of the Three Stooges styled your hair for the party tonight?"

Without missing a beat I responded, "Curly." Everyone laughed, including me. I felt my husband squeeze my arm and quickly move me to another room.

The little girl in me was just hoping that for once Daddy would love me just the way I was. All my life I tried to please him. I wrote him poems, invited him to sit with me on opening night of a play I'd written, named my firstborn child for him. But it was never good enough.

I wondered if God was like that, too. Over the next several months I found myself testing God. I stopped trying to perform for Him to see if He would withdraw His love from me. I quit all my jobs at the church, stopped all volunteer work for the school, and abandoned my writing.

I spent a lot of time at home in bed—crying. Surely He was disgusted with me because I was doing nothing for Him. But as I lay quiet and still on my bed, I felt His presence like never before. I pored through 1 John and realized His sweet love for me . . . and I was doing nothing to earn it . . . just being.

We can run ourselves into the ground trying to please our heavenly Father. What He wants from us first is our fellowship. Have you spent time "being" with your Father today? Or are you too busy "doing"?

Steps of Faith

Dear Abba Father, I don't understand a lot of things—my father, for one. Thank You that You are not like my father and will never reject or abandon me. I forgive my father and realize he is only modeling the pain his father gave him. Please let him know You love him, too.

Peace in Turmoil

*Peace I leave with you; my peace I give you. . . . Do not let
your hearts be troubled and do not be afraid.*

JOHN 14:27

I stared out my dining room window, waiting for the blue van to appear. *This isn't really happening.* Surely I would wake up and find this only a nightmare. *Where's Burt? Isn't he out of the bathroom yet?* I walked by the bathroom and heard my husband sobbing under the flow of the showering water. I'd never heard him cry before. *How did we get to this point? When did it all start to unravel?*

Bradley had just turned 13 when we first started noticing his rebellious, disrespectful behavior. Everyone said it was just "the teenage years" and it would pass. When Brad was 16 we were still waiting for it to pass. After many altercations with teachers, principals, policemen, and judges, we were at the end of our rope. All efforts at discipline had failed. Brad had rejected every offer of help from counselors and other concerned friends.

And so we prayed and waited . . . waited for God to show us what was wrong and what to do. He did.

The drug intervention specialist was to arrive in his blue van any minute. He was picking up our firstborn son and flying with him to a drug treatment center. My son knew nothing of the plan. Though my heart was shattering, I kept looking at Jesus. I knew somehow, some way, Jesus would do for my "prodigal" what I could not do.

Underneath the fear and pain His precious peace held me steady as I started to walk down the loneliest road I'd ever traveled.

Peace in the midst of the storm is the believer's inheritance. Are you in the midst of your own storm? Is your faith being stretched farther than you ever imagined? Turn to God. He is ready to offer you His peace.

Steps of Faith

Dear Shepherd of my heart, You know how much I love my children, but I know You love them more than I ever could. My prayer is that You will give me the faith to release each one to Your care when they are faced with a trial or heavy burden. I know You are faithful. Bless You.

Father to the Fatherless

*A father to the fatherless, a defender of widows, is God in his
holy dwelling. God sets the lonely in families.*

PSALM 68:5,6

*H*ow would you like to have had 26 children the first month
you were married?

Mrs. George Mueller had that and then some. In fact at times she had
hundreds of children to care for. George Mueller founded numerous
orphanages in nineteenth-century England. The Muellers' love for and
devotion to thousands of orphaned and abandoned children was
sparked by reading Psalm 68:5. They realized that as God's agents they
could provide for the needs of the "fatherless." So they rented a small
building and founded their first orphanage. In just a few short years they
had several homes and hundreds of children under their care.

Often the Muellers had little or no money for supplies. But their
faith in *Jehovah-jireh* ("The Lord will provide") is legendary. One
morning the Muellers had no food or money and the children were
waiting for their breakfast. Mr. Mueller said, "Children, you know
we must be in time for school." Then he simply prayed, "Dear
Father, we thank Thee for what Thou art going to give us to eat."
Suddenly there was a knock at the door. It was the local baker with
fresh-baked bread. He said the Lord woke him up at 2 A.M. to prepare it for them. After the baker left there was another knock at the
door. It was the milkman, and his cart had just broken down in front
of the orphanage. He needed to get rid of his milk.

Between 1838 and 1840, the Muellers were without sufficient funds
50 times, yet they experienced God's miraculous provision each time.

The Muellers were a living testament that God is Father of all.
Through His children He manifests His love and care to the "fatherless."

Are you lonely? Do you feel abandoned by your family or
friends? If you do, according to Psalm 68, God has a family for you,
one of which He is the Father—the church. If you are blessed with
friends and family, adopt a lonely person. Share your abundance
with a "fatherless" brother or sister.

Steps of Faith

*Eternal Father of all, thank You for adopting me into Your kingdom
through the blood of Your only begotten Son, Jesus Christ. And
Father, for those who do not have earthly fathers, protect them from
the dangers of this world. Give them a powerful sense of Your
guiding presence.*

Surest Sign of Love

*I have set you an example
that you should do as I have done for you.*

JOHN 13:15

T
U
E
S
D
A
Y

*S*miling, Katherine entered the sterile-smelling hospital room and gave Mrs. Evans' thin hand a squeeze. "Here you are, Mrs. Evans," she said gently to the frail woman as she gave her a tablet and a cool cup of water. "This will help you sleep through the night. Don't forget that tomorrow's a big day for you—we'll start your physical therapy. Your granddaughters would be *so* proud."

Katherine was working the night shift at the women's medical center downtown. Mrs. Evans, a tiny, soft-spoken elderly woman with delicate, almost transparent skin, had rung the nurse's station a moment before, weakly requesting pain medication. While some of the other nurses griped about the tediousness of their jobs, Katherine responded quickly. She knew that this medication was the only thing that allowed Mrs. Evans to sleep, granting her a short repose from the pain of the disease that was destroying her body.

Frequently Katherine reflected on the story of Jesus washing the feet of His disciples. Through that simple, humble act He had poured out to them the love of His Father. Due to the regulations of the public hospital, she could not talk to the women about "religion." However, if they questioned her about the reason for her peaceful assurance and loving heart, she shared her faith with them quietly. Through her imitation of Christ, many of the women Katherine cared for found a new hope—an assurance of a life that disease cannot disfigure and death cannot take away.

Whatever your station in life, you can ask God to reveal Himself through your words and actions. Sometimes the most loving thing you can do for someone is simply to listen. You do not need to be a great orator or zealous evangelist to lead others to Christ. When you imitate Him in compassion and kindness, you draw others to His redemptive love.

Steps of Faith

Thank You, Lord, for the opportunities You give me each day to show others Your love. Please reveal Yourself through my life and my treatment of people that I encounter at work, at home, or wherever You have placed me. I can only do this through Your grace, Lord. I love You.

Rosh Hoshana

You will . . . hurl all our iniquities into the depths of the sea.
MICAH 7:19

I asked my coworker, for whom I had prayed for months, "Sarah, would you like to take a walk at lunch?" A practicing orthodox Jew, her customs intertwined with biblical history. Sarah came so close to yet was so far from seeing Jesus as her long-awaited Messiah. As we traveled our regular route I said, "Tomorrow is *Rosh Hoshana*, isn't it, Sarah? Will you tell me about it?"

"Oh, it is a very happy day. We send cards to our friends to wish them *Shanah Tovah*—Happy New Year—and we eat apples dipped in honey. . . . You really want to hear about it? *Rosh Hoshana* means 'Feast of Trumpets.' The priests blow a ram's horn—a *shofar*—to call people to repentance so God will not judge their sin. My family and I observe the *Tashlikh*—'casting off.' We throw bread crumbs into the river—symbolizing our sin being carried away."

"It sounds very special. You know, Sarah, the Bible tells of a man who taught something similar to *Tashlikh*. His name was John and he was the very last prophet who called God's people to repentance. When he saw Jesus coming toward him he recognized Him as the Messiah and called out, 'Behold the Lamb of God that takes away the sin of the world.' And later, just as the prophet Isaiah foretold what Messiah would do, Jesus died in order to fulfill the Scriptures. All the sins of the world were cast onto Him and then He died to pay the penalty for those sins."

"Why do Christians believe Jesus is the true Messiah?" Sarah asked curiously. "My people are still looking for Him."

"Well, to begin with, Jesus fulfilled Isaiah's prophecies. But there is so much more. I would love to tell you about Him if you'd like."

You may have Jewish friends who are curious about your faith. As you begin to talk with them, you may want to brush up on the Old Testament. Ask your pastor to suggest a book or Bible study that describes how Jesus fulfilled prophecies about the Messiah. Another source for information is your local Christian bookstore.

Steps of Faith

Father, the Jewish nation still awaits the coming of Your Son, their Messiah. As I speak to my Jewish friends about You, help me to be sensitive in what I say and loving in all I do.

God's Fingerprints

Those God foreknew he also predestined
to be conformed to the likeness of his Son.

ROMANS 8:29

*M*ake something for me to remind me of you," my mother
said as she put a blob of clay in my six-year-old hands. Then Mom
pressed her thumb in the soft clay. "What do you see?"

"I see your fingerprint, Mommy."

"That's right, sweetheart," she affirmed. "But I want to tell you
about God's fingerprint. After God made the world and all the animals, He picked up a handful of dust and made Adam. Now we can't
create things like God did; we have to start with something. But just
like God pictures in His mind what He wants to make, you look at
that lump of clay there and picture what you want it to be. And then
you start poking and jabbing and make what you want it to be.

"Honey, God does the same thing with our hearts. When He
made us, He knew that He wanted us to be like Jesus. After we
receive Jesus as our Savior, God starts forming our hearts.
Sometimes it hurts! So, next time something hard comes along, say,
'Why, I think I'm noticing God's fingerprints on me!'"

I listened hard as I worked the clay. Later I proudly presented
Mom with my clay gift. "It's me with God's fingerprints all over me!"

Now, 30 years later, I truly know how to identify God's fingerprints. They are evident in the comfort friends gave when my best
friend died in an auto accident when we were 16, in my renewed
hope after a broken engagement when I was 22, in the joy I find in
my precious husband and two babies, in places of service and
people to love.

As I look at that little clay figure in my mother's china cabinet, I
smile. God is still fingerprinting me!

Do you realize that you have God's fingerprints all over you? As
you do something with your hands today, think about how you are
reflecting God's creativity.

Steps of Faith

Creative Father, thank You for the ways You keep working with me.
No matter how painful it gets, Lord, continue to shape my heart,
keeping it soft to Your touch until I look like Your Son.

Preparing for Worship

I love the house where you live, O LORD,
the place where your glory dwells.

PSALM 26:8

Sunday mornings used to be the worst part of the week for me. For a while I wasn't sure why. Now I know.

First of all, I wouldn't think about Sunday morning until Sunday morning. No one in the family knew what he or she was going to wear, including myself. Clothes always needed pressing, shoes needed polishing, and every pair of panty hose in my dresser had a run. It was chaos. By the time we piled in the car, I was frustrated with everyone.

Another factor was that my husband normally turned on one of the Sunday morning news shows. I am passionate about certain political and cultural issues, so if a topic caught my attention, I would usually end up glued to the television and get all worked up. I wouldn't be able to concentrate on anything else the entire morning. No wonder my Sunday morning worship experience was less than fulfilling.

A family conference set the direction for some much-needed changes. First, Sunday morning was planned on Saturday. We got everyone's clothes ready the night before; they just had to tell me what they were going to wear, which got them thinking about Sunday morning. Second, we decided on no television. Instead we played praise music.

Third, my husband and I agreed to pray together on Sunday mornings before we left our bedroom. We asked for God's blessing and protection and put Satan's forces on alert. Our home and our family were no longer going to be a Sunday-morning battlefield.

What are your Sunday mornings like? Do they put you in the proper state of mind for worship? Taking time to prepare yourself for worship before you get to church will make a vast difference in your worship experience once you get there.

Steps of Faith

Almighty God, thank You for the privilege of coming before Your throne in worship. How I regret the many times I have been distracted, exhausted, and flippant about my worship. Help me to prepare myself so I will have a sense of awe and excitement when I enter Your house.

F
R
I
D
A
Y

221

The Gift of Creativity

So God created man in his own image,
in the image of God he created him. . . . God saw all
that he had made, and it was very good.

GENESIS 1:27,31

*W*hile recently visiting my sister-in-law Michelle, I decided it was time to confess to her—face-to-face—the envy I had been harboring against her.

"Michelle, I think you should know that I've secretly despised and resented you for many years," I said. "Please forgive me."

Michelle, somewhat stunned, replied, "What have I done?"

"Not *done*. *Do*. I am not talking past tense . . . or maybe I am," I stammered. "Just look at this house. You not only made all your draperies and bedspreads, but you also refinished all these antiques. And don't think I've forgotten that you designed your wedding invitations and your wedding gown. And now you're painting a mural for your church's hundredth anniversary! How do you think that makes me look to the in-laws?"

After a pause, I said, "It's just that you're so creative, so artistic. You make everything beautiful. I assassinate everything I touch. Maybe I'm 'creatively challenged.'"

Michelle laughed and said, "Okay, it's my turn. First, no one can tell a story without a book in front of her better than you. And your letters! Everyone fights to read your letters because they're so funny and descriptive. And the ways you come up with to save money and time astound me. How do you think *that* makes *me* look to the in-laws?"

Do you think of yourself as a creative person? If you are a human being made in God's image, you are creative—whether you realize it or not. Keep in mind that your creativity may manifest itself in a number of unexpected places: in a garden, housework, teaching and disciplining your children, or managing your household finances. Thank God for the gift of His creativity—and celebrate it!

Steps of Faith

Author of Creation, Thank You for creating me in Your glorious image. I know that Your creativity is infinite, and mine is very finite. Help me, Lord, to celebrate this gift of creativity in ways that glorify You.

Dash of the Dachshund

*Give thanks to the LORD, call on his name. . . . Look to the
LORD and his strength; seek his face always.*

PSALM 105:1,4

*W*oof! LuLu, my dachshund puppy, barked at me to hurry, squirming impatiently and straining at the leash that held her back. It was early morning, and I had decided to take her for a walk, hoping that some fresh air would lift my mood. Since I had been laid off my job two months before, every lead had proved to be a dead end. I became depressed and discouraged. I had also recently broken off a long-term relationship with the man I thought I would marry. *Why, Lord?* I wondered. *Why all this now? Don't You love me anymore? Everything is going wrong.* My quiet time with God, which had previously brought me such great joy, had dwindled to a few hurried minutes of prayer each night.

As LuLu and I walked through the still-dewy grass and down the street, I tried to teach her to "heel" and walk quietly by my side. Instead she ran circles around me, occasionally rolling on the ground trying to dislodge the small green harness I had put on her. That harness was what saved her a few minutes later when she scampered toward an oncoming car. I drew her in sharply, my heart pounding. Undaunted, she resumed her frenzied investigation of her surroundings, completely ignoring me. *Why won't she mind me?* I thought in frustration. *I'm trying to teach her these things because I love her. I wish she would trust me and listen to me.*

Suddenly I realized how I had been struggling against the Lord's instruction. I wanted things to work out *my* way, in *my* time. All He asked of me was trust and obedience—because He knows what is best for me.

The Lord sometimes closes certain doors for us, but we cannot be blessed until we quit knocking on all those doors and look to Him instead.

Steps of Faith

Lord, how can I ever doubt Your love? What seem to be setbacks to my plans may be part of Your ultimate plan for my life. I'm afraid my desires are not always in accordance with Your will. Forgive me and help me to give thanks as I discover what You want me to learn from these circumstances.

Sanctified Dating

It is God's will that you should be sanctified: that you
should avoid sexual immorality; that each of you should learn
to control his own body in a way that is holy and honorable.

1 THESSALONIANS 4:3,4

I am one of those people who has learned a lot from my mistakes. In fact, it took a painful divorce to draw me to Christ and show me that God has something to say about love, sex, and dating. I must admit that I wasn't too thrilled about getting back into the dating scene. Frankly, I was scared to death. I didn't want to make the same mistakes again.

I suppose my first husband, Jeff, and I were the typical seventies couple. No one had ever heard of AIDS, and "free love" abounded. I was on the Pill—how convenient. We had sexual intercourse on our second date. We hardly knew each other. We thought if the sex was great, the relationship must be great. Neither one of us gave God a thought. We carried that mindset into our marriage and the rest is history.

But God is good. He's given me a second chance. I have started dating a man I met in my singles' Sunday school class. Steve has learned the same lessons I have—the hard way. So we're taking things *very* slowly. In fact, after three months of dating, we haven't even kissed. Instead we spend a lot of time talking, just getting to know each other. After three months, I think I know Steve better than I knew Jeff after 17 years.

At times I've wondered if I'm falling in love with Steve. A couple of nights ago he asked if I would pray with him about our future. I thought my heart was going to burst. And as we prayed, it occurred to me that we were doing it the right way: being joined spiritually in prayer before ever contemplating being joined physically. That's sanctified dating.

Unfortunately the "free love" culture has created millions of slaves to immorality and misery. But the good news is that God is ready to break the chains. Have you had to learn the hard way about sanctified dating? Ask Him to heal you and set you free to enjoy a pure dating life.

Steps of Faith

Oh God my Father, I praise You for Your power to set me free from
all of my sins, especially the intensely debilitating sin of sexual
immorality. Father, I want to live a life that's holy and honorable,
and I can do that only in Your power. Thank You, Father.

A Team Effort

So don't be afraid; you are worth more than many sparrows.

MATTHEW 10:31

$\mathcal{M}$om, are we going to have to be homeless because Dad got laid off?" David asked. "Jason Phillips down the street said that's what happens to people when they lose their jobs."

"Don't worry, honey," Beth answered. "You can trust Daddy and me—we won't let that happen."

Beth smiled. David's fears were very real and so were her own. But underneath the fears was the bedrock confidence that the Lord would meet their needs. For now, they needed to pull together and play as a team.

"But David, Daddy and I do need your help with something. . . ."

"Sure, Mom, what?"

"During your Little League game, what would you do if it's the bottom of the ninth, your team is down by three runs, the bases are loaded, and your best friend is up at bat?"

"I'd holler and scream and root him on and say, 'You can do it!'"

"Well, honey, that's exactly what we need to do for Daddy right now. Daddy really needs to know we're rooting for him—that we're a team! Daddy's a great hitter, but he's feeling tired and a little scared—you know how that feels?"

David grinned and nodded his head. "I sure do!"

"What are some things you think would cheer Daddy on?"

"Well . . . probably if I turn off the lights when I leave a room . . . and if I don't ask for money when I don't *really* need it."

"Sure, that's a start. But the most important thing, David, is just to remember that Daddy loves you very much, and he wants us all to trust Jesus to provide a job for him."

If a member of your family is going through a time of unemployment, you will either be drawn together or pulled apart. As a "team," make the choice to work together, supporting and encouraging each other in love.

Steps of Faith

Oh God, my Provider, thank You for using this time to develop our foundational confidence in You. Draw us together as a family, calm our fears, and sweeten our spirits. Help us to look to You as the "Giver of every good gift."

W
E
D
N
E
S
D
A
Y

Distortions

My flesh and my heart may fail, but God is the strength of my heart and my portion forever.

PSALM 73:26

I sat huddled on the floor beside the bed, hugging my knees. I knew that if I moved my hand just a few inches, I could reach the handle of the small gun my husband kept sandwiched between the mattress and box springs of our bed.

How did I get here? What is the source of this rage inside me? Surely Christians don't have such destructive feelings. I must be a terrible Christian. I know I'm a terrible mother. I mean, what kind of a mother would scream at her kids and spank them so hard simply for making a fort out of the sofa cushions?

Then I lay sobbing beside the bed, hating myself. The kids would be better off without a mother who would fly into a rage over their simple boisterousness.

My fingers were edging under the mattress when the phone rang. I answered it. It was a friend inviting me to walk around the block with her. I could bring the kids over to her house and her older daughter would babysit.

We walked all right—until dinnertime. To test the water, I hesitantly revealed bits and pieces of my shameful behavior. She listened without judgment and told me some of her struggles with unresolved anger. In the account of her long journey to emotional health and spiritual rebirth, I could clearly see how God worked.

God is good. Because of my friend's encouragement, I got the help I needed. The bitter roots of my rage were exposed and healed. My relationship with God went from one of distant uncertainty to a trusting intimacy. Today other relationships are healing, and I have great patience and tenderness toward my children.

Sometimes we adopt distorted images of God because of how we were treated as children. Once those pictures are corrected, we have a clearer picture of God's attributes and can see ourselves as God sees us: precious children who make mistakes but who are gladly forgiven.

Steps of Faith

Dear God, thank You for saving me from my worst enemy—me. Slowly but surely, I see You exposing more and more of my heart to Your healing touch. Please continue to show me Your truth that sets me free and give me opportunities to show others the way to that same freedom.

First Five Minutes

A cheerful look brings joy to the heart,
and good news gives health to the bones.

PROVERBS 15:30

*I*t's a wonder my husband didn't run away from home.

Jack and I have three boys, aged six, eight, and nine. I am an elementary-school teacher. After 3 P.M. our home resembles a zoo.

Jack has a high-pressure job as a production manager. His shift ends at 3 P.M. Just about every afternoon he would drag himself into a chair, plop himself in front of the tube, and tune out.

It was driving me crazy. Couldn't he see that I needed help with all the laundry and dishes? Plus I wanted to tell him about my rough day and the students that were giving me trouble. And usually one of the boys needed "a talkin' to"—or worse.

This greeted Jack every afternoon. Then one day my neighbor Dottie was over when Jack came home. She witnessed the whole routine. Later, as we chatted in the driveway, she paused. I could tell she had something to say.

She shared the secret of the "first five minutes." During her 40-plus years of marriage, Dottie tried to be aware of what her husband, Emory, was exposed to during his first five minutes home. She did her best to see that the house was relatively quiet and in order, with the children doing homework or playing outside. Sometimes she would light a candle or have a glass of iced tea waiting for him. Most of all she would greet him with a smile and take time to listen to his concerns before she unloaded hers.

Thank God for Dottie and her sweet wisdom. Since then I have taken her advice and see to it that Jack comes home to a sanctuary instead of a zoo. And my small services to him during those crucial five minutes make all the difference in the way our evenings go.

What greets you when you walk through your front door can have an impact on your state of mind for the rest of the day. If you want your home to be a refuge from a chaotic world, you must think ahead and invest a little time. Beauty and order are good for everyone's mental health.

Steps of Faith

Lord, I know that first impressions are important, but perhaps I haven't applied that knowledge to my own home and family. Help me to treat them with the same regard I would a special guest.

The Ugly Duckling

Man looks at the outward appearance,
but the Lord looks at the heart.

1 SAMUEL 16:7

After hours of searching the mall, Sherry found "it"—baby-blue satin, with bows on the shoulders, and in my price range. The perfect dress for "the big event"—her first junior-high dance.

"Go try it on, honey!"

Coming out of the dressing room, Sherry tearfully whispered, "It doesn't fit. I'm so fat."

On the way home, I realized that not only had my daughter's shape changed without my notice, but so had her self-image.

"Honey, the dance is two months away. Let's work at getting into that dress!"

She brightened a little. "For sure?"

A new routine began around our house. Gone were pizza and cookies, here to stay were rice cakes and carrots. I packed Sherry's lunch with yogurt and fruit and notes like, "Jesus loves you and so do I. You can do it!" We would "power walk" around our neighborhood (after dark so her friends wouldn't see her with her mother!). While we walked, we'd talk about school and friends and that blue dress. I would tell her often how precious she was—and how beautiful God had made her.

On the evening of the dance, Sherry proudly walked down the stairs in her new blue satin dress. In her countenance, I noticed an emerging young woman who believed in her heart that in God's eyes, she was beautiful—inside and out.

Do you know someone who is waging an uphill battle against weight loss or a harmful habit? Pour some courage in him or her by sending them encouraging notes that focus on success.

Steps of Faith

Lord, so many people need cheering on. With the strength You give,
use me to be an encourager. Help me to be aware of people who need
a reminder that You are faithful.

Running on Empty

*The LORD will call you back as if you were a wife
deserted and distressed in spirit—a wife who married
young, only to be rejected.*

ISAIAH 54:6

*P*erhaps if I had been 28 instead of 18 when I married Dan, things might have been different. Perhaps not.

Although I thought Dan was the most exciting and sophisticated man alive, things never ran smoothly. After a brief honeymoon period, I got pregnant, and then Dan lost his job. I was hormonal, he was depressed. I needed an extra measure of love and encouragement from Dan, and he needed it from me. Yet we were both so self-consumed that we couldn't sense the needs of the other.

When Dan finally got a job, he threw himself into it with everything he had. Nothing else mattered, including me and our child. He even stopped going to church with me. He became a different man.

After our second child, our sex life disintegrated. Dan wouldn't even touch me. Eventually he would hardly talk to me, except to criticize my housekeeping or my increasing weight. (Food had become my closest companion.) I was overwhelmed by the thought of the slightest task. I felt like a car trying to run on an empty gas tank.

My faith in God was the only thing that kept me from going crazy. When I finally sought some professional help, I slowly began to understand how depression was hurting me and my marriage.

I wish I could say that Dan joined me in therapy and has been miraculously transformed into the prince I thought I'd married. He has not. However, I am encouraged. God has faithfully poured His Spirit of love, joy, and peace into my empty tank. I no longer run on empty.

When should you seek help for depression? According to Brenda Poinsett in her book, *Understanding a Woman's Depression*, it's when you can't pinpoint the cause of your depression and despair; you're having delusional or suicidal thoughts; your health and sleep habits are being seriously affected; your marriage, family, or job is suffering. Depression is a treatable illness for those who want help.

Steps of Faith

*Lord of Life, my life certainly hasn't been the fairy tale I imagined it
would be. Please help me, Lord, to rejoice in the blessings You have
given me, and to be alert when feelings of depression begin to
encroach.*

229

The Presence

The salvation of the righteous comes from the LORD;
he is their stronghold in times of trouble.

PSALM 37:39

Chestnut Elementary School was the last place I thought I'd ever see armed policemen and metal detectors. Only schools in the crime-ridden inner city needed such drastic measures, or so I thought.

Then nine-year-old Miles Hawthorne, son of a deacon in our church, was shot as he rode his bicycle home from school. He had reported a drug deal he'd witnessed on the playground the day before. After three days in ICU he died.

After the shock wore off, our community mobilized into action. With the help of the PTA, parents, teachers, and school administrators began networking for the safety of the children. We set up a directory of students and parents. We got to know our neighbors and could readily tell who belonged in the neighborhood and who didn't. We looked out for each other.

Parents who were policemen or counselors volunteered their time and worked with us. Other parents, like myself, took one morning or afternoon a week to "be a presence" in the hallway and classroom, or on the bus and playground. And as these parents got more involved with their children's lives, we began to seek help from another, more significant "Presence." We began to pray. Mothers, fathers, teachers, even some of the students started to gather once a week to intercede for the safety of Chestnut Elementary School.

That was four years ago, and there has not been another incident involving guns or drugs. The Presence made a difference. And, praise the Lord, last week they dismantled the metal detector and put it in storage!

No school is exempt anymore. Drugs and violent crime have seeped into some of the best schools in the safest neighborhoods. And parents and students are scared. If you are in a similar situation, consider networking with concerned teachers and parents. And don't forget to call upon the Presence!

Steps of Faith

Heavenly Father, I praise You for being a refuge for my family in a world that seems to grow more and more dangerous every day. Please shield my loved ones from harm, and in times of trouble may we always seek Your help and protection.

Spiritual Mothering

For you yourselves know how you ought to follow our example.

2 THESSALONIANS 3:7

God has blessed me with two mothers: a biological mother and a spiritual mother. I've known my biological mother all my life. I've known my spiritual mother, Janelle, for just a few years.

Janelle and I met at the bank where we work. She is 23 years older than I am. My husband, Kirk, and I had just moved to the area. We happened to join the church Janelle and her husband attend. Janelle and I quickly became friends.

One morning I heard some women on a Christian radio show discussing "spiritual mothering." It was the first time I had heard the term "Titus 2 woman." My heart yearned for someone like that in my life. I couldn't help but think of Janelle.

After praying about it, I decided to ask Janelle to be my mentor. I was a little nervous at first—as though I was proposing marriage to her!

Janelle agreed to pray about it. Two days later she accepted the job. But she warned me that she took this role seriously, that this relationship would mean some work for both of us.

As I shared my disappointments, fears, and weaknesses with her, Janelle was able to discern how to pray for me and with me. All of her counsel was based on the Bible. We had lunch once a week, during which we would pray and recount any spiritual defeats and/or victories. And I would recite—*verbatim*—the verse she had assigned me to memorize!

Janelle will never replace my biological mother, but the spiritual standard she has modeled for me has strengthened my resolve to become a mentor myself. I know God is already preparing that special "spiritual daughter" for me.

Ninety percent of moral failure among the pastorate stems from counseling women alone. That is why there is a new emphasis on women's ministries, especially woman-to-woman ministries. If you want to learn more about mentoring, read *Women Mentoring Women* by Vickie Kraft.

Steps of Faith

Thank You, Lord, for the love and counsel You provide by means of the older and wiser women in my life. Bless them for the interest they show in my life. And when You think I'm ready, lead me to a young woman to whom You can offer love and guidance through me.

231

Dark Clouds

Many advisers make victory sure.

PROVERBS 11:14

*E*velyn was always the first person to send a get-well or birthday card. She eagerly lent an extra shoulder in the church nursery. And with Evelyn, you enthusiastically shared news like "I got the job!" or "He proposed!" as well as your deepest burden. Her response was always the same. She said, "I will talk to the Lord about it." To her, the act of prayer was as natural as conversing with her husband. A widow for decades, that was certainly the case.

But for months now, Evelyn has not been herself. A little sadder, a lot quieter—she stays at home more than usual. That's why we were so pleased when she came to the Tuesday morning Bible study. Women, young and old, sincerely told her how good it was to see her. But it wasn't until we began our study of Elijah's depression in 1 Kings 19 that Evelyn divulged what had been so heavy and so long on her heart.

"A few months ago, a dark cloud rolled over my life," she explained. "I felt overwhelmed with even the most daily problems. I prayed, cried, confessed, and pleaded with the Lord to show me why, but I only got worse. When my daughter visited she insisted I see a doctor, but I refused. After all, 'the Lord is enough,' I thought. But soon I had no choice. My health was deteriorating. To my surprise, the doctor discovered my depression had a chemical cause. The medication he prescribed righted the imbalance and within a few days, the dark clouds blew away. And yes, the Lord is enough! He supplied the answer!"

Do you suffer from unexplained depression? It is not "un-Christian" to seek medical help or counseling. If a doctor or counselor can offer genuine insight or solid biblical advice, get it!

Steps of Faith

Creator God, You formed our intricate parts and wove our physical and emotional and spiritual parts all into one body. We are fearfully and wonderfully made! Because my body is your temple, please give me wisdom to know how to treat problems correctly. I trust You to lead me to solutions and the right kind of help when I need it.

Beauty Abused

Like a gold ring in a pig's snout is a beautiful woman who shows no discretion.

PROVERBS 11:22

*O*ne Saturday after shopping, I tried on my new outfit for my husband, Roger. It was for a party some new business associates were having, which called for something other than what I had in my closet. I had decided to be fashionably daring—and it backfired. One look at Roger's face and I knew instantly that he didn't like my outfit. But for some reason he wouldn't discuss it. Then and there I decided to return it.

Later in the evening Roger told me what had been bothering him. I'll never forget what he said: "I'm not angry with you for buying that outfit; it's really okay. But that sheer blouse reminds me of something one of my coworkers wears sometimes. Hers is so sheer and so low-cut, I don't know where to look. I'm so sick of women who come to work, and sometimes even to church, wearing tight leather miniskirts, see-through blouses, and low-cut dresses. Why, just this week, one of our young clerks wore some sort of tank top that looked like a lacy slip. She had on a jacket, but I thought she'd forgotten her blouse!

"You know I'm not a pervert—I'm a healthy, red-blooded man, and I love you very much. I don't want to think about other women that way. Still, most men are visual creatures. It's hard for us not to notice and let our imaginations roam. Don't these women realize what they're doing to our minds when they wear clothes like that?"

Evaluate your wardrobe and your motivation for wearing it. Do you take care that you will not be a distraction? Or do you set out to attract attention? What you wear and why you wear it reveal your character—and your heart.

Steps of Faith

Holy Father, thank You for the plumb line of Your Word. So often areas of my life don't square with it, and then I seek Your strength and wisdom to obey it. Father, please show me my heart when it comes to my motivation to be attractive to others. Help me to dress in a way that glorifies You and does not cause anyone to sin.

F
R
I
D
A
Y

233

Angel in Pigtails

*The LORD is close to the brokenhearted and saves
those who are crushed in spirit.*

PSALM 34:18

Dear Helen:

I am writing to thank you for your precious Anna. Who would have dreamed the Lord would use my four-year-old neighbor to give me comfort from my deep depression!

Since my dear Robert died last month, I have sat in his rocker in the family room and stared at the clock on the wall. Sometimes I would sit there from early morning until after the sun went down. It got so bad that I couldn't even get out to go to the doctor.

Last week I began to get frightened. I cried to the Lord, "I need help!" Well, He sent a little angel in pigtails and pink overalls to my door. She held out a fist of black-eyed Susans (I think she picked them from the Nelsons' garden!) and asked if she could come "visiting." For a long time we sat silently in the family room. Her little legs swung in time with the pendulum clock's ticktock, and she gazed wide-eyed around the room. Then she did a wonderful thing— she scooted off the piano bench and walked over to me. She ever so gently touched my cheek and said, "I miss Robert, too," and her brown eyes welled with tears. She crawled up on my lap and I held her tightly. My heart suddenly felt overwhelmed with sadness and comfort, and then the tears came. Little Anna and I rocked and cried until the long shadows came through the window and I sent her home.

Thank you, Helen, for sending your little angel to me— the Lord used her tender heart to bring me back to life!

Love, Marilyn

Do you know someone whose grief and depression are caused by the loss of a loved one? You may not know what to say to her. She may not want you to say anything. Sometimes the best way to show that you care is simply to be with her and share her pain.

Steps of Faith

Comforting Father, when my heart is overwhelmed with grief, thank You for Your presence. I am also very sure that You want me to be a comfort to others. Give me wisdom to know when to be silent, when to speak, and what to say.

Guilt by Association

How long will you love delusions and seek false gods?
PSALM 4:2

All my life I dreamed of growing up to be just like her. She was beautiful and kind. She was revered in her church and community. Her house was neat and clean, and she seldom raised her voice in anger. Her husband was devoted to her, and her children respected her.

She was my mother. So it was natural for me to assume I would become the same kind of wife and mother.

I don't know what went wrong. I tried so hard to be like her. But ten times a day I caught myself saying and doing things Mother would never have said or done. My house was a mess, my children talked back to me, and there were days when my husband, Jay, tolerated me at best.

What was wrong with me? I felt guilty all the time, and it was stressing me out. I was always comparing myself to my mother and, to make matters worse, other people were, too. One summer day Jay and I hosted a family barbecue. I overheard Aunt Missy cluck, "You'd never know she was Millie's daughter. . . . And Millie's potato salad was much better." I hid in the laundry room and cried for an hour.

It took several years before I could separate myself from Mother and learn to accept myself, warts and all. I stopped trying to be her and worked on learning who I am, what my strengths and weaknesses are, and what I want to do about it—no apology.

I will always love and appreciate Mother, but I have finally given myself permission to be the woman God wants me to be. Even though my floors don't sparkle, Aunt Missy doesn't like my potato salad, and no one calls me Saint Lisa, I'm giving my family the best I can be—the real me, not the shadow of another woman.

Do you find yourself stressed out by guilt? Many women admit that guilt is a driving force in their lives, and the stress it causes is eating them alive. Ask God to help you sort out your guilt feelings. Accept who you are—God has.

Steps of Faith

Loving Father, I used to think life was going to be so easy. I had the perfect picture of what my life would be like when I grew up. Now that I have, please give me the faith and patience to exchange my perfect picture for Your perfect plan—and all the challenges it may hold for me.

Priorities

Though you have made me see troubles, many and bitter,
you will restore my life again.

PSALM 71:20

T
U
E
S
D
A
Y

The guilt was bad enough after the divorce. Every time one of the children brought home a bad grade, argued with a sibling, or played the stereo too loud, I somehow thought it was my fault.

But it was the pressure that almost killed me—the pressure of trying to be both father and mother, along with being a full-time employee. I was up every morning at 4:30 A.M. and usually got to bed around midnight. I knew I couldn't last long at this pace.

The problem was that I had a neurotic need for perfection. I rationalized that a spotless floor, home-cooked meals, and hand-knitted sweaters would compensate for what I was unable to give to my children. When I thought I could no longer cope, God sent a friend to help me come to my senses.

I met Martha at work, and we discovered we have a lot in common—especially all the trials of single motherhood. She told me that she keeps a list of what she has to do each day, prioritizing each item. (Mopping and knitting are seldom on her list.) When she can afford it, she pays for luxuries like dry cleaning. To save time she cooks on the weekends and stores single portions in the freezer.

Time for herself is also a priority. Martha has arranged for her sister to watch the children on Saturday mornings. She belongs to an exercise class and maintains a few close friendships.

Martha admits that all the responsibilities overwhelm her at times, even to tears. But that brings her back to her first priority: time in prayer and reading God's Word. She says it's the foundation of her life, the only priority that is as constant as it is refreshing.

Divorce is traumatic—especially with the added pressures of being a parent. Find ways to relieve the pressure and give yourself the time you need to sort out your feelings and regroup. And don't be afraid to ask for help. Listen to the suggestions your friends and family offer.

Steps of Faith

Heavenly Father, Your Word promises to restore and comfort those who have suffered many trials. I claim those promises for every single mother out there. And when I come upon a single mother, give me a heart filled with mercy.

A God of Precision

*The eyes of all look to you. . . . You open your hand and satisfy
the desires of every living thing.*

PSALM 145:15,16

Like most other Christians, I have undergone tests of my faith
in God. And like most other Christians, there are several where I
have to admit, "I flunked."

My problem has never been a lack of faith in God's power and
sovereignty. I don't doubt His ability to do anything, and I am
soundly convinced that He alone is in control of the universe. The
area in which I fail to trust God has to do with His *desire* to work on
my behalf. Sometimes I wonder, *Does God really care about my life?
Does it matter to Him whether my husband is miserable in his job? Why
should He help us sell our home when so many people are living in
poverty? God has already given us eternal life; why should He be concerned with the mundane details of my life?*

I suspected that God was mainly interested in people who were
doing "big" things for Him—soul winning, gospel spreading, policy
making—things that influenced the course of events on a large scale.

Until I saw a spider. As I drew up my bedroom window shade, I
noticed a rather large spider spinning a web on the other side of the
window. I watched, fascinated, as the spider released a barely visible
silken strand, at the same time working the strand into its web.
Methodically and consistently, the spider formed a perfect octagon
and then began the process all over again with another strand.

As I watched that tiny creature, I realized that God cared infinitely
and lovingly about details. Nothing was too great for Him, and
nothing was too small to escape His attention. It was all part of the
same plan.

When we claim to have faith in God's sovereignty, we are
asserting the truth that every atom of matter is under His control and
has a purpose in the scheme of the cosmos. He is a God of precision
as well as power.

Steps of Faith

*Father, when I behold the mighty works of Your hands on the earth
and in the heavens, I know that same faithfulness extends to the
details of my life. Increase my confidence in You by helping me recognize Your work in my life.*

237

Single, Not Separate

Delight yourself in the LORD.
PSALM 37:4

I'm single, in my thirties, and I've never been married, though I'd very much like to be someday. There are some disadvantages to being a "spinster" (quite an unglamorous word, compared to its counterpart, "bachelor"), but I can honestly say I am content, most of the time, with my life as it is. Except for this one small area.

I think the term *singles* is fine if you're talking about tennis or ice-cream cones, but not people. In my church there are two types of adults: singles and couples. I go to a singles Sunday school class, participate in singles social activities, and attend a singles Bible study. Don't get me wrong: I am very grateful for the fellowship opportunities, and I've made many good friends through them. I realize that single and married people have different interests and concerns.

The problem is that when we singles are singled out, our singleness becomes the focus of the group. In our singles group I feel as though there is an underlying assumption that we are all there to find mates, not to enjoy fellowship with other believers. In our singles Bible study we concentrate mainly on dealing with the problems of being single. I think being in a study with married people would help us focus less on ourselves.

I enjoy being with my married friends, and I've learned a lot from them about how to live with and love another person "for better or for worse." Marriage may one day be a part of God's plan for me. Until that part of the plan unfolds, I am as whole and complete as any human being can be. But exposure to strong examples of Christian marriage can only help as well!

Singleness does have its advantages, but it can be hard at times, just as marriage can be hard. Single and married Christians have much to offer each other in terms of encouragement, support, and friendship. They should be encouraged to have fellowship together within the church. What can you do to integrate these two groups in your church?

Steps of Faith

Father, You know the deep desire within my heart to glorify You whether I am married or single. Help me to enjoy the single state and to serve You in ways I might not be able to if I were married. In times of loneliness help me to find all I need in You.

Evidence of Grace

*Let us not become weary in doing good, for at the proper time
we will reap a harvest if we do not give up.*

GALATIANS 6:9

*E*vidence of Grace" is a music ministry made up of Thom and
Robyn Holmes, Donnie and Nora Mauldin, and Jim and Sue Putney.
About two or three weekends a month, after a full week of "tent-
making," they pile into Thom and Robyn's van and travel throughout
the southeast to minister to troubled teens in youth detention cen-
ters or in prison. They're back Sunday morning so Thom and Donny
can lead worship in their respective churches.

On the road Robyn works the soundboards and joins Nora in
prayerful intercession for the band and the audience. Jim is on elec-
tric guitar, while Sue plays the mandolin.

Thom and Donnie are in the spotlight. They strum their guitars,
sing, and share their testimonies and the love of Christ. Though they
joke about their ponytails and leather jackets, they know they're
sending a powerful message to their audience: Christ is interested in
who you are on the inside, not what you look like on the outside.

And that message is received. Hundreds have been saved and
continue to follow Christ after "Evidence of Grace" leaves.

Once I asked Robyn where she finds the stamina and strength to
keep up Evidence of Grace's pace. Her answer surprised me. Along
with their daily devotions and prayer, Robyn said all she and Thom
need to do is watch the evening news. "There are so many acts of
teen violence. Hearing about all the shootings and stabbings in our
area motivates us to reach out to these people. It's obvious they're
hopeless. They feel like they have no purpose. We want to tell them
that God has a purpose for their lives."

Statistics show that baby boomers are notorious for not keeping
commitments. But there are exceptions. If you're a born-again boomer,
how faithful are you in your service to the Lord? Your faithfulness to
your calling will inspire others to discover their own gifts. Then they
can reach out to those hurting people who need to hear about Jesus.

Steps of Faith

*Lord of hope, I praise You for the lovingkindness You have faithfully
poured out on me all these years. You are more loyal than a best
friend. Let me show You how much I love You by serving You faithfully. Show me how I can demonstrate "evidence of grace" to those
around me.*

F
R
I
D
A
Y

239

Time Alone

I said, "Oh, that I had the wings of a dove!
I would fly away and be at rest—I would flee far away."
PSALM 55:6,7

*M*y husband, his staff, and the members of the church think it's my annual retreat. However, I secretly call it my annual "treat." It's a secret because a pastor's wife and mother of four isn't supposed to want to get away by herself, except for super-spiritual reasons. But that's not true!

On every third Thursday afternoon in July, I pack my Bible, a pad of paper, some praise tapes, some classical music, my needlework, my favorite low-fat snacks, a mystery novel, a rented copy of the movie *Gone With the Wind*, cutoff shorts and T-shirts, and my cat, Bama. And it's off to the mountains—alone!

It's usually during the drive up there, or on the way back, that the Lord ministers to me the most. It's quiet in the car, and I can hear His voice much more clearly. That's why I keep the pad and pen out—and I record what He tells me. I also spend a lot of time singing His praises and counting my blessings. Sometimes Bama chimes in.

Before I get to the cabin, I buy some other groceries, along with a gallon of my favorite frozen yogurt. (My family eats only "real" ice cream.) Once settled, I take a hot bubble bath, read my book, and drink a tall glass of iced tea. Heaven! Then, that night or the next, I curl up with Bama and a box of tissue and watch *Gone With the Wind*, which I could never watch at home without numerous interruptions.

The rest of the time is filled with sleeping late, long walks, setting some goals—along with Bible study and prayer.

I know this doesn't sound spiritual enough to some, but that's okay. The Lord and I know the emotional, physical, and spiritual benefits I obtain from my annual summer treat.

Do you schedule an annual summer "treat" for yourself? If a weekend is too long, consider just a night away. Even if you aren't a pastor's wife, you can benefit immensely from the time away from the daily pressures of home, work, and family.

Steps of Faith

Father, thank You for understanding the pressures I face every day.
I love my family more than anything, but sometimes I simply need
to be alone. Help me to know when the time is right.

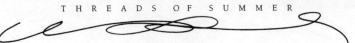

The Forerunner

You have heard that it was said . . .
"Do not murder, and anyone who murders will be
subject to judgment." But I tell you that anyone who
is angry with his brother will be subject to judgment."

MATTHEW 5:21,22

*F*or most of my life I internalized my anger. On the outside I looked calm, meek, and even-tempered, but on the inside I was raging. Because I didn't know how to process anger, I simply buried it and held onto it.

For instance, if someone offended me at work, I would harbor a grudge and go out of my way to avoid that person. If a clerk was rude, I wouldn't shop in that store. And if a family member crossed me I would pout, cop an attitude, or withdraw for a while.

Then Bill and I married. As much as I loved him, within a few years I wanted to escape. So many things he did made me angry. He didn't handle our finances in the best way. He wasn't always prompt, and he refused to let me know if he was going to be late coming home. He would often ask me to pick up something he had forgotten at the store. I considered all this rude and disrespectful. I nagged. I sulked. Nothing happened. His behavior got worse. I got angrier.

Shortly before our fourth anniversary Bill told me that if we didn't get help he would leave. He said my constant disapproval was literally killing the love he felt for me. Half the time he didn't know what he'd done to make me angry. He couldn't stand it any longer.

By God's grace I was receptive to Bill's plea. When I realized that I could actually lose my husband, I was horrified. The next day, I made an appointment with our church counselor. During the last few months, she has helped me understand and confess my anger for the sin it is. Now I won't be guilty of murdering our marriage.

Do you harbor any anger toward anyone? If you do, ask his or her forgiveness. Then ask God to forgive you and enable you to love him or her.

Steps of Faith

Eternal God, I know Your Word is true, and sometimes its lessons are extremely difficult. Pour out Your grace upon me. Rescue me from any sinful anger and replace it with Your precious and powerful love.

A New Season

I will say of the LORD, "He is my refuge and my fortress,
my God, in whom I trust."

PSALM 91:2

*J*an was aghast as she left the doctor's office with the news that at 43 she was experiencing menopause. Her mind reeled at the implications. She was too young. This wasn't supposed to happen for years! She'd read that with "the change," as menopause was often called, the aging process accelerates sometimes with negative effects.

Most women she'd encountered in this phase of their lives were at least seven years her senior. She filed through her memory of experiences and old wives' tales she had heard from her circle of family and friends.

She recalled her mother throwing open the windows on a cold day in Vermont because of hot flashes. And hadn't her father laughed at her mother tossing the blankets off her side of the bed when the temperature dipped below freezing?

Jan wondered if her husband would be laughing at her soon. She began to feel less than whole and worried that the special intimacy she shared with her husband would not continue.

When she got home, she took time to sit awhile and look at the beauty of the mountains and valley before her. A calm began to still her racing thoughts. She recalled the promises of God to bless her into old age. A peace and tranquility settled over Jan. She gazed at God's creation and pondered His love and care for her during this next season of her life.

Can you trust the same God who got you through the throes of adolescence to get you through menopause? God doesn't promise that our lives will be free from challenges and trials. But we can find comfort that God gives us a future in which we can walk free from fear.

Steps of Faith

Dear Lord, thank You that we are fearfully and wonderfully made and that You meet our individual needs for security and freedom from fear. Help us to walk daily in Your promises for our lives, overcoming each new challenge that arises.

Secure in Him

*What good will it be for a man if he gains the whole
world, yet forfeits his soul?*

MATTHEW 16:26

*A*s I was reading a newsmagazine, an advertisement caught
my attention (as good ads are intended to do). It was an ad for a
financial planning and investment company. It showed a man, about
35 years old, playfully holding his little boy. The remarkable thing
about the photograph was the way the man was looking at the child.
It was a look that said, "As long as I'm here, nothing is ever going to
harm or threaten you. You'll never have to be afraid. I promise."

The copy in the ad used phrases like "long-term stability," "personal commitment," and "peace of mind," which are things you'd
want to hear from a company that you pay to handle your savings.
But what struck me was the subtle way the ad played on the most
deep-seated fears of parents: What if I can't afford to send my children to college? What if something happens to me? Who will see
that my family is provided for? Will I have enough money for retirement, or will my children have to look after me? The ad successfully
married the ideas of protection and security with money, further
promoting the myth that if you have enough money, you'll never
have to worry about the future.

As they get older, most people do believe that security means
financial security. The challenge to us as Christians is to allow God's
principles to guide our financial planning for the future, because
only He knows what it will hold. Fear can make us hold on too
tightly to our money, and not give generously. Then we miss out on
opportunities to bless others and be blessed ourselves (in more ways
than financial). If we use wisdom and choose obedience, God will
always provide what we need. Our future is already secure in Him.

Now there's a good title for an advertisement!

It would be foolish indeed to spend money with no thought for
future needs. But it would be just as foolish to plan, save, and invest
without consulting the Lord as to what our priorities should be.

Steps of Faith

*Father, as I grow older and my responsibilities seem greater, help me
resist the temptation to rely on my finances for security. There is no
such thing as security outside of obedience to You.*

Kid Talk

When I was a child, I talked like a child, I thought
like a child, I reasoned like a child.

1 CORINTHIANS 13:11

*P*arenting is rough—especially when you're a grandmother. My children are doing exactly what I said I'd never do when I was their age, and what they said they'd never do. They expect too much from their children. And I have to keep my mouth shut!

It boils down to having reasonable expectations—and properly communicating those expectations to each child. Harry and I expected too much. Why we thought a three-year-old should think, behave, and speak like a six-year-old is beyond me. And the six-year-old was supposed to act like a ten-year-old. It was as though we had put all our hopes and self-worth into our children. And did we lay on the guilt if they didn't make us look and feel good about ourselves. Therefore my children have struggled with perfectionism or a perpetual lack of ambition almost all their lives.

Oh, that I could go back and make it all right—like a good mom. But that was another one of my mistakes. I thought that by trying to solve their problems for them, I was communicating how much I loved them. Actually, I was telling them I didn't think they were capable of doing much—at least not without me. Even today they have little confidence in their ability to think and act on their own.

I'd love to talk to my kids, not as their mother, but as an interested bystander. I'd remind them that parenting takes time, patience, wisdom, and prayer. But most of all it takes love—1 Corinthians 13:4-8 love. With that kind of love a parent is free to affirm the child's unique part in God's creative plan.

What are you communicating to your children? Are you equipping them to mature into stable, independent adults? Examine your heart and ask God to give you wisdom. Pray that He will help you become a parent that enables, not disables.

Steps of Faith

Father, thank You for my children. I know they are a gift from You that comes with a tremendous amount of responsibility. Grant me the love and wisdom necessary to mold them into adults who love and serve You along with those around them.

Choose Joy

Shout for joy to the LORD, all the earth.

PSALM 100:1

*O*ne of the devil's chief annoyances is the joy that Christians experience. He can neither understand it nor have it himself; so he sets out to steal as much of it from us as he possibly can. And so often he is successful only because we allow him to trick us into believing that we deserve to be angry, or offended, or upset, or resentful. (See Ephesians 6:11.) He does this by presenting certain lines of thought, which we then choose to follow. You may recognize some of the following as familiar thought patterns. Treat them as "alarm signals"—warnings that the Enemy is out to steal your joy.

"I made a mistake years ago, and now my life is ruined."

"I wonder why God gives so much more to some people."

"This is typical of him! It's just like the time he . . ."

"Why did my mother/father do that to me?"

"Nobody has noticed that I'm doing all the work. No one ever offers to help."

"What could it hurt just to look?"

"What did she mean by that comment?"

"That's the third time he's done that and I haven't said anything. If I did that, he'd be complaining about it."

"No one will ever find out."

"I've been going to this church for a month, and no one has come up to introduce herself to me."

"I don't deserve to be treated like that."

"If I were God. . . ."

Entertaining such thoughts only leads to your misery, and then to the misery of others. Instead, spend the time in prayer, and choose to be joyful!

God doesn't promise that we will always be happy; but He does promise that we will always have joy. Meditate on the differences between temporal happiness and everlasting joy.

Steps of Faith

Father, so many times I have chosen to make myself miserable when I could have had joy. Help me to recognize thought patterns that are destructive and to reject them before they take root.

245

Adultery Hurts

You shall not commit adultery.

EXODUS 20:14

*K*eith was charming and funny, and he entertained everyone in our office with his stories. He was also married and had two children. I admired him as the model of the kind of man I eventually wanted to marry.

During one of our projects, Keith and I started getting coffee together, then lunch. Eventually we were meeting after work "to talk." Keith began telling me about his marital problems. How he wished he'd met me before he married. How I was the only person who really understood him.

W
E
E
K
E
N
D

At that point I knew the relationship was wrong but rationalized it with the fact that we hadn't "technically" committed adultery. However, God's voice was very strong. The Friday night I told Keith I would not see him again outside of work, he accused me of being heartless and selfish. It was 1 A.M. when he got home. He told his wife whom he'd been with—and that he loved me more than her or the children. She told him to move out.

I hadn't been the first.

By Monday morning, the whole office knew. My guilt and shame were indescribable. I had played a part in breaking up a marriage. My Christian witness was compromised. I knew God was grieved. And as the child of a broken home myself, I knew the heartbreak, the insecurity, the emotional pain, and even the financial hardship those two children were facing. I was overwhelmed with grief. My involvement with a married man might not have been physical, but it was adultery all the same. I knew God would forgive me, but I also knew there would be consequences for everyone involved, innocent and guilty alike. When would I be able to forgive myself?

What harm does adultery cause? It destroys the home, trust, and personal value. It leaves permanent scars on its victims. It cheapens the gift of sex. God knew this when He gave Moses the Ten Commandments. Do you know it well enough to never fall into adultery's trap?

Steps of Faith

Holy God, it's clear You gave the Ten Commandments for the benefit and protection of Your people. Thank You. Keep me mindful of their power and purpose, especially in a day when they seem to be ignored.

THREADS OF FALL

Reflecting

Reflecting

The seasonal changes punctuated by Fall are evidence of the cycle of life in God's beautiful plan. All the energy of the growing season is being harvested, and the world quiets itself for a season of rest and renewal. The leaves falling from the trees signal a type of death, but we know that new life is just a few months away. In 1 Corinthians 15:42 we read, "So will it be with the resurrection of the dead. The body that is sown is perishable, it is raised imperishable; it is sown in dishonor, it is raised in glory; it is sown in weakness, it is raised in power; it is sown in a natural body, it is raised in a spiritual body."

That thought is exciting, not just for the hope of eternity with our Lord, but for today. We can experience an abundant harvest of God's goodness and live each day reflecting the glory of God. A seed falls to the ground and waits for the new life Spring will bring. Plant seeds of goodness now and watch for the harvest. Celebrate the reality of knowing the living God by sharing His blessings with others. And not just by giving tangible things. There is no greater gift than to pray a blessing for your spouse or your children.

Be specific when you pray. It helps if you know of special needs in others' lives and can quietly wait to see how God works.

Most things in this world are out of our control. However, the God who spoke the world into existence has promised that He hears us when we pray, so we may ask for His blessing for us and those we love and plant seeds of blessing to all we know.

Reflect on the blessings of God in your life.

Let Go, Let God

The mind controlled by the Spirit is life and peace.

ROMANS 8:6

$\mathcal{A}$t Marian's first 12-step group meeting at her church, she heard the truth about "hitting bottom" and decided she didn't want to go there. But she also heard others share their stories of being rescued from the pit and thought, *If they can do it, I can do it!*

With determination, she got a sponsor and began to work the program one day at a time. In no time at all, she was "white-knuckling" it, trying in her own strength to stop her compulsion. She called Darlene, a member of the group, who listened sympathetically and then said, "Marian, if you could do this yourself, you would have already done it. Read Step One."

We admit we are powerless—that our lives have become unmanageable. To Marian, that sounded like complete defeat. She called Darlene again. "Do I have to actually do Step One?"

"There's no other way. Now read Steps Two and Three," she said.

Step Two—*We believe that only God can restore us to sanity.* Step Three—*We turn our will and our lives over to the care of God.*

"Darlene, this is crazy! I'm a Christian. I've given my life to God already!"

Her friend's only comment was a curious "Oh?"—then silence.

"Well, okay, if I was really trusting God, I wouldn't be in this crisis, right?"

Darlene helped Marian understand the first three steps, then added, "This shorter version helps me remember: 'I can't. God can. And I think I'll let Him.'"

Although Marian was a Christian and she sincerely had turned her life over to the Lord, she kept taking back certain areas she wanted to control. Through the Christ-centered 12-step group at her church she learned how to "let go and let God" have His way in her life.

Steps of Faith

Dear Father, thank You for teaching me how to release control, especially in my weakness, and give it to You. Even if I have to do it over and over again, a hundred times a day, thank You that You are teaching me to be willing.

M
O
N
D
A
Y

Finding Wisdom

If any of you lacks wisdom, he should ask God.

JAMES 1:5

*I*n these days of so many choices, so much information, and such strong influences all around us, it's a real challenge to know what is the right thing to do. Simply stated, wisdom is knowing how to live God's way—the right way! We all want to be wise, but how do we achieve that?

First, we've got to want it. Proverbs 2 says to esteem wisdom like treasure; Psalm 111 tells us that the source of it is the "fear of the Lord." Our love for His character and our respect for His authority motivate us to want to live life His way, so the key is getting to know Him.

Next, we've got to choose it. God's wisdom is always best in the long run, but we will encounter some difficult moments in walking it out. We've got to make the gut-level decision that says we're going to live this way no matter what it costs us.

Then, we've got to ask for it. James 1 promises that if we ask for wisdom, God will surely give it to us. But we must ask both in confidence that He will give it, and in commitment to follow through on it (see verses 6,7).

Finally, we've got to search for it in His Word. We also have the teachings and examples of believers who've gone before us; we can learn from their mistakes and take their counsel.

Last, we must seek out the wisdom He's deposited in those around us. Titus 2 points us to our big sisters in the Lord as a source of womanly wisdom. Ask the Lord to guide you to an older woman—someone who has the fruit of the Spirit in her life and relationships. Ask her if she would be willing to be a source of wisdom and counsel for you, and then take advantage of this treasure.

God promises His wisdom will guide, protect, and nurture us. He's expressed it through His Word and will apply it to our lives by His Spirit. All you need is there for the asking . . . so ask!

Steps of Faith

Father, I want to be a wise woman. I commit myself to seeking out Your wisdom and living by it; please guide me through Your Word and by Your Spirit.

Don't Look Back

Teach us to number our days aright, that we
may gain a heart of wisdom.

PSALM 90:12

*T*he night before my thirtieth birthday I cried myself to sleep. I couldn't believe my twenties were gone. I hadn't yet accomplished many of my goals: publishing a book (I hadn't even written one!), taking tennis and swimming lessons, getting in shape, and starting a family.

I didn't get a lot of sympathy. My husband had turned 30 months before and it never fazed him. Everyone older than me said, "Thirty's nothing. I wish I were still that young!" The only people who understood were my sister, who had been through it herself, and my girlfriends, who would soon be there.

What disturbed me most was how I felt. Why was I filled with such regret? I had a wonderful husband, a loving family, good friends, two sweet dogs, a nice house, a great church—and the list went on.

I also had the love of Jesus Christ. Around 2:30 A.M., I asked Him to forgive me and thanked Him for all my blessings. He reminded me that I had a whole life ahead of me to walk with Him.

That was some time ago. Now I'm a little wiser and much more active. I am taking swimming lessons and I have two children's books in process. I am grateful for each day and live life where I am, not where I'm not. Ephesians 5:15,16 is my motto: "Be very careful, then, how you live—not as unwise but as wise, making the most of every opportunity."

If you're not content with the season of life you're in, think about what makes it so unique. Is there potential for a new career or better education? If your children are in school, you could volunteer for that charity you love. If you're an empty-nester, you and your husband can get to know each other again. Whatever passage of life you're in, don't look back. Right now is God's gift to you.

Steps of Faith

Dear Lord, You've given me one life to live on this earth. Help me
to live it without regrets—and with Your glory in mind.

A Good Leader

Do nothing out of selfish ambition or vain conceit, but in humility consider others better than yourselves.

PHILIPPIANS 2:3

*K*atie, the leader of our writers' group, began our meeting with prayer, asking the Lord to help us evaluate each other's work in an encouraging and positive way. While she prayed, I asked the Lord to keep me from being defensive when the group critiqued my short story.

"Does anyone have any news?" Katie asked.

"I do, but it's bad," Debra said. "I got two more rejection letters this week. I'm beginning to wonder if God is trying to tell me something—like, 'Quit writing.'"

"I'm sure that's not it at all," Katie said, touching Debra's hand. "You have a real gift for inspirational articles. You just haven't found the right magazine yet. Don't give up!"

Next, Doreen said that two of her greeting cards had been accepted. "That's great!" Katie exclaimed. "We thought those cards would sell."

The time came to critique my short story. I was so nervous. I knew Katie would give me an honest evaluation based on years of writing and editing experience. She began, as always, with positive comments: my dialogue was believable, my main character well-developed, my details realistic. And when she pointed out things that needed improving, she did it so gently that I didn't feel hurt or defensive.

When the meeting was over, I thanked Katie for her encouragement. Now I was actually excited about the revising I'd have to do. And, believe me, it takes quite a leader to get me excited about revision!

Good leaders motivate, urging and spurring people on to a common goal. They humbly correct, gently showing people a better way. They commend, praising and encouraging people for a job done well. If you're a leader, do you make it a practice to do these things? Where could you improve?

Steps of Faith

Lord, I want to be a good and humble leader. I want to encourage and motivate people and not be afraid to help them see where they can improve. Please help me do so.

It's My Choice

The wise woman builds her house,
but with her own hands the foolish one tears hers down.

PROVERBS 14:1

*M*y arms pumped and my pace quickened as my words punctuated the morning air. "Give me a break, Lord! It's not like I wake up and say, 'I think I'll nag Robert today!' I just remind him! Why does he respond like that?"

Robert's angry words over breakfast echoed in my mind: "Stop treating me like a child, Sara! You are not my mother!" Stinging, harsh words—and a harsh look as well.

Determined, I challenged the Lord, "I'm not going back to the house until You show me what's at the bottom of this!"

I often talk to God on my morning walk. Sometimes it's the only quiet part of my day. On this particular morning I wasn't prepared for what happened next. I sensed God was talking to me: *"Robert is speaking the truth."*

"Well, yes and no," I contradicted. "It's true I am not his mother, but it's not true that I was treating him like a child!"

"You may not have intended to treat him like a child, but that's how Robert feels when you constantly remind him about things."

"Ouch!" My insides flip-flopped as I walked back to the house to apologize. The Holy Spirit had revealed the truth. I had to act on it.

Your attitude plays a large part in whether you are building people up or tearing them down. You wear many hats every day— wife, mother, daughter, employee, sister, friend. In some relationships you may be a builder; in others, a destroyer. Ask God to give you attitudes that build.

Steps of Faith

Dear Father, I want to be a builder in the lives of those I love. Teach me to get my attitude right and to be a blessing to others. Help me correct attitudes that bring people down. Replace them with the building blocks of acceptance and love.

F
R
I
D
A
Y

Tough Lessons

For we are God's workmanship, created in Christ Jesus.

EPHESIANS 2:10

*S*arah blinked back tears as she halfheartedly rinsed the last of the dishes. Her heart ached for her son as he labored over the bright-colored booklet that was his homework. "I just can't do it, Mom," he announced, his voice full of despair. Sarah straightened herself with new resolve.

"Honey, you've worked hard enough on your reading today. Go on out and play. I've got a call to make." She dialed the number on the card that had been taped to the refrigerator for the past several weeks. "Hello, Learning Center? I'm hoping you can help me with my son, Christopher, who seems to have a reading problem. . . ."

Unfortunately, there's a huge influence on us today to derive our self-esteem from performing well instead of from studying the Bible, which secures our uniqueness as a beloved son or daughter of the Father. For the child who does not find academic success easily, we must be especially determined to create a positive identity within them.

Here are a few steps to begin that process:

- Remind yourself to focus on achieving a godly character and loving relationships rather than solely academic success. In any area, pushing your child to achieve at a level he or she was not created for will only wound and cause stress in your relationship.

- Seek professional advice on how to best assist your child's learning process. Find someone who is full of hope for your child and will help you strategize on how to maximize your child's learning abilities.

- Discover and develop your child's abilities and interests in other areas. Help your child feel successful somewhere!

- Make time to enjoy your children for who they are. Our pleasure in them is foundational to their sense of well-being and the truest reflection of their heavenly Father's perspective.

In order to help our children become their best, we've got to face their difficulties honestly and get whatever help we may need to create plans for their growth. Are you willing to take those first steps?

Steps of Faith

Father, help me to appreciate the children You've given me and to do whatever it takes to nurture them to their fullest potential in every aspect of their lives.

Teaching Wisdom

The child grew and . . . was filled with wisdom.

LUKE 2:40

I marched down the hallway, ready to correct Jordan on the same problem for the third time in the same day. I shot up an angry question: *What do I do with this kid, Lord?* Immediately, a question came to my mind: *Have you taught him what he needs to know in this area?*

Ouch! I realized we had told Jordan what we wanted him not to do, but we never explained what we did want and why. An energetic nine-year-old, Jordan was learning rules, but he wasn't really growing in wisdom.

Later, as my husband, Cliff, and I prayed, God reminded us that He has given us biblical principles to help us understand what He wants us to do. Knowing how to apply these principles in everyday situations requires wisdom, and that's what we must teach our children.

We first looked at Jordan's most common areas of misbehavior. We asked ourselves: what does God want changed in this area, and why is that so important? What is God's wisdom on this? We began to pray for those positive qualities and spent time talking and praying with Jordan about them.

We read stories and verses from the Bible. We looked for both the positive and negative examples in TV shows and favorite stories. When Jordan misbehaved, he received consequences for poor choices, but we also reviewed his positive behavior, asking him what he could have done differently and how that would have affected the outcome of the situation.

In teaching Jordan about wisdom, we saw our son's sense of purpose and confidence rise. He was no longer simply trying to avoid negative consequences but making an effort to become a young man of wisdom, growing in his ability to know what God wanted him to do—and doing it!

God has given us the instruction and understanding we need for fruitful, joyous lives. If you are a parent, it is your privilege to seek out His principles and help your children grow in their ability to apply His wisdom to their lives.

Steps of Faith

Father, help me to live by Your wisdom as an example to my kids and as an expression of my love for You. Enlarge my capacity to absorb Your wisdom.

255

Abraham's Seed

If you belong to Christ, then you are Abraham's seed,
and heirs according to the promise.

GALATIANS 3:29

I've always felt fortunate to be raised in a strong, loving family. Although I had the same problems as everyone else in high school, I was never overwhelmed by my insecurities. As a young adult I didn't need to embark on a quest to "find myself." I thought I knew who I was. I belonged to a moderately observant Jewish family. We went to synagogue on the Sabbath and kept all the major holidays. But what seemed more important than our religious beliefs was our family identity within the community. I never felt a greater sense of belonging than I did on family occasions; often my grandparents would tell stories of our ancestors in Russia.

All of that changed this year. I came to know Jesus (or *Yeshua,* as He is called in Hebrew) as the Jewish Messiah, and as my Lord and Savior. The people in my new fellowship tried to prepare me for the difficulty of telling my family about my decision. I knew that I would probably face rejection. In fact, my parents told me that none of the family would have anything to do with me if I chose to worship the "Christian God." I know it hurt them terribly to say that, and I'm sure they didn't think I would adhere to my new faith.

But once I knew *Yeshua,* I couldn't turn my back on Him; and He has been faithful to me in every way. I found that my true identity is, and always has been, with Him. I was a slave to sin, unable to choose to do right, unable to please God in any way. *Yeshua* has given me the only freedom I've ever known. I'm now a child of God and a joint heir with *Yeshua.* I know the Jewish Messiah—the only Messiah. And since *Yeshua* was also rejected by His own people, He knows how I feel. He gave up His identity, so that I might find mine in Him.

Jesus does not ask us to forsake our identity and take on a new one in Him. Rather, He makes it possible for us to claim our true identity as children of God—which was His plan from the beginning. Do you know who you are in Him?

Steps of Faith

Father, whatever I may give up in this life to follow Christ cannot compare with what He gave up for me in His life on earth. He laid aside His rights as Your Son so that I could share in His inheritance.

Price of Peace

Blessed are the peacemakers,
for they will be called sons of God.

MATTHEW 5:9

*M*y 11-year-old son wanted to put a bumper sticker on our car that said "Visualize World Peace." When I told him he couldn't, he wanted to know why. I didn't want to tell him simply, "That's a New Age concept" without some explanation, so I tried another approach. I said, "Mark, that's an important question and I really want to give you a good answer, but I need some time to think about it. I'll tell you tomorrow, okay?"

Mark was agreeable. "Sure, Mom."

What was so wrong with the exhortation to visualize world peace? Wasn't anything that encouraged peace good? The problem was, my generation had embraced two false ideas and popularized them. One was that people were inherently good and would choose to do the right thing if they were sufficiently educated. Hence, peace could be achieved by man's efforts alone. The other popular idea, or value, was one of supreme selfishness. Hence, peace could be achieved through mere visualization. There was no need for personal sacrifice.

God sent His Son on a peacemaking mission. He was successful, but at a great price. Peace between man and God was realized through the suffering, shed blood, and death of Jesus. Now He commands us to follow in His footsteps and be sons of God by making peace with one another. That goal will not be realized by adopting some passive state of mind, but only through the death and crucifixion of our sinful desires on a daily basis.

So I told my son this: "God wanted peace so much that He sent Jesus to make peace between Himself and us. If we could have peace just by visualizing it, then Jesus wouldn't have had to die. So I've got an idea. If you want a bumper sticker about peace, that's okay. You can make it yourself. It should say, 'Blessed are the peacemakers.'"

As Christians, we are all called to make peace in a world whose ruler is the enemy of peace and love. We will surely be opposed, perhaps persecuted, for our efforts at peace. But Jesus has called us "blessed."

Steps of Faith

Father, people everywhere say they hope for peace, but lasting peace can come only through Jesus Christ. I look forward to the day when all the nations on the earth will acknowledge that Jesus Christ alone can bring peace.

WEDNESDAY

257

Love and Marriage

May you rejoice in the wife of your youth.

PROVERBS 5:18

*M*ommy, tell me again why you are kidnapping Daddy for the weekend," Joel begged, his eyes shining with the excitement of it all. I rehearsed the plan with him again, knowing full well that his nine-year-old buddies would soon hear every detail.

I had made weekend-getaway plans, coordinating an extra day off with Craig's manager. My parents would stay with the children until we returned Monday evening. I'd waited to tell Joel until Craig had left for the office that morning. Melissa, our toddler, wasn't sure what was going on, but I knew she'd be thrilled when Paw-Paw and Grammie arrived.

Actually, it was my folks who had encouraged the getaway. "Honey, when's the last time you and Craig took time for a weekend by yourselves?" Mother asked when they were visiting us the month before. "You owe it to those little ones to spend some time together!"

"Every marriage needs a jump-start now and again," Dad chimed in, giving me a knowing wink. Actually, it was that wink that gave me the idea to surprise Craig. I decided to make all the arrangements, then "kidnap" him after work!

Now, Joel was waiting for an answer.

"Honey, I'm surprising Daddy with a special trip because I want to spend time with him, just the two of us. When you are married, you'll understand."

"I know, Mom. You and Dad have to figure out what to talk about after all of us grow up and leave home, right?"

"Well, something like that!"

When we take the time to strengthen our marriage, we are investing in the lives of our children. We are building a foundation that will allow them to grow up secure in their parents' love. It also doesn't hurt them to know they cannot have our undivided attention all the time!

Steps of Faith

Heavenly Father, what a blessing you have given us in the covenant of marriage. Help us to make our marriage better by making special times for one another.

Be Still and Know

Be still, and know that I am God.

PSALM 46:10

"Do you hear Him?" Aunt Josie asked. I was seven years old and a brand-new Christian, and it was the last night of my two-week summer stay with her. We were sitting on her screened porch with our eyes closed. I strained my ears trying to hear—I didn't want to let her down.

"Does He sound like crickets?" I asked.

"No."

I closed my eyes tightly and listened harder. Nothing. I opened my eyes and looked over at Aunt Josie. Even now, 20 years later, I can still see her sitting there with her blue eyes closed and a sweet smile on her face. I didn't know that would be my last visit with her before she died. I only knew that she could know God if she sat still and concentrated hard enough.

"I want to hear Him! And I'm being very still—I'm just not knowing."

She leaned over and hugged me. "You'll get better, Franny. It took me a long time to learn to make my mind and my heart still—to shut out all the distractions—and to spend time with God."

"How do you do it, Aunt Josie?"

"I start thinking about the things He's created, like my dogwood trees, rosebushes, those crickets you hear, the sky and stars. I think about how strong He is and how much He loves me. Then I think about all He's given me and I thank Him: for my job, my house, my family, you. And I thank Him that I'm one of His children because Jesus is in my life. He makes me love Him and want to spend more time with Him."

"That's why I have to be still, right?"

"Yes. Being still is a way to focus your mind on Him and His goodness. You'll learn. Just keep practicing, you'll learn."

Be still and know God, whenever you can, wherever you can: five minutes here and there. At your desk, on the way home from work or errands, during lunch, or after dinner, when you lie down, when you wake up. Don't let television, noise, books, or conversation erode your time with your Lord. Be still.

Steps of Faith

Father, You are God, all-knowing, all-powerful. Thank You for loving me enough to allow me to come into Your presence. Thank You for wanting me there.

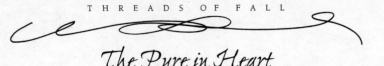

The Pure in Heart

Blessed are the pure in heart, for they will see God.
MATTHEW 5:8

*W*hen I was 11 years old, a routine eye test at school determined that I was almost legally blind. No one was more surprised than I. I didn't realize I had blurry vision. I thought I saw just like everyone else. It wasn't until I walked out of the optometrist's office with my first pair of glasses that I realized how little I'd actually been seeing. Everything was so sharp and clear. I could now see the individual leaves on the trees and blades of grass in the yard. (They'd been green blurs in the past.) I wondered how much I'd missed in life simply because I couldn't see properly.

About that time I became aware of how Pastor Sanders saw God everywhere and in everything. In almost every sermon he recounted experiences from the previous week that were filled with God's presence and power. As much as I enjoyed his stories, I couldn't relate to them. I didn't see God in anything. It began to bother me.

During Vacation Bible school that following summer, I realized the condition of my heart. I was a sinner in need of a Savior. I couldn't save myself from sin, but the Good News was Jesus had already done it for me on the cross. I knew He was what I needed and asked Him into my life.

A funny thing happened when Jesus moved in: He fitted me with spiritual glasses. As I grew in my faith, I began to see more and more of God all around me. The more I saw, the more I realized how much I'd been missing simply because I couldn't "see" properly. And Pastor Sanders' stories now had a whole new level of meaning—because I, too, could see God.

Can you see the presence and power of God around you? If not, you may want to check your spiritual vision, which is directly affected by the condition of your heart. The pure in heart see God today in the earthly realm and will see God in eternity in the spiritual realm. Ask God to create a pure heart in you (Psalm 51:10-12).

Steps of Faith

Father in heaven, I praise You for all Your mighty and wonderful works around me. What a joy it is to see Your presence in my life and my circumstances. Keep my heart pure, devoted only to You and Your will for my life.

Wonderful Words

*Do not let any unwholesome talk come out of
your mouths, but only what is helpful for building others up
according to their needs, that it may benefit those who listen.*

EPHESIANS 4:29

Shut up, stupid!"

These words startled me enough that I pulled the car onto the shoulder of the road. I glared into the backseat where Sean, my six-year-old, was berating his three-year-old sister, Lindsay. She was sobbing. I counted to ten in my head, knowing what I said would set the tone for the rest of our two-hour trip to see my mother. I turned the car off and climbed into the backseat, cuddling Lindsay in my arms.

"Sean, tell me what you said to your sister," I said finally.

Sean tried to defend himself, "But, Mom, she was—"

"Sean." My voice was firm. "Just tell me what you said."

"I told her to shut up." Sean was no longer belligerent.

"Sean, when you said those mean words, they hurt Lindsay. Remember how Jesus said kind words even to unkind people? Jesus would never want you to say words like those to Lindsay."

"I'm sorry," Sean replied, his bottom lip quivering. "I was just mad at her for eating all the Fruit Loops."

"Will you tell that to Lindsay?" I had tears in my eyes now. How many times had I lashed out at others because I was mad?

After Sean apologized to Lindsay and hugged her, I hugged him. "You know, I say mean things sometimes, too, because I get angry. So let's help each other. If you hear me say angry words, you remind me what kind of words Jesus wants to hear, and I'll remind you. Okay?"

"Okay," Sean agreed. "We'll both be careful about what we say."

Words can heal wonderfully or wound terribly. When we are angry, it is especially difficult to control the flood of thoughts threatening to rise through our throats. But the little ones are listening. Make sure the words they hear are good, true, and right.

Steps of Faith

Word-Giver, thank You for the mighty gift of words. May I always honor You with this gift as I bless and encourage others with my words.

Blessing with Words

An anxious heart weighs a man down,
but a kind word cheers him up.

PROVERBS 12:25

*W*hen Madge, a seasoned seventh-grade teacher who attends our Sunday school class, inherited an unruly sixth grade, we all watched to see what would happen. Madge knew this term would be difficult and had asked us to pray. Some of the bigger boys had already been in trouble with the law. Pete, the acknowledged ringleader in the group, was rude, disrespectful, used profanity loudly and often, and sported an attitude of superior indifference to all authority figures—especially female teachers.

I didn't attend church for much of that year because I was nursing my mother in another state. When I returned, Madge was one of the first people I encountered. "How's school going?" I greeted her. "Have you had to suspend any of those troublesome students yet?" I was only half jesting.

To my surprise, she countered, "Oh, school is going great! Most of my students are exceptional in many ways, and I thank God for sending them to me!"

My curiosity aroused, I said, "But Madge, I thought your class was made up of all those difficult youngsters. How is it that now you say they're 'exceptional'?"

With a big smile, Madge responded: "Several of them were difficult at first, but two things made the difference. First, prayer. I make it a practice to pray for each child every morning. And I say something encouraging to each one every day. Words of blessing will eventually penetrate the toughest veneer. Now, all my kids are doing their best. I'm pleased with them and they're pleased with themselves."

Are you speaking words of blessing and encouragement to others—or do you say negative words that actually do harm? Ask God to help you bless others by your uplifting and encouraging words.

Steps of Faith

Father, help me to speak kind, cheerful words to others today—those words that will build people up and encourage them. Enable me to be a blessing by speaking blessings to people.

Making Wise Choices

Seek first his kingdom and his righteousness, and all these things will be given to you as well.

MATTHEW 6:33

*O*n a shopping trip to a crowded mall, I stood on the escalator, rehearsing my mental list. Suddenly my eyes met those of a woman descending on the other side. Surely that wasn't Mary, a college acquaintance from ten years ago. I was almost sure it was, but her appearance shocked me! Sallow, dry skin had replaced the once-flawless complexion. The thin, hunched shoulders spoke defeat and resignation.

In college, Mary had been a glamour queen. Her radiant blonde beauty stood out in every group. I remembered being concerned when she began dating Jack Webster, a sophisticated young man who spent his spare time in off-campus bars where drugs and alcohol were prevalent. When I arrived at the next floor, I turned immediately and went back down. Mary had waited.

"Mary, I'm so glad to see you!" I gushed. "How have you been?"

Before answering, she cast a furtive, downward glance: "Oh, Claire, I've thought of you so often these past years! I remember those long conversations we had about life and religion back in college. I made some really bad choices. I think if I'd listened to you my life would be different!"

My heart raced as I reached out and drew the slight figure into a hug. How limp and frail she seemed!

"Mary," I whispered, "let's get a cup of coffee and talk. It's never too late to start making good choices."

Every day we make choices. Often they involve choosing to go either God's way or the world's way. It's easy to do what everyone else is doing but difficult to stand alone. Ask God to help you make wise choices that will honor Him and avoid remorse and regret later on.

Steps of Faith

Father, thank You for the ability to choose. Strengthen me to make wise choices that glorify You and benefit others. As I seek guidance through Your Word, may my choices be an example to others.

Elohim

For the Lord your God is God of gods and Lord of lords,
the great God [Elohim], mighty and awesome.

DEUTERONOMY 10:17

*T*he cappuccino machine had sat, unused, on our kitchen counter for years. I had tried making some once or twice, but it never tasted right. Then I lost the instructions.

Last winter Phil and I invited his supervisor, Ross, and his wife, Wanda, over for dinner. Wanda was an elegant beauty and had an air about her that attracted and intimidated me. She was filled with a certain love and joy I'd never known.

When Wanda saw the machine, she said excitedly, "Oh, I just love cappuccino! Are you going to serve some with dessert?" That had not exactly been my plan, but wanting to impress her, I said I would.

Even without the instructions I got the espresso brewing after dinner. When it stopped dripping, I assumed it was ready. But the pressure for the milk frothing was still at full force when I disengaged the container.

The last thing I remember seeing—before the explosion—was Wanda's mouth dropping open in horror.

After we cleaned up everything, I nervously joked that the Big Bang theory had been proven in my kitchen. A whole new conversation opened. We began talking about the Big Bang theory and other theories of creation.

Wanda told me why she believed in God, the almighty *Elohim,* the Creator of the universe. I knew in my heart that her words were true. Over the weeks we became friends and she led me to Christ.

She also taught me how to make a great cup of cappuccino.

How well do you know God? The best way to get to know Him is to learn the names the Bible uses to describe His character. The name *Elohim* is used in Genesis 1:1, describing the almighty, infinite, creator God. He is sovereign and omnipotent. He controls the universe. He is there for you, even when your life seems out of control.

Steps of Faith

Jehovah Elohim, what an awesome God You are! You are my Creator, the one true God, great and glorious, almighty and everlasting. Thank You for all You have done for me. You, the Sovereign God of the universe, are also my Savior and my Friend.

Loving Conversations

*Two are better than one, because they have a
good return for their work.*

ECCLESIASTES 4:9

The telephone was ringing—it was Mary. We always find time to talk and encourage one another. Sometimes the daily chores and stress of life can feel overwhelming, but having someone to share my burdens with brings a sense of peace to my life.

Mary sounded distressed. "Martin is going to be very unhappy with me when he gets home tonight. I don't know what to do!"

"What's wrong?" I asked, concerned.

"I promised Martin I wouldn't use the credit card any more. We are trying to get out of debt! I couldn't resist the sale on exercise equipment at the sport shop today. I pulled out the charge card automatically without thinking about the consequences until I came home."

We talked about her anxiety and prayed for a peaceful discussion with Martin. I promised to go with her to return her purchases. We also talked about her impulse buying and how she might restrain from those kinds of splurges in the future. I related to her struggles because I had struggled with the same issues in my life.

Sometimes we meet at Mary's to talk over a cup of hot cocoa or walk around the neighborhood. We enjoy our quiet chats about things that concern us. We know there are no quick answers; none are expected. All we know is our hearts always feel a little lighter when our souls are soothed by kind words from one another.

Has God placed someone unique in your life to share your heart with? Look at the opportunities He places before you for loving friendships. The love of a friend will be returned over and over again.

Steps of Faith

Father in Heaven, thank You for blessing me with a dear, committed friend. Thank You for a friend who is able to keep confidences. Give me the wisdom to discern when it is appropriate to speak and when it's appropriate to be a good listener.

That Woman Again

A wife of noble character who can find?
She is worth far more than rubies.

PROVERBS 31:10

Oh no, I groaned. *Not that Proverbs 31 woman again!*

Fortunately, the Bible-study leader didn't notice my dismay. *What does that Proverbs 31 woman have to do with my life?* I was tired of comparing myself to her and falling short every time.

The leader gave us five minutes to rewrite verses, modernizing the Proverbs 31 woman's tasks. My head was swimming with challenging phrases: "works with eager hands . . . sets about her work vigorously . . . does not eat the bread of idleness. . . ."

I couldn't imagine the Proverbs 31 woman watching daytime television or chatting on the telephone. I doubted she would go "recreational" shopping, either, if her house looked like a tornado had hit it.

The time was up and one by one, women began to read their descriptions. "She gets up while it is still dark to have her quiet time with the Lord." *Hey, I do that!* "She shops at the farmer's market to get the freshest produce for her family." *Yeah, Lord, I do that, too!* "Her lamp does not go out at night as she uses the hours after the children are asleep to fold laundry or finish her mending while watching television." What a great idea! Now I was taking notes. I could accomplish many tasks while watching television. And with a longer phone cord, I could chat with a friend while cooking dinner or doing the dishes.

I was feeling a lot better! Besides, I had something the Proverbs 31 woman did not have, I chuckled to myself. A name!

Do you have trouble relating to women in the Bible? Consider doing a character study on one you admire. Much can be gained as the Holy Spirit reveals qualities that are desirable, no matter what century you live in.

Steps of Faith

Father, teach me from Your Word as I look closer at the lives of other women who have loved You. Use their lives to instruct me in a fresh, new way so that I may learn to love You more.

Awkward Moment

Jesus said to her, "Will you give me a drink?"
JOHN 4:7

*I*t was the one social event I truly dreaded. My husband's law firm was having a dinner, and spouses were invited. That meant a half-hour of mingling among 150 people before sitting down at a table with six people I had never met before. My husband was great at these functions; it was his living. I, however, was a stay-at-home mother of three children under age six.

Everything went as expected. Soon after the salad course, my husband was deeply engrossed in conversation with the real-estate attorney on his right. I listened in for a few moments and then my mind began to wander. Suddenly I had an abrupt thought: *Talk to the woman next to you.* I stole a few glances at her. There was no ring on her left hand. *Great,* I thought. *No husband, no children.* No particular current events of interest sprung to mind. What could I say to her?

She asked me to pass the salt. As I did, I said, "It's seven o'clock. If I were home now, I'd be up to my elbows in Mr. Bubble. What would you be doing?" I asked, smiling.

She smiled back. "I'd like to be doing the same thing. But my daughter is with my ex-husband this weekend."

Wrong question. "I'm sorry . . ." I stammered.

"Oh, don't be sorry at all," she said. "I'd much rather talk about her than business." We introduced ourselves; her name was Diana. She asked me how many children I had. After talking a little while, I learned quite a bit about her. We actually had a lot in common. Our fathers had both been in the military, and we had both lived overseas as children.

At the end of the evening, Diana and I exchanged telephone numbers and promised to be in touch. And I'm quite sure we will be.

There are two things that all people, no matter who they are, have in common: schedules and relationships. You can always, in any situation, start a conversation by asking about one of these things.

Steps of Faith

Father, I sometimes feel awkward because I don't know what to say. But Jesus did not initiate friendships by being a versatile conversationalist. He did it by showing people that He cared about them. Help me develop a knack for asking caring questions.

Know Your Enemy

*When [Satan] lies, he speaks his native language,
for he is a liar and the father of lies.*

JOHN 8:44

*T*wo years ago I witnessed the power of Satan's lies in the life of my daughter, Beatrice. Although I monitored some of what Bea was exposed to, I hadn't been discerning about it. In fact, I had made some naive assumptions.

There were the cartoons and sitcoms Bea watched as a child. Some were violent or mystical, in which characters called on "higher powers" for wisdom and strength. Others portrayed well-adjusted families that never went to church. There were also music, movies, fantasy games, magazines—even some classes at school!—that were filled with subtle (and not-so-subtle) lies about God, Jesus Christ, and Christians. All of these chipped away at her faith.

By the time Bea was 16 she was angry, sullen, and disrespectful. I thought it was hormones. Then her friends, interests, and taste in clothing changed. I sensed a hardening of her spirit. When she refused to go to church one Sunday, I told her she was grounded. That afternoon, when we returned from church, she was gone. In her room I discovered that she had torn up her Bible.

People from our church began praying immediately. Bea came home two days later, very shaken. I still don't know what happened while she was gone, but it was enough to make her go to our church counselor. The next few months were difficult but Bea finally came to trust Jesus Christ with all her heart and is growing in Him.

Satan tells lies. His favorite target is Jesus Christ and anyone who claims to follow Him as Lord and Savior. These lies are prevalent in our culture, and you must guard your children and yourself against them. Pray for and practice discernment. Know your enemy. Satan is the father of lies. Spend time developing your relationship with God, who enables us to walk in truth.

Steps of Faith

Father, keep me mindful that it was a lie from the mouth of Satan that ushered sin into the world. Show me his lies in regard to my family. We want no part of them.

Prayer for the Nelsons

For this reason I kneel before the Father.

EPHESIANS 3:14

*I*n my Bible the subhead for Ephesians 3:14–21 reads "A Prayer for the Ephesians." In my prayer journal, I've renamed it "A Prayer for the Nelsons." That's my family. I was one of the first Nelsons to become a "real" Christian. Sure, we all went to church regularly, just like we voted regularly and put out the trash regularly. But we were all "dead in [our] transgressions and sins" (Ephesians 2:1).

At 19, when Jesus became my Savior and Lord, I began telling the other Nelsons about it. My parents called it "teenage rebellion" and my brothers called me a "Jesus freak." That was okay. I knew God had a plan for my family, and I was to pray for them in a special way. The question was how.

I was reading through my Bible that year. My mother's birthday corresponded with the reading of the Book of Ephesians. That morning I read "A Prayer for the Ephesians" for the first time in my life. I began to cry because I wanted God to do for my mother what Paul wanted for the Ephesians. I recited the prayer out loud, putting my mother's name in the place of "you."

And that's when my secret birthday present began. I still prayed for my family daily, but on their birthdays I would fast and pray "A Prayer for the Nelsons" several times during the day, replacing "you" with his or her name.

That was 19 years ago. Since then, every member of my family has received Christ. I have my own family now and have extended "A Prayer for the Nelsons" to include my husband, children, nieces, nephews, and in-laws. And I know future generations of my family will be blessed. "To him be glory in the church and in Christ Jesus *throughout all generations,* for ever and ever! Amen!" (Ephesians 3:21).

Do you pray for your extended family on a regular basis? If you have a large family, you may want to write out all their names (and birthdays, if desired) and keep the list in your Bible. Praying God's Word for your family is the best gift you can give.

W
E
D
N
E
S
D
A
Y

Steps of Faith

Lord Jesus, You are able to do immeasurably more than all I could ask or imagine for my family. All praise and glory are Yours. Please fill my family "to the measure of all the fullness of God" (Ephesians 3:19).

"Oh No, Not That!"

*Impress them on your children. Talk about them when you sit
at home and when you walk along the road.*

DEUTERONOMY 6:7

$\mathscr{M}$y eight-year-old son, Brian, bounced into the kitchen and cheerfully announced, "Hey, Mom! I know what a condom is! Do you?"

Without skipping a beat, I matched his casual cheer with, "I sure do, but I'd love to know what you think one is!" We had a brief, friendly, open discussion and Brian was on his way down the hall to do homework.

How would you have responded? My "calm, collected" response was the fruit of years of "teachable moments" like this. I regretted that he had been instructed by an eight-year-old "expert" (I phoned the child's mother that night), but we can't completely shield our kids from such situations. As opportunities have come, we've given Brian clear answers about the boundaries of behavior in the area of sexuality.

We've not yet felt the need to give a detailed explanation on the "mechanics" of it, but the values of respect, self-control, and the fear of the Lord have been regular themes of conversation. The morality of sexuality is at least a weekly topic. We discuss everything from why we cover our bodies when we get out of the shower to why we don't laugh or use crude slang about private parts to commenting on a commercial that caught us by surprise with its sensual content.

To have both a biblical message and method in communicating values to our kids, we had to first develop healthy attitudes and an accurate understanding of sexuality ourselves. My husband and I had issues from our own pasts to resolve before we could address the subject without confusion. If envisioning these kinds of conversations with your kids raises your blood pressure sky-high, perhaps there are some points for you to bring to the Father for His healing touch. Ask for insight into the beauty of His plans for human sexuality.

Information is the easy part! It's the values underlying the boundaries we expect our kids to abide by that take regular, open, sincere communication, whenever and however the subject arises. Are you confidently prepared for those teachable moments?

Steps of Faith

*Lord, help me teach my kids to respect and appreciate the human
body as Your creation and to gladly abide by Your rules for sexuality.*

Feel So Loved

*All the ways of the LORD are loving and faithful for those who
keep the demands of his covenant.*

PSALM 25:10

*W*hen it became increasingly clear that Ben and I were falling
in love, I began to pray more than ever for guidance. I knew he was
the one for me. There was just one issue, and it was a big one: Ben
is paralyzed from the waist down.

Shortly after we married, Ben and I began to fight. Issues that a
"disabled" couple face are so different from those of normal couples.
It's a miracle any of these marriages survive. Ours has, and it's taught
me an amazing lesson about touch.

Countless times Ben and I would get in an argument, and a few
minutes later (while we were still stewing), Ben would need my
help. It almost always involved my touching him. If I was still mad,
my first reaction was to pull away. However, I knew I couldn't just
abandon him.

It never failed. The moment my flesh touched his, I could feel the
anger and tension evaporate. Even when Ben couldn't feel my touch,
just knowing I was touching him eased his tension as well. Within
minutes we were hugging or laughing—or both.

Over the years I've seen how touch works with other disabled
people, young and old. Because of wheelchairs and other equipment, the disabled aren't as accessible to human touch—but they
still long for it, even more than the able-bodied.

I've always made it a point to touch any disabled person I come
in contact with, usually on his or her hands, arms, or shoulders. I'll
touch the faces of only those I know very well. I didn't know how
much this was appreciated until my friend Mary, who is also disabled, said after I gave her arm a squeeze, "I love it when you do
that. It makes me feel so loved."

Is there a disabled or chronically ill person in your life? One of
the best ways to demonstrate the love of Christ is to begin affection-
ately touching him or her. It's normal to feel a little awkward at first,
but the moment you conquer that fear and do it, you will experience
the same joy that you are giving to that person.

Steps of Faith

*Dear Lord, thank You for the healing power of touch. Help me to use
it in my ministry to people who may not get touched very often.*

The Afternoon

He changes times and seasons.

DANIEL 2:21

$\mathcal{I}$ brought her lunch tray into the bedroom ever so quietly. Mom slumbered peacefully through Tuesday afternoon. The warm glow from the shuttered windows granted just enough light to dissipate the shadows. Setting the tray on the nightstand, I sat on the edge of her bed. *How many times have I sat here, looking into the face of a loved one?*

It was Michelle who first occupied this bed. She hung her horse-show ribbons across the shelf above her head. *Now she hangs her family's laundry out to dry.* I smiled. Melanie moved in next, displaying her own watercolor creations and springtime flowers. To keep with tradition, Marie moved in last, packing the room with giggling girlfriends. Her telephone resided on the shelf—that is, until a few months ago when my last little bird flew from my nest. On the shelf in their honor I now display a favorite photo of my three little birds, happily ignoring the camera in their playful embrace. I study their smiles and see traces of me in their expressions—as I see my own face in my mother's beside me.

Coming to live with us a few weeks ago, Mom seemed to know her days were passing. Smiling when spoken to, gentle in reply, quiet the rest of the time, she's no trouble at all. I suppose I could resent her arrival stealing my newfound freedom—but I don't. We are both exactly where we ought to be.

I smooth her soft white curls on the pillow. There won't be many more warm Tuesday afternoons. Soon this season, too, will change.

Do you ever catch yourself "wishing away" a period of your life? Living in the future is an especially common hazard for women. However, when you do, you miss what God is saying to you today. Instead of longing for what's ahead, enthusiastically accept all God is giving you today.

Steps of Faith

Lord, You have given me today. I anticipate receiving the good gifts that come wrapped in possibilities. I accept each one, be it easy or difficult, and say "yes" with all my heart for what You have for me.

The Offering

The LORD is good, a refuge in times of trouble.
He cares for those who trust in him.

NAHUM 1:7

I staggered into the kitchen carrying my purse, briefcase, car keys, and three bags of groceries and promptly unloaded them on my little kitchen desk. I let out a long sigh. From one job and its problems to another job with its problems. It never seemed to end.

After putting some clothes in the dryer, I put away the groceries and started supper. There were bills to pay and laundry to fold. And to make the evening even more interesting, I had to prepare my favorite recipe for a bridal shower! Who decided to have a shower on a *Thursday night* anyway? As I was reaching for a cookbook on my desk, I spied my old thesaurus. What was it doing there? Then I noticed a yellowed 3x5 card sticking out of it. It was my mother's recipe for Apple Bread.

Memories flooded my mind. *Has it already been five years?* My mother, who had battled breast cancer, made her final visit that Thanksgiving. I wanted so badly for us to prepare her famous Apple Bread together, like we had when I was a little girl. I searched diligently for the recipe, but I never found it. And I never got to make Apple Bread with my mother again. She died the following March.

Tears from deep within began to pour forth. I missed my mother. I wanted her back with me, to help *me* be a mother and everything else I was expected to be! Gradually, as I composed myself, I realized she already had. Then I had an idea: I'd make the Apple Bread for the shower! It would be a special offering in honor of my mother and all she did to prepare me to be a godly wife, mother, employee, and friend—a celebration of all the seasons (and seasonings) of life.

Life is a continuing series of changes. People and places flash before our eyes as though we're viewing life from the window of a bus. And life just keeps going. But God doesn't change (Hebrews 13:8). He will be with you at every stop, every turn, and every new experience.

Steps of Faith

Eternal God, how grateful I am that in a world that is constantly changing You are forever the same. You have seen me through so much, mere adjustments and major traumas, in my life. Lord, how I need You beside me through every trial of every day.

For Such a Time

"Let a search be made for beautiful young virgins
for the king. . . . Then let the girl who pleases the king be queen
instead of Vashti." This advice appealed to the king,
and he followed it.

ESTHER 2:2,4

*E*sther has been my favorite Bible character since Sunday school. I loved imagining myself as the beautiful and wise queen, whose faith and courage saved the nation of Israel from annihilation.

However, as I matured—in years and in my faith—my eyes were opened to certain aspects of Esther's story which I hadn't noticed as a child. For instance, I had naïvely thought King Xerxes had chosen Esther as his queen strictly because of her beauty and charm. But as I have learned more about the culture of that time, it seemed that Esther's beauty was not the only thing that won her the queen's crown.

As a member of his harem, she would be expected to please him sexually and in every other way. Though Esther was Jewish, she was living in captivity in a pagan country, under the rule of a pagan king. And King Xerxes was the type of man who would divorce a woman just because she refused to dance for his drunken friends. Such was the status of women in Persia at that time.

As I pondered this degrading treatment of women, I began to appreciate just how much courage Esther needed to approach the king. He had not summoned her for 30 days, and Esther (and probably others in the court) may have feared that she no longer pleased him. Would she forever be relegated to the harem?

But Esther put aside her fears and trusted God. She knew He had placed her in the role of queen for a reason and put her life in His hands.

Who you are, where you are, and who you know all play a part in God's overall plan for His creation. And the more you submit yourself to His will, the more He can use you. Consider Esther. Her obedience helped save the entire nation of Israel. Your faithfulness is capable of no less.

Steps of Faith

Heavenly Father, I am amazed how You use each of us and our individual gifts and circumstances to work out Your plan. When I think about Esther, along with her faithfulness and courage in her situation, I know I can be faithful in mine—but only by Your power.

Late Arrival

Because of the LORD's great love we are not consumed,
for his compassions never fail.

LAMENTATIONS 3:22

I don't know how it could have happened. Matt thought I had picked Rob up—I thought he had. As I turned into the school driveway, the street lights illuminated the vast, empty parking lot. There, under a lonely light, sat Rob. How could I explain how sorry I was? He had been sitting there for three hours, without dinner, without a jacket. What kind of a mother was I?

I pulled up alongside him. "Hey good lookin', want a ride?"

He didn't say a word but threw his backpack on the floorboard and slammed the door.

"Honey, I'm so, so sorry. Dad and I miscommunicated—we didn't forget you, we just thought the other had picked you up. I had something unexpected come up at work." Silence. I looked down at my rough-n-tough 15-year-old and saw the little boy I had known for so long. "Will you forgive us . . . forgive me?"

He didn't look up, so I stared straight ahead. I felt like I was drowning in the crashing flood of responsibilities—my family, my career, my personal sanity. Towering waves were breaking around me. And they overwhelmed my heart. Tears began to flow.

"I thought you had an accident. I was scared," Rob said quietly.

"Oh, honey. I'm so sorry," I cried softly.

Slowly, Rob looked up and a grin crept across his face. "Let's just remember this after I get my license and miss my curfew some night."

In spite of my tears, I giggled at my forgiving son. Grace. What goes around, comes around.

Do you ever feel squeezed in the vise of responsibilities of home and career? Do important things "slip through the cracks"? Invest some valuable time to determine what in your life is most valuable and what can change. Ask God for wisdom in discerning His priorities.

Steps of Faith

Lord, You have given me the joy of many avenues of service but sometimes I feel so overwhelmed! Give me Your eyes in distinguishing between the important and the negotiable challenges of my life.

Laws and Loopholes

When you are harvesting in your field and you
overlook a sheaf, do not go back to get it. Leave it for the alien,
the fatherless and the widow, so that the LORD your
God may bless you.

DEUTERONOMY 24:19

*T*he role of widow in Old Testament times was synonymous with desolation and despair. And you couldn't get much lower than a widow without a son, like Ruth or Naomi. Under the patriarchal system, women were not allowed to own property. So when Naomi's husband, Elimelech, died, all of his property passed into the hands of his relatives. Ruth and Naomi were doomed to a life of abject poverty and would have to count on the charity of others for the rest of their lives.

Abandoning Naomi was clearly the easy way out for Ruth. And though she was somewhat new to Judaism, Ruth understood the trials that lay ahead as she and Naomi made their way back to Bethlehem. Nevertheless she faithfully stayed with Naomi.

And God faithfully protected Ruth and Naomi. His care of these helpless women is evident in their story. First, God's law provided a means for them to gather food (Deuteronomy 24:19). And it would be while Ruth was gleaning in the fields that she would meet Boaz, a wealthy relative of Elimelech's and her future husband.

God's law—and an obscure loophole—were also the means by which Ruth and Boaz were allowed to marry. And Naomi knew the law. When Naomi noted Boaz's interest in Ruth, she had an idea. After discussing it with Ruth, Naomi utilized the ancient levirate marriage laws by offering Ruth to her late husband's male relatives. The next of kin chose not to marry Ruth, which made it possible for Boaz to do so. The property of Naomi's son automatically went to Boaz, who took both women into his household.

In the story of Ruth we see the faithfulness of one woman to another and God's faithfulness to provide for their physical needs through His devoted servant Boaz. Are you a Ruth, a Boaz, or a Naomi? Does your faith allow you to trust God to take care of you?

Steps of Faith

Father, thank You for the story of Ruth. The more I study it, the more I appreciate how You orchestrate the people and circumstances in our lives for Your purposes. I must confess that there are times when I waver in my faith in Your provision. Please help me to be as faithful as Ruth.

Driver's License

*Train a child in the way he should go, and when he is
old he will not turn from it.*

PROVERBS 22:6

I feel a little funny. Five minutes ago I willingly handed my car keys to my 16-year-old son, Stevie, and watched him slowly, carefully, pull away from the curb. A rather stern Motor Vehicles officer sat in my place beside him.

So here I stand under the "Test Begins Here" sign, a nervous mother clutching her purse and craning her neck to catch a glimpse of her baby rounding the bend.

Stevie has longed for this day. *Oh Lord, help him remember what he's practiced.* When he was six, he climbed into the driver's seat, inadvertently shifted the car into neutral and drifted down the driveway. All that was visible was the top of his crew cut. Thank goodness for the chain-link fence that interrupted his journey.

Nothing can stop him now. In two years or so, he'll be pulling out of the driveway in a car loaded with all the college necessities. Just a moment later, he'll be escorting his bride to their car through showers of rice and good wishes.

Will he be happy? Will he remember what we've taught him? Will he be a good husband and daddy? *Oh Lord, help him remember what You've taught him.*

Before I lapse into the chorus of "Sunrise, Sunset," I see our blue sedan rounding the bend and glimpse my bright-eyed boy in the front seat. Our eyes meet as he brings the car to a careful stop. He did it!

No matter what your children's ages, you are in the process of letting go. Instead of grieving the passing years, seize the time to teach your children what they need to understand for the next stage of their lives. Be excited at the unique role you have in preparing them for what's ahead.

Steps of Faith

Father, do You get excited when You see me ready for my next set of responsibilities? Thank You for preparing me along the way for Your plans for my future. Help me to walk according to what You have shown me.

Puzzled Pieces

Teach me your way, O LORD, and I will walk in your truth;
give me an undivided heart, that I may fear your name.

PSALM 86:11

*S*heila sat on the edge of the child-sized chair and grew more uncomfortable as the parent-teacher meeting progressed.

"And last, Robert doesn't seem to understand the importance of learning his states and capitals," Mrs. Thompson explained. "He is distracted during the lesson and disappointed with his quiz grades."

"Mrs. Thompson, Rob has struggled with rote learning his whole life," Sheila offered. "I've always found it helpful to try to make relationships within the information for him."

"I'm sorry, it's really hard to give the one-on-one attention that Rob needs," Mrs. Thompson responded sadly. "I just don't have the time."

Sheila left the school parking lot as frustrated as she had been when she was in second grade. *Rob learns the same way I do,* she thought. *He needs to picture in his mind what he must memorize—and even better, to feel it.*

Her eyes brightened as she swung the car around into the toy-store parking lot. After dinner that night, Sheila and Rob sat at the kitchen table. Spread in front of them were colorful wood puzzle pieces of the United States. "Pick up the shape of the state we live in, honey." Rob fingered the familiar outline of the state of Texas. "Let's put a star sticker on the capital. What's the name of the capital? Now, feel the top—what state would fit in there?"

We all need help at times "opening the window to let the light come in." What are the ways you learn best? Do you see these styles in your children? Because you know your child better than anyone else, you can be instrumental in helping him/her learn. Look for and be sensitive to the "windows" that open your child's understanding.

Steps of Faith

Lord, like the psalmist David, I plead with You to teach me Your ways. Make me sensitive to the way others learn and help me find creative alternative ways to communicate. As I read Your Word, may Your Holy Spirit guide me into all truth.

What Is Better

"Martha, Martha," the Lord answered,
"you are worried and upset about many things,
but only one thing is needed. Mary has chosen what is better,
and it will not be taken away from her."

LUKE 10:41,42

*T*he tiny village was called Bethany, and it was a day's walk east of Jerusalem. In it lived a family especially close to Jesus' heart: Martha, probably a widow; her sister, Mary; and her brother, Lazarus. At a time when it was increasingly hazardous to be seen with Jesus, they always welcomed Him at their house—and Jesus often took advantage of their hospitality.

On this particular day Jesus must have been talking about something that spoke to Mary's heart. Maybe it was a temptation she was struggling with, a person she needed to forgive, or maybe living with Martha was really testing her patience. Whatever it was, Mary loved Jesus and without hesitation sat at His feet knowing that what He was saying was much more important than anything going on in the kitchen.

On the other hand, "Martha was distracted by all the preparations that had to be made" (Luke 10:40), and in front of her guests complained to Jesus about Mary's refusal to help her. She wanted Jesus to condone her anger and set Mary straight. However, Jesus reproved Martha for being so intensely concerned about the mundane rather than the spiritual.

Are you a Martha—stressed out and resentful about all the domestic burdens you must bear alone? Or are you a Mary—tranquilly sitting at the feet of your Lord? Mary was unruffled by the tasks at hand or Martha's complaining. She wanted to receive everything that Jesus had to give. Jesus did not love Martha any less than Mary, but His pleasure at Mary's desire to learn was obvious. Are you faithful to learn from Him?

Steps of Faith

Almighty God, every time I read the story of Martha and Mary I feel a twinge of conviction. I try to be a Mary, but when I honestly evaluate my life, it seems I resemble Martha more and more. Why is it that, even though I know I'll feel better and probably even get more accomplished when I do spend that time with You, I get distracted and then stressed out, like Martha? Help me, Father, to choose what is better, like Mary.

MONDAY

279

Apples of Gold

*The tongue has the power of life and death, and those
who love it will eat its fruit.*

PROVERBS 18:21

*I*t was a bright, warm fall day, but my mood was black. I was
driving home from my grandfather's funeral, numb with grief. My
father had died only six months before, and I felt alone and very
angry. *Why does God seem so far away from me when I need Him the
most?* I wondered bitterly as I pulled into a fast-food restaurant outside of town.

Once inside, I immediately regretted my decision. The long line
moved slowly, and the family in front of me had several screaming,
grubby children. When I finally stepped up to the counter, I made
no attempt to conceal my irritation.

"Welcome to Speedy Burger. My name is Shirley. May I take your
order?" The heavily made-up woman behind the counter beamed at me.

I replied darkly, "I'll have a cheeseburger minus pickles, small
fries, and an apple pie."

"Will that be for here or to go?" she asked, her smile wavering.

"To go!" I snapped. "I'm in a hurry, and I've been waiting in your
line for almost 30 minutes."

As her smile vanished, I felt a twinge of guilt. When I handed
Shirley the money, she said quietly, "I hope your day gets better."

As I turned to leave, I got a sinking feeling in my stomach. I
turned back to the counter and faced Shirley. "I'm sorry I was so
rude," I began. "I was taking out my stress and frustration on you. I
apologize."

Shirley smiled slightly and said, "It's okay. It gets pretty hectic
around here too, but it's a steady job. You see, my husband left me
and our three small children, so I don't really have a choice. Anyway,
I appreciate you apologizing to me. It means a lot."

Words are powerful and can bless or destroy a person. Since we
all will be held accountable for our words, we will truly "eat their
fruit" someday, be it bitter or sweet. If you want your words to be
sweet, you must give Christ control of your tongue.

Steps of Faith

*Father, today I have many opportunities to speak words of healing
and hope to others. In my everyday conversation, help me to be kind
and encouraging rather than critical and strident. I ask this in the
name of Jesus, the living Word, who spoke God's love to me.*

Root of Bitterness

*See to it that no one misses the grace of God and that
no bitter root grows up to cause trouble and defile many.*

HEBREWS 12:15

Sandy slammed down the telephone receiver. Her heart pounded and hot tears burned in her eyes. Three years away from that man and he still knew what buttons to push. "I hate you!" she yelled at the telephone.

Will, her ex-husband, had been one of the biggest mistakes of Sandy's life. She met him when she was 20, right before he entered dental school. He swept her off her feet, and they were married two days before the fall semester began. She agreed to quit college and work to put him through school. Neither was a Christian.

When Sandy found out three months later that she was pregnant, she was elated. But Will told her to get an abortion. Sandy pleaded with Will, assuring him that they would manage. He said coldly, "We'll have plenty of time and money for kids after dental school. Just get rid of it."

Sandy was never the same after the abortion. Anger, grief, and shame consumed her. Even though the counselor at the clinic had assured Sandy it was just "a tissue mass," Sandy knew she was grieving over a baby whose life had been snuffed out just because it was inconvenient. Four years later, when the twins, Megan and Rachel, were born, Sandy began to regain a sense of purpose for her marriage and her life. But when the girls were about three, one afternoon Will came home early and told Sandy he was in love with another woman. His attorney would call next week.

She didn't think she'd ever forgive him.

Many circumstances can lay a foundation for bitterness to take root—injustice, deliberate unkindness, and violence are just a few. If there is a "root of bitterness" in your heart today, ask God to reveal it and help you learn to forgive as His Word teaches. When you do, His discerning power is released in your life and will enrich your relationship with Him and with others.

Steps of Faith

Lord, You taught us to pray, "Forgive us our debts, as we also have forgiven our debtors." That's tough for me to pray sometimes; but then I think about what You endured for my forgiveness. Lord, teach me to forgive as You have forgiven me.

W
E
D
N
E
S
D
A
Y

Washing

Wash away all my iniquity and cleanse me from my sin. . . .
Create in me a pure heart, O God, and renew a
steadfast spirit within me.

PSALM 51:2,10

*T*he young wife tenderly leaned over her husband in the wheel-chair. Her husband, severely brain-damaged as a result of an auto-mobile accident, lifted his head slightly and smiled. The woman straightened his collar and smoothed his shirt as she talked.

"I used to have a hard time accepting Bob's injury," she said, smiling as she looked at him. "And the hardest part was bathing my husband, wasn't it, honey?"

His eyes rolled slightly and he smiled as if to say, "You bet!"

She straightened and fought back tears as she continued. "He would stand in the shower and hold onto the towel rack while I scrubbed his back. All the while my tears mingled with the running water. My big, strong, handsome husband . . . now he couldn't do for me, I had to do for him. Even to the point of washing him."

The man shifted his weight in his wheelchair, unable to speak, only to listen.

"But all that changed when I realized that Jesus did the same—no, I take that back. He did much more when He washed me of the dirt and filth in my own life. Now I count it a privilege to give Bob a bath."

The young woman with the brain-damaged husband began to change her attitude toward bathing him as she meditated on what her Lord was doing for her every day. And in John 13:1-17 we see the Lord washing the feet of His disciples. What about you? How can you "wash the feet" of a friend or family member? And if you have an attitude problem, ask God to refresh and invigorate you.

Steps of Faith

Lord God, I know my hands and feet are soiled from everyday con-
tact with this sinful world. Wash me, make me whiter than snow.
Like David I ask You to create in me a clean heart. And I thank You
for the blood of Jesus that cleanses and makes me whole.

Breakfast

Share with God's people who are in need.
Practice hospitality.

ROMANS 12:13

$\mathscr{I}$ am one of those people who waits until the last possible second before crawling out of bed. I then spend the rest of the morning sprinting from the shower to the closet to the kitchen.

Needless to say, I am not a morning person. But wonders never cease, especially when God is in the picture. One morning I sat up in bed one hour before the alarm was to go off. I was wide awake. And I had this overwhelming urge to make breakfast!

As I measured, poured, and stirred, I began praying for my family and other concerns. Then I began praying for each member of the Bible study group that meets in our home. Among them was Miriam, and she kept coming back to mind. I sensed God wanted me to pray especially for her.

Soon everyone was on his or her way—still a little stunned, I might add. I was dressed and had 45 minutes before I needed to leave for work. I didn't know what to do with myself. Then there was a knock on the door. It was Miriam. Her eyes were puffy and red. She had been crying, pretty hard it appeared. She apologized as she walked in the door but said she had to talk to someone. I poured some coffee and offered her a warm muffin.

As she sipped her coffee, Miriam told me that her husband, Wayne, had been arrested for drunk driving the night before—his third offense. He was in jail. She wept as she described the anguish of living with an alcoholic.

As I listened, I prayed for wisdom. I also realized God had gotten me up early that morning and had me praying for Miriam for a reason. I thanked Him for enabling me to welcome into my home, without notice, a sister who needed someone to talk to.

How many times has God paved the way for you to be hospitable to a friend in need? Even though we have no way of knowing what's going on in the lives of other people, God knows. And He will use you to minister to those people if you submit to the Holy Spirit's nudgings—even when they go against your disposition.

Steps of Faith

Father in heaven, I know it is only through Your Son, Jesus, that I have the ability to serve others in my home. Help me, Father, to be sensitive to the needs of others. My home is Your home. Please send Your hurting children to me, and give me the wisdom to help them.

283

F
R
I
D
A
Y

Worth It

*For I am the LORD, your God, who takes hold of your right
hand and says to you, "Do not fear; I will help you."*

ISAIAH 41:13

$\mathcal{M}$y husband, Scott, is a quadriplegic. He broke his neck in a freak accident when he was 17 and became paralyzed from the chest down. He has almost no use of his hands but tremendous upper-body strength. He finished high school and college, and then passed the CPA exam.

Scott and I met when I was assigned to write a story about him for our local newspaper. As a reporter, I questioned him extensively about his injury and the struggles of a disabled person. But I got a peek past the wheelchair into his heart. A year later we were married. However, neither one of us was prepared for the adjustments that awaited us.

Scott, who had been dependent upon his parents for his daily care, now was dependent upon me (practically a stranger) for the rest of his life. That was overwhelming enough. But also, he had never allowed himself to grieve losing 80 percent of his body. All of his repressed fear, grief, and anger erupted like a volcano during our first year.

On the other hand I idolized Scott. I imagined him endowed with superhuman courage and strength of character. I also assumed he would worship the ground I walked on. So when he began to pelt me with angry words and accusations, I responded with twice as much shock, pain, and dismay. It is a miracle we are still married.

That was seven years ago. Scott and I can honestly say we are happy; we love each other; we would not want to be married to anyone else. We have seen how God has healed the anger, grief, and pain that dominated our marriage in the early days. Today, Jesus Christ dominates.

It has not been easy, but it has definitely been worth it.

Do you have a friend who is disabled or is married to a disabled person? That person's marriage encompasses a whole set of problems you may not be able to imagine. But don't let that scare you. Be sensitive to your friend's situation and needs. You don't have to be a social worker or marriage counselor. Just love her. Just show her Jesus.

Steps of Faith

*Faithful Father, when I think about what some couples deal with in
their marriages every day, I am ashamed for some of the things I complain about in mine. Forgive my ingratitude. Help me to reach out to
a couple with special needs and at the same time give my needs to You.*

Hot and Cold

*He who covers over an offense promotes love, but whoever
repeats the matter separates close friends.*

PROVERBS 17:9

How many times have I asked him to call if he was going to be late?
I thought. With each tick of the clock, my anger got hotter and the
dinner got colder.

My whole day had been like this. *Didn't I tell the kids to make their
beds?* The Bible study was poorly attended. (Figures—look who's
teaching it.) And when Sue called to say she couldn't babysit, I asked
her to recommend someone a little more reliable.

Pondering the cold mashed potatoes and hamburger steak, I felt
sorry for myself. Then I spotted my preschooler's memory verse on
the table. "Love . . . is not easily angered, it keeps no record of
wrongs" (1 Corinthians 13:5). I stared at the red crayon script and
heard His voice probing, "Child, is there something you need to talk
to Me about?"

Hot tears welled up in my eyes. "Lord, what am I doing? I love
these people—why am I so critical? I cringe at the words I can never
take back—thoughtless, critical words spoken because of my anger,
selfishness, or insecurity. Please forgive me."

"I will always forgive you, child. Now, are there others you need
to ask, too?"

Just then, Will burst in the door. "Honey, I'm so sorry—I got
talking in the parking lot, and then I hit traffic, and. . . ."

"It's okay, sweetheart. I'm just glad you're home. We can warm up
dinner. How was your day?" I embraced my speechless husband and
smiled behind his back.

What would you hear if you played a tape of all the words you
said yesterday? For every one of your loved one's faults, think of two
positive qualities that make you smile. Then, praise them—applaud
their efforts, compliment their character, do whatever you can to
commend them. Appoint yourself their cheerleader.

Steps of Faith

*Lord, when I think only of myself I become so critical. This sin robs
me of joy and fellowship with those I love, including You. Protect me
from myself, Lord. Make my spirit restless until I submit to Your
Word and choose to think on that which is lovely (Philippians 4:8).*

A Discerning Woman

"So give your servant a discerning heart to govern
your people and to distinguish between right and wrong."
The Lord was pleased that Solomon had asked for this.

1 KINGS 3:9,10

*C*assie Thomas decided she wanted to learn more about spiritual discernment. She'd heard other Christians talk about it, but she just wasn't quite sure what spiritual discernment involved. Was it a gut feeling? Was she supposed to hear some sort of voice or have a vision? Was discernment purely subjective, or did it involve objective principles as well?

Cassie thought about her life and some of the poor decisions she had made, even after praying for guidance. What had gone wrong?

Cassie began to think about some of the people she knew who had consistently demonstrated discernment in their lives. What was special about them? As she pondered this question, she realized discerning people were discriminating in their choices, patient, perceptive, and insightful. They loved God and clearly trusted Him to guide them in the right way.

Cassie shook her head as she admitted silently that she was lacking in these qualities, especially patience and trust.

Over the next few weeks, Cassie began to spend more time in her Bible, reading stories about people like King Solomon, who had been blessed with discernment. But of all of them, Deborah (Judges 4–5) stood out in her mind. What a woman! The more Cassie learned about Deborah and prayed, the more she sensed God giving her insight into questions and situations that she had never experienced before. She was becoming a discerning woman.

Have you ever longed to find God's will for your life or to know the truth about a situation? It's important that you do. That is why God has empowered you with His Spirit, the Spirit of truth, to help you work out His plan for your life. Meditate on today's Scripture readings, and ask God to bless you with a heart that trusts Him for guidance and longs to do His will above all else.

Steps of Faith

Author of all truth, I know that You have given me the ability to
know all truth through the gift of faith. I want to love You, Lord, with
all my heart and to always comply with Your will for my life. Please
guide me into all that is true.

The Impossible

Jesus looked at them and said, "With man this is impossible,
but with God all things are possible."

MATTHEW 19:26

*W*hen 21-year-old Heather Whitestone takes the stage, a hush falls over the darkened audience. The music begins and she floats as if on angels' wings, performing perfect pirouettes and effortless arabesques. Her arms lift in praise as she dances en pointe to "How Beautiful" by Twila Paris.

And how beautiful is Heather's ministry. The talent she expresses to the glory of God rivals that of any prima ballerina in New York. Unlike other New York dancers, though, Heather is deaf. But what a message she brings to the hearing world as she gracefully moves to the vibrations of the music, never missing a beat.

Heather did not learn sign language until she was in high school. Before then she utilized a method called ocupedics to learn to use what hearing ability she does have to communicate with an aural world. Through self-discipline, she has learned to read lips and speak with intonation and expression.

Heather's motto is: "With positive self-esteem, inner strength, courage, and God's help, the impossible is indeed possible." She uses these encouraging words to challenge herself as well as others.

Someone once asked Heather, "How do you deal with your handicap?"

She quickly responded, "The same way you deal with yours."

When the person looked puzzled, Heather carefully explained that everyone has a handicap, whether it is physical or emotional—hers is just a little more obvious. She sees her deafness as an opportunity to work hard and to trust God to turn her weaknesses into strength.

What is your handicap? Is it a hand that is crippled or made stiff by arthritis? Or is it something less obvious, like bitterness harbored toward a colleague, spouse, or family member? Ask God to reveal to you your weaknesses. Pray that He will give you the power to overcome your disabilities and use them to glorify Him, your Maker.

Steps of Faith

Dear Heavenly Father, You have accepted me just as I am, with all my imperfections. Yet my desire is to be more like Your Son, Jesus. I lay before You today my own handicaps, knowing that Your power is made perfect in weakness.

WEDNESDAY

287

No Thanks

*I will praise God's name in song
and glorify him with thanksgiving.*

PSALM 69:30

Melissa chattered away about her freshman college classes as we arranged the fall mums for our centerpiece. She was home for the holiday and I relished the time we had together.

"Mom, I really miss being home. I never thought I would, but I miss the family!"

"We all miss you too, honey!" I said. "In two short months, you've gone from living at home to life on your own—hey, I made a rhyme!" We started to laugh, then unexpectedly, Melissa's eyes filled with tears.

"I'm really homesick, Mom. I want to come home!"

"Oh, my!" I sat down abruptly, grateful that the ringing telephone absorbed Melissa's attention for a few minutes.

My heart sank. Life at our house had changed since Melissa had gone off to college. For one thing, Michael had moved into Melissa's room, which gave Matt his own room. Now that they weren't into each other's things anymore, they weren't squabbling nearly so much.

But that wasn't all. The tension over curfews and household chores "now that I'm 18" had gone with her to college. Quickly, I considered what was really best for Melissa. As her phone call was ending, I sent up a quick prayer, asking God for wisdom.

Then I wrapped my arms around her and gave her a big hug. "Honey, you can always come home," I reassured her, "but let's talk this through before you make any snap decisions, okay? I'll make some hot chocolate and you tell me what's been going on."

Often our problems with change are solved when we talk them over and pray about them with a Christian friend or family member. We can always be thankful that God knows what He is doing and directs our steps as we seek His wisdom.

Steps of Faith

*Dear Heavenly Father, I am grateful to You for those things I under-
stand and those I do not. Thank You for Your wisdom to face change
in my family as my children leave "the nest."*

A Simple Holiday

And whatever you do, whether in word or deed,
do it all in the name of the Lord Jesus, giving thanks to
God the Father through him.

COLOSSIANS 3:17

*B*eing a little ornery sometimes has its advantages. Like last Thanksgiving—I hadn't been feeling well and wasn't up to making my usual huge (and delicious) holiday dinner. Since members of my family were traveling to be with me, we decided to eat out—at the café on the square.

The more I thought about it, the more I liked the idea. With no food to make and no dishes to wash, we'd have more time to visit. It would be a simple holiday with everyone gathered around the fire—just like when I was young.

When Thanksgiving came, my family room was loaded with loved ones loaded with turkey from the café. My son built a roaring fire, and my daughter played hymns on the piano. Half the family didn't sing, the teenagers sulked, and the men were aching to turn on the TV for the ball games. It wasn't quite the atmosphere I'd had in mind, but I pulled out a little surprise anyway.

I called it "My Tribute to My Family." I said that I thanked God daily for my family, one by one. Next, I read a favorite memory of each of my siblings and their spouses. Then, I read to each of my children and nieces and nephews something that described what made them special. When I finished, everyone was smiling (even the teens). They all needed to hear that they were unique and that God and I both loved them very much.

Later, we declared that Christmas would be simple, too—simple gifts, lots of singing, the Christmas story, and plenty of time for each other.

Are the holidays so hectic at your house that God gets overlooked? Here are some ways to simplify and enrich your family's holiday season: scale down your activities or your cooking; volunteer at a homeless shelter or visit a nursing home; commit to spending more time together and with the Lord. Make this season one your family will never forget. Simplify the holidays; glorify the Lord.

Steps of Faith

Dear Father, with cooking, shopping, and parties, it's easy for us to get distracted and forget the purpose of the holidays. Help us focus on Your gifts and give You praise and honor.

F
R
I
D
A
Y

289

Christmas in October

Go to the ant . . . consider its ways and be wise!

PROVERBS 6:6

W
E
E
K
E
N
D

*M*y daughter, Meredith, had been married for almost two years. It was during that time that I went from being an "out-of-touch-with-reality dinosaur" to the "sage mother who understands all mysteries."

According to Meredith, her first Christmas as a new bride had been a disaster. She had assumed Christmas cooking and baking was a no-brainer, especially since her mother had managed it all these years. Now she was sitting at my feet.

"Bottom line: Don't start at Christmas," I began. "Start in October." I told Meredith that I make lists of the Thanksgiving and Christmas meals, cookies, candy, desserts, and side dishes for the inevitable potluck supper parties. The trick is remembering that an extra $150 doesn't magically appear in my checking account. I have to work into my grocery budget things like turkeys, hams, chocolate chips, red food coloring, powdered sugar, Christmas tins, paper plates, and napkins.

Beginning in mid-October, I start looking for specials on these items. (It means the family may have to sacrifice a bag of cookies or eat dried beans periodically.) Slowly, but diligently, I stock up on these items as the holiday season approaches. It takes some discipline.

I buy the Thanksgiving and baking ingredients first. For the last 23 years my sister, Connie, and I have met the weekend before Thanksgiving to organize the family dinner and do our Christmas baking. (Meredith has never joined us.) We wrap up our goodies and put them in the freezer.

Meredith listened wide-eyed. When I finished, she asked if I would help her make her lists! And could she bake with Connie and me later that month? Wonders never cease!

When do you begin your Christmas preparations? The idea is to prevent budget-busting or overspending on food when you're already spending money on gifts. Ask God to help you begin thinking practically, like an ant.

Steps of Faith

Lord of all, thank You for the lessons I can learn from the ant. Grant me diligence and discipline to prepare for future demands on my time and money, especially at Christmas, so I can focus more of my attention on You and the gift of Your precious Son.

That Little Voice

So I strive always to keep my conscience clear
before God and man.

ACTS 24:16

*P*ieces of the shattered crystal pitcher surrounded me on the concrete patio. I was sobbing. I hadn't meant to break it. I'd only played with it for a little while in my clubhouse. To me, it was the most beautiful treasure in my parents' house. Now it was destroyed.

After Mom made sure I wasn't hurt, she swept up the glass. Then we went to her room to talk. As grieved as I was about the pitcher, I was also afraid of the certain punishment to come. I couldn't stop crying. "Now, honey," she said gently, "can you tell me why you were playing outside with Mommy's good pitcher?"

"I don't know," I wailed. "I just wanted to play with it in my house."

"Didn't I tell you once before that you were never to play with it? And you must have climbed up pretty high to get it, didn't you?"

After I nodded in agreement, she asked, "What did you tell that little voice?" When I looked at her with a puzzled expression, she said, "You know, the one that said you shouldn't be climbing on the kitchen counter or taking the pitcher outside. What did you say?"

I knew what she was talking about—my conscience—even though at age eight I didn't know what it was called. Ashamed, I whispered, "I said, 'She'll never find out.'"

Forty years later my conscience still talks to me. And I still sometimes foolishly answer with, "So-and-so will never find out," or "It won't hurt anyone," or "It's just a little." That's usually when the Holy Spirit reminds me of a shattered crystal pitcher, a weeping little girl, and a wise and loving mother.

Do you listen to your conscience when you're tempted to sin? Have you ever tried to argue with it? If you are a Christian, your conscience is the Holy Spirit's "megaphone." Submit to His warnings and direction. It's for your own good.

Steps of Faith

Heavenly Father, I praise You for the power of my conscience during times of temptation. Help me to always be willing to follow Your voice and know Your will.

Why We Lie

*A false witness will not go unpunished, and he who
pours out lies will perish.*

PROVERBS 19:9

Several years ago a book called *The Day America Told the Truth*
revealed that 91 percent of Americans lie regularly. One in five of us tell
a conscious lie every day. When we choose not to lie, it's usually not
because we believe it's wrong but because we're afraid of getting caught.

Other findings indicate that two out of three Americans don't see
anything wrong with lying. And sadly, a third of Americans believe
a pastor has lied to them.

Why do so many people lie? Here's a list of possibilities:

- *To get their own way.* People want to manipulate other people and situations to their advantage.

- *Feelings of inferiority.* Lying helps some people cope with their sense of
inadequacy. It makes them feel accepted and better about themselves.

- *To avoid consequences.* Whether it's to avoid a spanking, being
grounded, flunking a test, being fired, or losing an election, people
will lie.

- *To maintain a certain image.* A product is hailed as superior to other
brands. Neighbors lie about income and overextend themselves financially to live a certain lifestyle. A husband lies to calm his wife's suspicions.

- *For material gain.* Padded expense accounts, underreported income on
tax returns, and deceptive advertising are very common forms of lying.

- *It's a way of life.* Some people are such habitual liars they aren't aware
when they're lying.

The words of Alexis de Tocqueville should give us pause:
"America is great because she is good, and if America ever ceases to
be good, America will cease to be great."

Lying may seem like the solution to someone's fears and problems,
but that's the biggest lie of all! The Bible says that "the truth will set you
free" (John 8:32). If you have any sort of problem with lying, confess it
right now. God will forgive you and give you power to walk in truth.

Steps of Faith

*Merciful Lord, forgive our nation. Pour out Your Spirit of truth and
repentance. Ignite a revival in our country. And Lord, let it start with
me. I want to be a woman of truth.*

T
U
E
S
D
A
Y

Tornado Trust

I have told you these things, so that in me you may have peace.
In this world you will have trouble. But take heart!
I have overcome the world.

JOHN 16:33

Last summer a tornado ripped through our town, picking up and tossing more than 20 houses into a gigantic pile of pickup sticks. The wind's force was terrifying. The destruction was catastrophic. The death toll was three.

Although we were only on the fringes of the storm and our home remained intact, the intensity of the wind and rain was frightening as we sat in the basement praying that it would soon pass. How helpless we were in the face of calamity. Sleep was out of the question.

But God was there. We rehearsed the time when Jesus slept in the boat while the storm raged around Him. And of course we remembered what happened next. Awakened by His fearful disciples, Jesus calmed the waves and commanded the wind to cease.

After the calm, the disciples asked themselves, "Who is this man, that even the wind and waves obey Him?" The answer is that He is God! Our Lord, strong and mighty!

The tornado graphically reminded me of my utter helplessness in the face of calamity. At times, I have felt just like the fearful disciples. But a calm assurance sweeps over my trembling faith when I remember the rest of the story. The one in whom I trust controls the wind and the waves!

When was the last time you felt totally out of control? In a storm? In a personal crisis? When those times come again, remember that the one who controls the wind and the waves also wants to speak peace to your heart.

Steps of Faith

Lord, at times my faith fails just like that of the disciples and I begin to fear. Thank You for understanding my weaknesses. Now empower me with mighty faith in Your mighty power that controls everything that touches my life.

293

Mother, Not Martyr

That will make your load lighter,
because they will share it with you.

EXODUS 18:22

I was in a great mood as I skipped up my front steps after my Saturday morning with Ann. Then I opened the door. The clutter of the family room assaulted me: laundry, books, computer games, CDs, magazines, soft-drink cans, a bowl of soggy cereal, a golf putter, and four pairs of smelly sports shoes. And there, wallowing in the filth, were my four children and their father!

I silently, stoically began picking up the mess. I had to manually lift the arms and legs of different offspring to reach some of the clutter. No one got the message. When I vacuumed, I actually had to nudge their bodies out of the way with the vacuum cleaner, like I was operating a bulldozer. But the only reaction was that my oldest son groped for the remote control and punched up the volume.

My husband finally noted the tears that were pooling in my eyes and motioned me to the kitchen. Once we were alone, I started to cry.

He let me vent my frustrations and then lovingly reminded me that all I needed to do was tell him what to do and when. He apologized for being a part of the problem instead of the solution. Then he set about creating a solution.

He suggested that we had become lax with the kids and their household chores. And he was right. Sometimes it seemed so much easier just to do it all myself than to plead with or convince them to do the work. It was time to delegate.

Later that afternoon, we had a family meeting. Chores were reassigned, rules and rewards carefully explained.

Women are nurturers by nature. Left unchecked, that nurturing aptitude can cause a woman to try to do more than she can or should be doing. If you are a busy mother of older children, it's time to start delegating some of your responsibilities. The work will transition your children into adulthood and give you more time to enjoy your family.

Steps of Faith

Loving Lord, You know how much I cherish my family. I want to enjoy their company, not constantly nag about chores. Please give me the wisdom to delegate the work so that we will live in a pleasant home and have time to enjoy one another.

The Lilly Cause

They shared everything they had.

ACTS 4:32

Lilly could always be found at the corner of Jefferson and East Main, about a block from the office where I worked, drinking a cup of coffee and reading the newspaper. From her appearance, I guessed she probably ate once a day, bathed once a week, and changed clothes once a year. She kept all of her belongings in a shopping cart, organized in plastic grocery bags. She also had two African violets that bloomed year-round.

Throughout the year, but especially at Thanksgiving and Christmas, our office would periodically collect food, clothes, and money for Lilly. I must confess that even though I always contributed to the Lilly Cause, I slightly resented it. I wondered why Lilly's circumstances didn't improve. *Probably drugs or alcohol,* I reasoned.

Then last Thanksgiving, a coworker and I were appointed to deliver the gift to Lilly. We had canned goods, secondhand clothing, and about $50. When we handed it to her, she had tears of joy in her eyes. My throat choked with emotion although, at the same time, I suspected Lilly's response was an act.

After Christmas the owner of the diner at Jefferson and East Main told us Lilly was in the charity hospital in the advanced stages of breast cancer. She died in April. At the funeral we heard story after story, from street people to clergy, describing how Lilly had distributed food, clothing, and money to women at the various shelters. She kept just enough to buy her coffee, newspaper, and basic items. God had given her so much, she used to say, and she wanted to give too.

I was ashamed of myself and my cynicism. Only God knew how much Lilly had taught me about trusting Him to use what we give to others.

Have you ever wanted to give but not had much to give? The widow in Luke 21:1-4 did. Most people—sometimes even those who do not know the Lord—want to experience the pleasure of giving. Be sensitive to that need the next time someone unlikely wants to minister to you.

Steps of Faith

Giver of all gifts, how grateful I am that You have given me the desire to give. To me, it is just more evidence that I have been made in Your image. Help me acknowledge that need in other people when they reach out to help me.

Chaperon: Unwanted

Whoever wants to become great among you
must be your servant.

MARK 10:43

*O*h, Mother, how could you?"

But I had. I had willingly chosen to destroy my daughter's social life for years to come. I had volunteered to chaperon her youth group's Christmas banquet. "It's not like I called Mrs. Singer and asked to be a chaperon," I argued defensively.

"You could have said you were busy or sick," she whined. "Oh, Mom, I'll be the only girl there whose mother is serving punch! I'd rather die!"

Sigh. Gone were the days of hands reaching up to me over the church nursery gate or first-grade cupcake parties. *This is a normal part of growing up,* I reasoned. *Hormones, adolescence, and peer pressure. No need to let my hurt feelings complicate matters.* But I couldn't keep the pain away. A part of me longed to hold my little baby girl in my arms again, to read stories to her, to see her face light up when I walked into a room. . . .

When I realized my eyes were misting over, I shook off my self-pity and said a quick prayer. On the night of the banquet the church fellowship hall had been magically transformed into a "Winter Wonderland." And my daughter had been transformed into a radiant princess (with braces). As a compromise, I agreed not to wear my name tag, cutting off all ties with Kristen for two hours. But that couldn't stop me from admiring from my punch-table post the little girl wearing my pearl earrings, carrying my silk purse, and holding my heart forever.

Have you ever served in a ministry with a pure and giving heart, yet your motives were totally misread by others? If so, don't let that misunderstanding rob you of your joy of service. God intimately knows your heart's desires.

Steps of Faith

Lord, You know how I long to serve You. I must admit that some-times it is hard when others don't appreciate my service. Help me to remember it is You I serve and Your approval I desire.

W
E
E
K
E
N
D

One Step at a Time

The Sovereign Lord is my strength.

HABAKKUK 3:19

*A*s I closed the car door, the handle came off in my hand. *I hate this car. It's a piece of junk.* But I couldn't do anything about it. Dave had been recently laid off and was starting his own company. We had not planned for this setback and had little savings in the bank. We might have to sell our house.

Then I got a call from Trevor's teacher. He had thrown a floppy disk across the room and hit her in the backside. His attention problems were not getting any better. She suggested medication.

I was breaking out in hives every other day. The doctors could not explain it. The constant itching and irritation made me crabby. *Why me, Lord. Why me?* I immersed myself in His Word for answers. One day I read Habakkuk 3:17-19: "Though the fig tree does not bud and there are no grapes on the vines, though the olive crop fails and the fields produce no food, though there are no sheep in the pen and no cattle in the stalls, yet I will rejoice in the LORD, I will be joyful in God my Savior. The Sovereign LORD is my strength; he makes my feet like the feet of a deer, he enables me to go on the heights."

In those years of what seemed like never-ending crisis, I leaned totally on Jesus. I got through one day at a time, just doing the next thing and not thinking of my misery. I learned about the faithfulness of God to meet my needs in His timing. I learned to recognize His sovereignty in the day-to-day events of my life.

God allows what He does for an eternally significant purpose. Hopefully, like Habakkuk, we can learn to trust Him when everything looks and feels frightfully grim, remembering that in our weakness, He is made strong.

Steps of Faith

Dear Heavenly Father, thank You for teaching me how to trust You. Thank You for using seasons of suffering to build and shape the character of Jesus in me. Thank You for Your Word that continually lights my path and brings me hope.

M
O
N
D
A
Y

Floods of Joy

*If there is a poor man among your brothers in any of the towns
of the land that the LORD your God is giving you, do not be
hardhearted or tightfisted toward your poor brother.*

DEUTERONOMY 15:7

Last July my family watched and prayed as the waters of the Flint River in Albany, Georgia, were about to crest—and the rain just kept pouring. Through the eye of a television news camera, we saw the devastation, the emotional trauma, and the loss of life and livelihood, along with the kind of courage and generosity that disasters of this magnitude generate.

We also witnessed a minor miracle. Andrew is my 11-year-old. He wanted to buy a new video game system that cost $150. He had been mowing lawns, washing windows, and sweeping all summer to earn the money—and saving every single cent. In fact it had been difficult to get him to tithe from what he had earned. My little tightwad had saved $132.66.

Then Andrew took an interest in the Georgia flood victims. He asked questions about where those people would live or get food and clothing. When I told him that many of them had lost everything, I could see something in Andrew's face. Could it possibly be compassion?

After supper one night, Andrew came into the kitchen with his money box. I could tell he had been crying, but he didn't look sad or upset. Then with a big smile he told me he wanted to send his money to the people in Georgia. They needed it more than he did, he said, and it was what Jesus would have done. "Mom, you know what?" he asked, his face beaming. "I bet there's a kid down there who lost his video game system in that flood. Maybe this money will help buy him a new one!"

Have you ever experienced the joy of sacrificial giving? It's one of the greatest testimonies of the gospel of Christ. When you pry your fingers off of a worldly object that enamors you and sacrifice that thing to another person in need, you will be blessed beyond any measure. Try it.

Steps of Faith

Lord Jesus, You are the most generous person who ever lived. And according to Your Word, when You were asked to give the greatest gift, You gave it with deep joy—and some tears. Lord, I want to reach a point in my walk with You where I will demonstrate a giving heart to the world, no matter what the cost.

The Gift and the Giver

*We loved you so much that we were delighted to share
with you not only the gospel of God but our lives as well,
because you had become so dear to us.*

1 THESSALONIANS 2:8

*U*p until the time I had my first child, I worked in a convalescent home for people in the advanced stages of multiple sclerosis. MS runs in my family, so I have a special place in my heart for anyone suffering from its effects.

As in most hospitals and nursing homes, Christmas can be one of the most depressing times of the year. Many of these patients have been neglected, even abandoned, by their families. They have no hope, no purpose, no joy.

As a new Christian, I was determined to make that Christmas different. I wrapped small, inexpensive gifts and placed them in a basket. My plan was to walk into a patient's room, offer a gift, and then tell about the greatest Gift ever given. At this point the patient would want to know more about Jesus and God's love and he or she would then pray to receive Christ as Savior. Joy would fill the halls of that convalescent home. I couldn't wait.

To my dismay, it didn't happen. Ironically, each patient accepted the cheap trinkets wrapped in shiny paper, but only two were interested in the greatest Gift of all—the Good News.

My heart was heavy as I left the convalescent home that cold, gray December afternoon. I thought I had failed. Then I felt a stirring in my heart as though God were saying, "Now you know how I feel. The world will gladly receive My smaller gifts, but very few are interested in the gift of My Son. But don't grieve. You have not failed, and no time has been wasted. It will all be used unto My glory."

Volunteer work can be one of the most fulfilling aspects of your life. However, in many cases you may not see the fruit of your labor, especially if the work involves evangelism. First, be certain it is the work God has set aside for you. If it is, you can trust that it will bear fruit—eventually.

Steps of Faith

Everlasting Father, how it must grieve You when people reject the gift of Jesus Christ for the world's baubles and trinkets. Give me a heart that will not only always recognize the best You have to offer but one that also longs to share that gift with those You bring into my life.

WEDNESDAY

Coming to Term

*Rescue those being led away to death; hold back
those staggering toward slaughter.*

PROVERBS 24:11

*F*or almost 16 years I lived a lie. Only my husband and I knew the truth, but when we began discussing having children, I knew I couldn't be a mother until my past had been healed.

At 14 I had had my first abortion. By 21, I had had three. When I confided this to a friend, she suggested that volunteer work at a crisis pregnancy center might help me deal with my past. I decided to try it.

Training as a counselor forced me to confront the truth of my abortions. It hurt. But all along I felt the Lord telling me, "This is the truth, and it will set you free. Your healing has begun."

My healing had indeed begun, and it took about three years. Since then I have become involved with many young women who come to our center looking for help. Each one is special, but I'll never forget Lana. As we waited on the results of her pregnancy test, I shared the gospel with her. She prayed to receive Christ and decided against an abortion. But she would not consider adoption.

Over the next months, Lana and I worked together to find her a doctor in her area, a shepherding home where she would live until the baby was born, and agencies that would provide baby items, like a crib and high chair. Two months before she was due, she asked me to be her labor coach during the delivery. In March 1992, Sam was born, and I was there to celebrate the miracle of God's deliverance.

Although I will always grieve over my three abortions, God has used them to help me relate to the women who come to our center. They are desperate—they want immediate solutions. He has given me the ability to love them, even if they choose the abortion option. It's the unconditional love that God has shown me and has taught me to show them.

Whether you have had an abortion or not, God can use you to minister to women having a crisis pregnancy. And there is a shortage of people who are willing to invest their lives in these women. Are you willing? Ask God to show you His will in this matter.

Steps of Faith

Merciful Lord, I thank You that through Christ Jesus there is no condemnation for me or anyone else (Romans 8:1). Help me to remember that, Lord, when I reach out to help someone who has sinned—and who may be in sin. That's where You found me. And I will forever be grateful.

THURSDAY

Snowed In

*A man's steps are directed by the LORD. How then can
anyone understand his own way?*

PROVERBS 20:24

See you tomorrow," I said and I hung up the phone. I hadn't seen my sister in six years, and finally I had found a weekend when we could meet. Jeff had agreed to keep the kids.

What? There goes the power! The kids came running into the kitchen. "Oh goody, where are the candles? Can we make snow cream? Will we toast marshmallows? When will you build a fire in the fireplace?" they chorused.

I looked out the window and saw squalls of snow swirling around. This was strange . . . and certainly not predicted. *Lord, please don't let this interfere with my trip tomorrow.*

The snow kept falling—eight inches in eight hours. This was not the usual ground dusting of a southern snowfall. Jeff was unable to come back in town from his business meeting. The airport was closed. I was sick. How could I get to Susan in Chicago? As the kids played outside in the snow, I sat by the fire, wrestling with the Lord. After much prayer, I'd reached the "not my will but Thine be done" acceptance of whatever He had in mind.

The kids and I hauled wood inside and I made another batch of hot chocolate. We built a snowman and an igloo, and slid down the back hill on cookie sheets. In front of a roaring fire we put together puzzles and played games day and night for the next two days.

I missed my visit with my sister, but I would take nothing in exchange for the fun time I shared with my kids.

God seems to test us at such inconvenient times! When was your most recent time of testing? Did you feel different about it going in than coming out? Most of us do. When you can get to the place where you have no mind in the matter, He can begin to unfold His beautiful plan for your life—and you will welcome the tests!

Steps of Faith

Dear God, thank You that You know best—always. Thank You for the wonderful three days of "captivity" with my children. We will have those fun memories to feed on forever. Increase my faith and wisdom, Lord, to the point that I will be ready for any test—at any time.

Safe in His Hands

He who dwells in the shelter of the Most High will rest in the
shadow of the Almighty.

PSALM 91:1

I was lying in a hospital bed, sick and in pain. Many well-intentioned friends came to visit me, but my mother turned them away. I was in no condition for visitors. We kept the phone on because my father or my husband would be calling, but the incessant ringing was unnerving.

Before my mother decided to turn the ringer off, a coworker called. I decided to talk with her for just one moment. She let me know she was praying for me. I expressed my appreciation. Then she said, "I would like you to read Psalm 91. When you do, just imagine our heavenly Father beside you, shielding you from fear and pain."

After we said goodbye, I asked my mother to read the psalm to me. As she read the words of this beautiful praise poem, I felt as if God was speaking directly to me:

> He who dwells in the shelter of the Most High
> will rest in the shadow of the Almighty.
> I will say of the LORD,
> "He is my refuge and my fortress,
> My God, in whom I trust." . . .
> He will cover you with his feathers,
> and under his wings you will find refuge;
> his faithfulness will be your shield and rampart.

I had never felt more comforted. The words of God's provision and protection strengthened my heart, reminding me of His presence. In every situation, I can be sure He is orchestrating His perfect plan in my life, and the end result will be beautiful music.

Is there someone you could touch today to remind her of God's love and protection? People who are hurting physically or emotionally need a blessing from you. Take the time to see the need in those around you.

Steps of Faith

Heavenly Father, thank You for Your love and protection in my life.
Please make me aware of how I can convey Your message of hope to
others who need it.

Carrie's Blessing

Now I want you to know, brothers, that what has happened to me has really served to advance the gospel.

PHILIPPIANS 1:12

*C*arrie caught my eye my first week at the Tuesday morning women's group at our church. She was a beautiful woman who had a warm light around her face that testified of a close relationship to Christ. I could tell from her car, clothes, and jewelry she was "comfortable."

Frankly I was a little intimidated by her at first; however, all the other women seemed to love her and many spent time talking privately with her. During our Bible study, Carrie usually was the one who had discovered some new, deep truth in the Scripture. When she shared an insight or experience, a hushed awe filled the room.

After awhile, this began to bother me. I wondered why Carrie, who couldn't possibly know what real life was like, always had someone sitting at her feet, hanging on every word she said. My resentment festered. Why was God blessing Carrie so much, even spiritually?

Then one day at the grocery store my eyes were opened. There was Carrie with her 14-year-old daughter, Wendy, who was severely retarded. I later learned that six years earlier Carrie and Wendy had gone "underground" to escape an abusive husband and father. After years of hard work, Carrie was able to start a small Christian publishing company in her home, which God was prospering.

I was immediately convicted. God has given each of His children special talents and gifts. And each of us has our own burdens and sorrows. I want to learn to trust my heavenly Father to be content with what He chooses for me.

Have you ever caught yourself desiring someone else's blessing? Whether it's material or spiritual, to do so is to covet. When you do that, you take your eyes off all God has given you and lust for what you think you deserve. That fills your heart with envy and ingratitude. Give God thanks for all the blessings in your life—and in the lives of others.

Steps of Faith

Father, forgive me for the times I covet the blessings of others and fail to recognize the abundant blessings in my own life. Help me to turn my blessings into blessings for those around me.

303

M
O
N
D
A
Y

The Search

You are not your own; you were bought at a price.
Therefore honor God with your body.

1 CORINTHIANS 6:19,20

*W*hen my mother was 19, she got pregnant. She and my father quit school and married, but when I was two he left. We never saw him again.

Of all the emotions that ricocheted around our little apartment, guilt was the most piercing. Even as a toddler, I remember sensing that Daddy had left, and Mommy was always crying, because of me. As much as I tried, I could never do enough to change things. I began to believe there was something dreadfully wrong with me.

By the time I was eight, I had a weight problem. Mom was so wrapped up in working and trying to find a husband, she didn't regulate my diet. So I ate a lot of junk. Soon I was turning to food for comfort and companionship. It was always there for me.

When I was in high school, interest in boys motivated me to lose weight. I lost 40 pounds in three months. The boys started calling. What I wasn't prepared for was the pressure for sex. I wanted so badly to be loved by a "man." Certainly that was the key to happiness.

Only by the grace of God did I escape high school with my virginity. When I was 16, my friend Nanette asked me to a youth event at her church. We stayed up all night singing songs, playing games, and eating snacks. At one point a man presented the gospel. Then we broke up into groups and discussed what he said. I listened intently, hearing for the first time how much God loved me, how valuable I was to Him, and what my sin cost Him. That night I prayed to receive Christ.

Day by day God continues to bless and heal me, even after 22 years of walking with Him. Many wounds have healed; many questions have been answered, but not all. However, there is no question about God's love for me. All I have to do is look at the cross.

Human beings long for security and significance and often forget (or never learn) their true value (John 3:16; 1 Peter 1:18,19). Do you ever question yours? Look at the cross. You were bought at a very high price.

Steps of Faith

Precious Father, thank You for paying the ultimate price for my salvation. No one else could have done it for me. And if I ever begin to feel insignificant, remind me of the cost of my ransom.

Giving Back

*If anyone does not provide for his relatives, and
especially for his immediate family, he has denied the faith
and is worse than an unbeliever.*

1 TIMOTHY 5:8

*S*ighing, Janice walked into the kitchen where her mother was washing dishes. Her mother handed her a dish towel. "Thanks for helping your dad and me get the house ready for your grandmother. I know you wanted to go to the mall today instead." She paused. "Grandma has been so lonely since Grandpa died, and she's so frail. I think her moving in with us is the best thing for everyone."

Janice hesitated. "Me too, Mom. It's just that I liked having the upstairs all to myself with Joan at college. I don't mean to be selfish, but with Grandma staying in Joan's room, I won't have any privacy anymore."

"Honey, we're all going to have to make sacrifices, including your grandmother. I'm sure she'd rather stay in her house with her own things and her friends nearby, but this is her home now. We need to show her that we want her here."

"I do. It's just that everything will be different."

"Yes, it will. But think about all she's done for us. Remember when you and Joan had the chicken pox and Grandma came to stay so I could go to work?"

"Yes, and that summer Dad had back surgery."

"Right. She stayed for two weeks, cooking and cleaning and caring for Dad during the daytime. Do you know why she did these things?"

"She loves us."

"Yes, and we needed her."

"Like she needs us now," Janice said, nodding. "Well, I guess the least I can do for my grandmother is give up a little privacy."

Will you be caring for elderly parents soon? Prepare your family for the change by talking to them about it ahead of time. Try to anticipate how your lives will be different, and remember to emphasize how your lives will be better.

Steps of Faith

Dear Father, thank You for my parents. Show me how I can best care for them while caring for my own family. Show me how I can make this time with them special. I know that my doing so will bring You honor.

Flip Side of Success

*The fear of the LORD is the beginning of wisdom; all who follow
his precepts have good understanding.*

PSALM 111:10

Sue settled into the soft, cool leather of the first-class recliner.
What a treat! She had taken a "bump" from her scheduled flight in
order to get the free-flight coupon—and she landed in first-class!

Now it was time to think. Two days of interviews with a presti-
gious law firm had left her head spinning with affluence—an outra-
geous salary offer and endless amenities—more than she had ever
dreamed of during her grueling graduate years. What was there to
decide?

Well, she really liked what she was doing now. *You've got to be kid-
ding,* she scolded herself. *Working in a downtown legal rights "clinic" is
not exactly success. Maybe not . . . but there is something about helping
those who desperately need hope . . . and the Lord always meets my needs.*

For the first time, Sue noticed the woman seated beside her. *A real
first-class regular,* she mused after a side-glance at the executive suit
and leather attaché. Then Sue heard her companion sigh—a long,
painful sigh—and noticed splattering tears on her linen-suited lap.

"Is there something I can do? My name is . . . " Sue touched her
neighbor's sleeve.

The sad executive turned and offered her hand, "Claudia . . . nice
to meet you." She forced a smile and wiped her running mascara.
"Just part of running in the rat race. I guess I expected it to be different."

In the next hours of conversation, Sue learned the flip side of
"success" and realized she had a lot to think and pray about before
she called the law firm with her decision.

Think of the most successful people you know. What is it that
makes them successful? Now determine what would make you feel
successful. The Bible says success is simply faithfulness in doing
God's will. In that light evaluate your level of success. Don't judge
success by salary or status but by God's Word.

Steps of Faith

*Lord, in the world's evaluation, Jesus would not have been consid-
ered successful, and yet He is who I want to be like. With each decision I make, give me the discernment to know Your will.*

Shrinking the Secrets

I will give you the treasures of darkness,
riches stored in secret places.

ISAIAH 45:3

$\mathcal{N}$ow let's go around the circle and tell what gifts God has given us." Judy was an excellent Bible teacher, but for the life of me, I didn't know why we were doing this exercise. The women started round the circle, "I have the gift of teaching and I enjoy using it to teach children."

Another said, "I have a gift of mercy and I love working at the nursing home, caring for older people." I started to hyperventilate. What was I going to say? Then I heard Judy call my name.

"Francie?"

"Oh, well, I . . . hmmm . . . thick hair."

"Excuse me?" Judy looked befuddled.

I burst out crying. "I don't have any gifts unless you consider my thick hair. I'm not good at anything."

The women spent the rest of the Bible study trying to convince me of my gifts, none of which I could see. I had the self-image of an earthworm. After the study, Judy gave me the name of the counselor at her church. I mumbled something about an important appointment, then hurriedly left. I felt exposed, and I never wanted to see those women again.

Judy's exercise was the key that unlocked a flood of unwanted feelings. I isolated myself and tried to find a way out of my depression by myself. No way—I needed help.

During the next year, with the patience and understanding of Judy's counselor friend and my supreme Counselor, I was able to sort through a lot of painful experiences that had left me scarred and feeling worthless. With a healthier self-esteem and God buoying me, I began exploring my gifts. Writing is one. Voilá!

God will bring to light the sick and deluded secrets within our heart—the fear, the anger, and the hurt—that have conditioned us to act and react in certain ways and that sometimes prevent our accepting His love and forgiveness. He wants us to walk in the fullness of His promises. But we must humble ourselves to ask for help.

Steps of Faith

Dear God, thank You that You love me enough to teach me the truth about my heart. Even though it hurts to face these painful feelings, please don't stop Your refining process until I look like Jesus.

F
R
I
D
A
Y

Home Work

*I have brought you glory on earth by completing
the work you gave me to do.*

JOHN 17:4

*T*hree years ago the company my husband, Dru, works for went through a corporate reorganization. And when the business downsized, so did Dru's paycheck. (The only other option was unemployment.)

Dru started clearing $350 less each month. This came as quite a blow to our household budget. After considering the alternatives, Dru and I decided that I would try to earn some money working from our home. That decision was easy enough; the big question was, "Doing what?" So Dru, the children, and I started to pray for guidance.

The next week I hosted a baby shower for a friend. Several women I had never met attended. One of them asked me where I'd bought the curtains in the family room and kitchen. After admitting that I'd made them, I was stunned when she asked if I'd be interested in making some for her. I knew I was on to something.

"Interior Appointments" is the name of my little business. I help my clients select the pattern and fabric for curtains, pillows, and upholstery, and then whip them out on my machine. I set my appointments around my family's schedule and get most of the sewing done at night after the children are in bed.

Financially, it has kept us in the black. In fact, some months I make well over $350.

Cottage industries are a major trend in the business world, and in most situations working out of your home benefits everyone. Have you ever considered it? Accounting, cake decorating, writing, nursing, desktop publishing, laundering and ironing, and educational consulting are just some of the possibilities. Brenda Hunter's *Home By Choice* and Donna Partow's *Homemade Business* are excellent resources for helping you start your own cottage industry.

Steps of Faith

Father in heaven, Your Word is clear that we are commanded to work. Whether we're paid for it or not, You are glorified through our work. If it is possible for me to earn money by working in my home, please guide and protect my family and me as we seek Your will in this matter.

Brenda

*[Pursue] the unfading beauty of a gentle and quiet spirit,
which is of great worth in God's sight.*

1 PETER 3:4

$\mathcal{T}$he first time I saw Brenda she was sitting with her husband, Randy, in the sanctuary. The low roar of the preservice chatter hung over them, unable to penetrate their quiet meditation. I knew these people were special.

Three years later Brenda, Randy, and I traveled to Chile with a group from our church. On that trip I watched the gentleness and love they showed each other. My throat tightened when I thought about my own marriage.

During the trip, Brenda and Randy sort of adopted me. One day I casually mentioned some advice a psychic coworker had given me. They went ashen, and as soon as we got home, Brenda, Randy, and I were in the pastor's office. It was clear to them that I needed help. The pastor assigned Brenda to me as a mentor.

Brenda and I spent many hours together. I began to see the contrast in our spirits. Hers was so gentle, peaceful, calm. Mine was full of bottled-up anger. We worked on combating that pain with prayer and God's Word.

One day I wept as I told Brenda that the night before my husband had said I was ugly. She held me and assured me that Scott had been speaking in anger. Then she smiled. "Did you know that Randy doesn't find me a knockout? It wasn't my physical beauty that first attracted him to me."

I was flabbergasted. "But he dotes on you," I said sniffling. "You're one of the most beautiful women I've ever seen."

She blushed and chuckled. "Honey, if you look at me real close, you'll see I'm rather plain. And you're right: Randy loves me dearly; but the beauty you both see is the Spirit of Jesus in me, nothing else."

Titus 2:3-5 exhorts older women to "train the younger women." If your heart is yielded to the "meekness and gentleness of Christ" (2 Corinthians 10:1), ask God to lead you to a young woman who needs to learn about "the unfading beauty of a gentle and quiet spirit."

Steps of Faith

Dearest Lord, I invest a lot of time and money in superficial beauty and superficial relationships. Help me to invest more of that energy in what counts for eternity. Lead me to a woman who will be willing to join with me in a mentoring relationship.

Zip Your Tongue

Let your gentleness be evident to all. The Lord is near.

PHILIPPIANS 4:5

I stirred the pot of stew on the stove and tried to picture Jerry driving home on the freeway. I knew he was listening to a worship tape, letting his cares and worries evaporate into the evening air. He shared this strategy with me a few days ago after one of my routine "explosions" when he arrived home late after a long day at the office.

Today I can't even remember what triggered my irritation, but he got it full in the face when he walked in the door. I remember hearing myself ranting and raving, and all the while, I was aware of his tender, peaceful gaze. He never responded in anger to me. Finally I couldn't stand it anymore and blurted out, "How can you be so calm?"

He told me about his "strategy." "Every day, I use the time when I'm driving home to pray and release all the frustrations of my day. I want to be at peace when I come home to you. It's a gift I want to give you," he told me, without a hint of condemnation or condescension in his voice.

What a gift!

Jerry models this gentleness to me and the children and now we practice his "strategy" daily, too. While I prepare dinner, I "unload" on the Lord and get my heart and spirit settled before Jerry arrives. At the same time, Joey and Jordan, our busy seven- and nine-year-old boys, have a quiet time. They call it their "time out with Jesus."

Believe me, our dinnertimes have been much more pleasant as a result.

What's your strategy for responding to your family in gentleness? Have you noticed a need to practice a gentler way? Have you "exploded" in anger only to vow, "Never again, Lord"? Have you asked God to help you?

Steps of Faith

Dear God, You said that gentleness is a fruit of the Spirit and I confess, Lord, that I can't produce this on my own. Please change my heart and teach me to respond with a gentle word instead of wrath.

The Retreat

*Jesus left there and went along the Sea of Galilee. Then he went
up on a mountainside and sat down.*

MATTHEW 15:29

*E*very evening Jason comes home, grunts a greeting, gropes for
the evening newspaper, heads to the bedroom, shuts the door, and
disappears for about an hour. Our bedroom is off-limits during "the
retreat."

The one time I dared to trespass, I found Jason lying on the bed
with the newspaper draped over his head. He wasn't sleeping, "just
thinking," he mumbled. When I asked him if he'd like to talk about
it, all he said was that he'd be out when supper was ready—and for
me to close the door on my way out.

I have friends whose husbands behave similarly. One stares at the
evening news, not saying a word, for an hour. Another plays solitaire
on his computer. My sister's husband runs five miles every night.

I resented the retreat. I felt rejected, and nothing I said would get
Jason to change. It was during our women's prayer meeting that this
subject came up. Sherry and her husband, Don, had gotten in a fight
about his daily retreat, and she was asking for wisdom. Many of us
could relate.

As we prayed, Nancy began to thank Jesus for His hard work
among the masses. He must have been exhausted, even frustrated at
times, when the day was over. She could see why He would need to
get away.

Aha! If Jesus needed to break away after finishing His work, our poor
husbands certainly did! It was a major revelation in our little group.

So today, when Jason comes home, I give him a smile, a kiss, and
the newspaper, and then send him down the hall. I know a happier,
more focused, and rested husband will emerge in about an hour.

Dr. John Gray, author of *Men Are From Mars, Women are from
Venus,* says most men go into their "caves" after work to sort out the
events of the day, think about their problems, and come up with
solutions. To offer a man advice at this point is to signal to him that
you don't believe he is capable of solving problems on his own.

Steps of Faith

*My Father, when I consider the life of Jesus, I learn that He always
took time away to rest, meditate, and pray. I know my husband
needs time apart as well. Please make me sensitive to his need for
solitude and refreshment.*

W
E
D
N
E
S
D
A
Y

311

Three Cheers for Mom

Let us discern for ourselves what is right;
let us learn together what is good.

JOB 34:4

*G*inger adjusted her cap and gown for what seemed like the hundredth time. Was that really her in the mirror? In a few moments, she would be a college graduate! She'd done it! Tears filled her eyes. Seven long years, but she had worked hard. Today was her graduation day!

The ceremony itself was a blur, but later, at a party in her honor, she asked her family to stand with her "because they've earned this diploma as much as I have. Let me tell you about the sacrifices they made. . . .

"Dwight, for the last seven years, you have carried out more trash and done more dishes, more weeding, and more shopping than in the previous 20 years of our marriage. You encouraged me and when I wanted to give up, you held me as I cried.

"Kathryn, thank you for bragging about me to your friends when I got an A on a paper, for taking me out for a Coke so we could catch up, and for bringing my grandchild to the library to see her Granny studying.

"Mike, thanks for doing extra errands, ironing your own clothes and not complaining, and giving up time on your computer so I could write my research papers.

"Chris, your ability in the kitchen amazes us all! We have loved your 'experiments,' your home-cooked meals, and your fancy cakes to celebrate each class successfully completed! That's a lot of cakes over the last seven years!" She patted her stomach where a few extra pounds had been added.

"I love you all. Thanks, guys!"

Ginger learned a valuable lesson in tackling a lengthy project, such as continuing her college education. She recognized that others enabled her to succeed. She learned that without their sacrifices and help, she might have given up or failed. Are you willing to give someone that kind of support? Or receive it?

Steps of Faith

Dear God, allow me to show my appreciation to those who help me succeed. And open my heart so I am willing to continue my own education if You lead me that way.

Trail of Rejection

Do not reject me or forsake me, O God my Savior.
Though my father and mother forsake me,
the LORD will receive me.

PSALM 27:9,10

*N*o one would ever have guessed it. I didn't even suspect it until after I married him. Philip Colter, star football player and all-around fun, lovable guy had suffered rejection most of his life and was deeply depressed.

Phil's father was an alcoholic. When he was ten, his parents divorced. Phil grew up feeling inferior to his older brother, Patrick, who was "perfect"—at least according to both of his parents. Nothing Phil did could compete with Patrick's accomplishments.

Phil had told me about his family, but I never considered the toll it had taken on him. Shortly after we married, I began to notice outbursts of anger followed by days of moodiness and withdrawal. To make matters worse, his father was terminally ill, and Phil was miserable in his job. There were days that he cried on his way to work.

An exam showed that there was no physical or chemical problem. When I began to suggest counseling, he adamantly refused. I prayed constantly for Phil and our marriage. Then one day a friend told me about the book *Making Peace with Your Past,* by Dr. Tim Sledge. When I began to read it, I knew it was God's answer to my prayers. And when Phil finally read it, he could identify the coping techniques of every member of his family—including himself!

Phil's family still lives with the pain of the past, and we continue to pray for them. In the meantime Phil has steered off the trail of rejection and depression into the Lord's arms of unconditional acceptance and joy.

Is your husband depressed but you don't know how to help him recognize the signs? Some symptoms are excessive sleep, weight loss or gain, disrupted relationships at home or at work, crying, withdrawal, and lack of desire for sex. Ask God to open his eyes to his depression. When He does, even though most men would prefer to read a book that addresses this problem, it's often necessary that he seek help from a Christian professional.

Steps of Faith

Almighty God, it hurts me to see my husband hurt. If he is suffering from depression, Lord, please open his eyes to it and give him the wisdom to seek out the appropriate kind of help. Guide him and protect him. He's very much loved and needed.

Brian's Secret

Let your gentleness be evident to all.

PHILIPPIANS 4:5

*T*here is a six-year-old boy in my church named Brian Carpenter. His parents, Tom and Jeanne, are close friends of mine. Everyone in our little church knows Brian. You can't miss him. And once folks meet Brian, they're never the same—they've been touched with the spirit of gentleness.

Brian has a rare syndrome called Lissencephaley, making him one of the fewer than 1,000 known cases of this condition in the world. The latest research shows that Lissencephaley may be the result of a deletion of the seventeenth chromosome during the gestation period. The average life expectancy of a child with Lissencephaley is the middle teens.

According to Jeanne, Brian is at the physical and mental level of a four-month-old child, with less upper body strength and head control. He wears diapers and is transported in a wheelchair. Because of his condition, Brian occasionally suffers seizures and respiratory problems. His chest becomes congested, and when he has a "good cough," Tom or Jeanne must use a suction machine to clean out the mucus from his throat and mouth.

So how does a boy like Brian, who is constantly surrounded by the harsh realities of his disabilities, generate gentleness in others? By loving and trusting others first. He can't speak and he can't smile, at least like we do. But there is a peace and sense of security that surrounds him when he looks into your eyes. He melts all fears and suspicions and leaves you relaxed, your heart filling with compassion and a new kind of joy.

It's Brian's secret that's really no secret at all.

Why does the fragility of some bring out gentleness in others? Little babies, the elderly, the infirm—all must be handled with gentleness and care. However, if their care becomes a burden to us, we may not always be so gentle. If you care for a "fragile" person but feel like you're at the end of your rope, cry out to God for help. He is a God of gentleness.

Steps of Faith

Almighty Father, although You are mighty, You are gentle as well. And thank You for being gentle with me and all my failings and helplessness. Please make me more sensitive to the "fragile" people you've brought into my life. Help me to be as gentle with them as You are with me.

The Difference

*What do you prefer? Shall I come to you with a whip,
or in love and with a gentle spirit?*

1 CORINTHIANS 4:21

*E*leven years ago my sister-in-law Kathy and I started a company out of my garage in which we design and produce educational toys. Today we have 36 employees and a real office, but one thing hasn't changed over the years: we continue to run our company according to biblical principles. We even hold a 30-minute chapel before lunch on Mondays.

Because of the nature of our business, we have seasonal rushes. Hiring temps is convenient and cost-effective, and when we don't have any more work for them, the agency informs them that the job is over.

Then there was Cynthia, a temp who worked with us for several weeks. Her enthusiasm about our products and her hard work were contagious—even I was susceptible. But to my disappointment, she was neither a Christian nor interested in chapel.

When the rush began to wind down, we knew Cynthia would have to go. Everyone loved her; many of us witnessed to her about Jesus and prayed for her salvation. And we hated the idea of her getting that phone call from the agency. It seemed too cold.

On that dreaded day, I called Cynthia into my office. My heart ached as she greeted me with her open smile. I sincerely thanked her for all her hard work and gently told her that today would be her last day.

I could tell Cynthia was struggling with a mixture of emotions, but she maintained a cheerful demeanor. She finally said, "Thanks for telling me yourself, Jill. No one has ever done that for me; I feel . . . respected. I knew this place was different—but I didn't realize how different it was."

The world is not a gentle place. That's why Christians stand in stark contrast to the world when they show tender consideration for the feelings of others. That's gentleness. It's one of the fruits of the Holy Spirit, so it resides in the heart of every believer. How gentle are you?

Steps of Faith

Dear Father, Jesus Christ told us that He is "gentle and humble in heart" (Matthew 11:29). I confess that my heart is sometimes full of anger and arrogance, which rear their ugly heads at the worst times. Forgive me, Father. I want to be gentle to at least one person today.

Gorilla Lamp, Etc.

He who covers over an offense promotes love.

PROVERBS 17:9

T U E S D A Y

*A*s the big day neared, I dreamed about a beautiful wedding and a happily-ever-after life as Mrs. Christopher Hodge. I also dreamed about Mr. Christopher Hodge himself—but not exactly in a way he appreciated.

I couldn't wait to change him. I knew just the kind of man he needed to be. Don't misunderstand; I was in love with Chris, and we both knew our marriage was God's will. However, throughout our courtship, I had made a mental list of everything that needed "improving." For instance, he watched too much television, especially baseball; he didn't read enough books; and his taste in ties was too conservative. Worst of all, his prized possession was a gorilla lamp. Its base was a coconut carved and painted to look like a gorilla. (That thing was not going to see the inside of our apartment!)

I started dropping subtle and some not-so-subtle hints. Then three weeks before the wedding, as we were buying some things for our new apartment, I made a snide comment about the gorilla lamp. Chris was unusually quiet for the rest of the day. Later, something I said (probably another little hint) made him explode. I'd never seen him so angry, but I'll always remember what he said: "I am not your construction project! If you can't accept me, then I can't marry you!"

"Project Chris" was aborted immediately. Today, fifteen years later, Chris hasn't changed much, but at least the gorilla lamp has been moved from our bedroom to the boys' room!

Is your man an "improvement project"? A woman's nature is to improve things. What you may consider help and guidance will probably be perceived by your man as criticism and rejection. And that will usually make him angry and defensive. Instead, reassure him of your respect and unconditional love.

Steps of Faith

Almighty God, I confess that I have tried to "improve" almost every man in my life. Please give me wisdom to know when to major on the majors and minor on the minors.

Burning Joy

*You, O LORD, keep my lamp burning; my God turns
my darkness into light.*

PSALM 18:28

Last April, Floyd was sent to Miami for a week-long business trip. After discussing it with his supervisor, he got permission to take the children and me along. A whole week in a beachfront condo—paid for by the company!

Well, that might be great if your children are old enough to enjoy the beach and pretty much take care of themselves. All three of ours are under five, the last one being a "surprise." And after one day, I could see that the trip wasn't going to be the "upper" that I needed; in fact, I could feel a familiar sense of hopelessness beginning to drown me. Caring for the children left me exhausted and frustrated.

During the afternoon of the third day, I took the children down to the baby pool. As they played, I chatted with a young woman who appeared to be about my age. Her nephew was splashing and kicking along with my kids just like part of the clan.

After a while, Marie opened up and told me that she didn't have any children. She and her husband had tried for years, had conceived, and she'd given birth to a boy, Joseph Andrew. When Joe was four, he was diagnosed with leukemia. He died less than a year later. After years of tests and many prayers, Marie and her husband had not been able to have another child.

No pithy words of consolation or wisdom came. My shame muted me. I weakly stammered a promise to pray for Marie, and when she left, I couldn't take my eyes off my beautiful children.

Sometimes just your perspective on a situation can trigger depression. Do you have any depression triggers? Common ones are marriage, career, children, and financial status. It's easy to allow the negatives to overwhelm us and rob us of our joy. Ask God to shine His light on your "trigger" and make you see the blessings to which you may be blinded.

Steps of Faith

Dear Lord, You are the eternal light of the world. Thank You for all the many blessings You have given me. I don't know why I should be so fortunate. I certainly don't deserve anything from You. Continue to show me how blessed I am, even during those times when I can't see it.

WEDNESDAY

317

The Reunion

Above all else, guard your heart,
for it is the wellspring of life.

PROVERBS 4:23

Fifteen years. It was hard to believe. Thoughts and emotions raced through my mind as Doug and I boarded the jet bound for my hometown and my high-school reunion.

Actually, the thoughts and emotions had been racing for days . . . weeks . . . years . . . dare I say 15 years? I had never completely forgotten my first love, Stan. Whenever I got depressed or angry at Doug, I dreamed about what life would have been like with Stan. Stan and I had broken up on graduation night. I was convinced we would be miraculously reunited, but he married Kelly, and I married Doug, my sedate, predictable husband of 13 years. How different he was from Stan, the charmer, the ladies' man.

I would have walked into a minefield of emotion and temptation if I hadn't confided in my friend Christy. After we talked and prayed, I saw how my thoughts and feelings for Stan were wrong. I confessed my sin and thanked God for Doug and for our marriage.

The night of the reunion, I silently prayed as Doug and I entered the hotel ballroom. Before I knew it, Stan was at my side . . . slobbering drunk. As I tried to make intelligent conversation, all I felt was revulsion. By the time Doug and I left, Stan had been shoved or slapped by several women. I was no longer impressed.

Then I looked at Doug as if I were seeing him for the first time. *Now this is a man!* I thought about his integrity and tenderness. I was so proud to be his wife. Suddenly I couldn't wait to get him inside our hotel room!

Do you have sexual fantasies about someone other than your husband? Do you hope your spouse leaves you so you will be free? If so, you are at high risk for an affair. Confess your sin and ask God to protect your mind. Discuss with your spouse the emptiness you feel—which he may also feel. Consider getting Christian counseling. Remember that God will give you the ability to do His will (1 Corinthians 10:13).

Steps of Faith

Lord God, I praise You and thank You for Your protection in my life. Your Holy Spirit has given me the strength to have victory. Teach me to prepare in advance for those temptations to which I am most vulnerable.

Just a Little Pinch

A prudent [woman] sees danger and takes refuge,
but the simple keep going and suffer for it.

PROVERBS 22:3

Pap smear. Even the name of the test sounded unappealing. And now that my oldest daughter, Ansley, was ready to have regular gynecological examinations, I wanted to do all I could to inform and prepare her.

Ansley and I have spent time together discussing the biological changes she is experiencing. And she's made it clear that she isn't too excited about having a pap smear—especially the first one.

"What's the big deal?" she asked me one day in the car. "I mean, will I *die* if I don't do it?" she added a bit sarcastically.

"I don't mean to scare you, honey, but, yes, you could die. You see, a doctor performing a pap smear takes a sample of cells from your cervix, the entrance of your uterus, and places them on a slide. They are sent to a lab and examined. Doctors do this to identify any precancerous cells. Before pap smears, when the cancer was discovered, it was usually too late. Many women died."

"Wait a minute, Mom. Are you saying I could have this test and then find out I'm dying of cancer?"

"That's highly unlikely, Ansley. Not at your age. Plus, today's technology is so advanced. We really should thank God for pap smears."

"Well, I'll thank Him after the thrilling experience," she noted. "I guess now you're going to tell me that a pap smear doesn't hurt, just like you used to say those shots wouldn't hurt. *'Just a little pinch!'*"

I felt my face flush. *That's what all the doctors say before a pap smear!*

"Mom. Mom? What's wrong? Why are you blushing?"

A regular pap smear is your greatest weapon against cancer. To ensure the most accurate reading, have the test done when you're not menstruating, empty your bladder right before the exam, avoid douching, vaginal lubricants, tampons, or vaginal contraceptives at least 48 hours before the test. And when it's time for your daughter's first pap smear, educate her and calm her anxieties by honestly answering all of her questions.

Steps of Faith

Loving Father, millions of women have been spared a painful death because of this test and others like it. Thank You. Help me to see the works of Your hands in every aspect of my life—and then to thank You for them.

319

Gospel of John

Blessed are the pure in heart, for they will see God.

MATTHEW 5:8

*W*hen I walked into the church that Friday night, one of the first people I saw was a man sitting in the back of the church in a wheelchair. He was looking straight at me, smiling, so I waved and smiled back to him. I took my seat at the end of a row near the front and began praying for my husband and his band as they set up. We were there to lead a special worship service that night before we took part in an evangelistic outreach with the church the next day at a state park.

A few minutes later there was a tap on my shoulder. I turned around to see the man in the wheelchair. I was a bit startled but smiled and said hi. He showed me an alphabet and numeral chart with a sign that read: "My name is John. I have cerebral palsy and I can't talk, but I can communicate with you." He then pointed to the letters and numbers.

One of the first things John communicated to me was that he was 42 years old. "No way!" I said, laughing. He started laughing and kept pointing at the numerals "4" and "2" and then at himself.

The next day I was surprised to see John at the park. As my husband's band played, John diligently distributed gospel tracts. I could see people's amazement as he wedged a tract between two twisted fingers and lifted it up to them. *How wonderful*, I thought, *John can be part of the outreach, too.* We heard everyone laughing as John, by using his chart, told jokes and shared the gospel.

Meeting John changed my life. He showed me that God can use anyone to share the gospel, even those who have disabilities. All He asks for is a willing heart.

Any believer can share the gospel of Jesus Christ with unbelievers. Ask God to make you a vessel of His grace and help you develop your unique approach. Sharing your testimony is a great start. Try writing it out in your own words, then whittle it down until you can share it in three minutes or less.

Steps of Faith

"Create in me a pure heart, O God, and renew a steadfast spirit within me" (Psalm 51:10). When I think about all the junk that usually occupies my heart, I long for purity and holiness. Surround me with Your beautiful grace, Lord. I want the world to see You in me.

This Present Light

Through the blessing of the upright a city is exalted.

PROVERBS 11:11

Like thousands of other Christian readers, I consumed Frank Peretti's novels *This Present Darkness* and *Piercing the Darkness*. Never before had an author so vividly illustrated the continuing warfare between the "ministering spirits" (Hebrews 1:14) and "the spiritual forces of evil" (Ephesians 6:12). After reading those books, I began to realize that my behavior, my faith, and my prayers really do make a difference in the world in which I live.

In 1989 a group from my Sunday school class decided to do an extracurricular study of *This Present Darkness*. Using our Bibles, we studied the principles of prayer and spiritual warfare and then applied them to our lives, families, and neighborhoods. Each of us began to see results—some immediate.

Our "Ashton" is a city in the south encircled by an interstate highway. We'd seen our crime and divorce rates skyrocket over the last several years. Plus, there'd always been a brooding sense of corruption in our local government.

We decided to "take the city" for Jesus. Once a week, we would meet to pray for our city—for our businesses, schools, officials, churches, and families. Since then we've seen our streets become safer, the divorce rate lessen, and corrupt politicians replaced by godly ones.

Today we are beginning to see true revival in our city. And as more people commit to pray for the city, more fuel is added to the fire of the revival. It's an awesome spectacle to behold. We're witnessing the present darkness being overcome by the eternal light.

Do you pray for your community and its leaders? Did you realize that when you walk in the light of Christ you actually bring blessings upon your family and your community? Meditate on Proverbs 11:10,11 today and share these verses with your family, friends, and Sunday school class. Encourage them to exalt your community through their righteousness.

Steps of Faith

My dear Father, thank You for the community in which You have placed my family and me. Please bless and protect our leaders, teachers, policemen, churches, and families from Satan's attack. Pour out a spirit of repentance and revival, Lord, and give me diligence in my prayers.

And Live She Did

*When anxiety was great within me, your consolation
brought joy to my soul.*

PSALM 94:19

*H*er picture still sits on my desk by my computer. She's beautiful, her radiant smile telling the world, "Life is great!" She's wearing her favorite sweatshirt, which reads: "Give me some chocolate and nobody gets hurt."

A picture may be worth a thousand words, but this one would have never betrayed the fact that Myra had only a year to live.

And live she did. Never once during her battle with ovarian cancer did Myra say, "I'm dying of cancer." Even when she tenderly broke the news to those of us who worked with her, Myra underscored the fact that she was *living with* cancer.

And live she did. In spite of the pain, the drugs, the wigs, the smell of death, the needles, and yes, the fear—Myra wrested control of this uninvited guest and laid down the law. She changed her diet, even giving up chocolate. She studied everything she could about ovarian cancer, learned the medical terminology, and conversed with her doctors as a partner in a battle. And when she wasn't enduring another round of chemo or was so weak from its aftereffects she could hardly speak, Myra was determined to live life to the hilt.

And live she did. No one could do lunch like Myra, but then *everyone* did lunch *with* Myra. She had every possible coupon for every known restaurant in town. One hour wasn't enough. The time flew as she had you screaming with laughter or listening in silent awe as she shared God's latest treasure to her from His Word. In the face of death and pain, He had taught her how to *live* with cancer.

And live she did.

Are you living with a chronic illness? Whether it's terminal or not, be positive and take as much control of the illness as possible. Ask one or two close friends to pray for you and with you about the details of your illness, including your fluctuating emotions.

Steps of Faith

Heavenly Father, You promise that when I experience anxiety, Your consolation will bring joy to my soul. Several times in the past You have fulfilled that promise in my life. When I face fear and pain again, give me a heart of joy, one that makes the world know that my trust is in You.

Deaf and Defiant

Expel the wicked [woman] from among you.
1 CORINTHIANS 5:13

Renee was the newcomer to the Tuesday night Bible study that met in my apartment. We had met at a singles conference and discovered we worked in the same building. She was nice, but I never got the sense she was exactly "on fire" for the Lord.

One day as Renee and I met for lunch, I could tell she wanted to tell me something important. And before our salads were served, I had already heard more than I could stand. Renee was seeing a man from her office—a married man. She recounted how they had started out as friends, but then began having lunch alone together, holding hands, meeting after work. She was quick to point out that they had not had sex, so they hadn't committed adultery.

I told Renee that they had indeed committed adultery to a degree, and explained why from a biblical point of view. My words fell on deaf ears. She protested that they hadn't and that no one was getting hurt. Renee insisted that this man was the one for her; he had simply married the wrong woman. God cared about her happiness, didn't He? And anyway, even if they were sinning, God has promised to forgive them, hasn't He?

I couldn't believe my ears. I tried to explain to Renee that God will not be mocked by one of His children. As long as she was defying her Father, she was cutting herself off from Him. Continued sin would bring unfortunate consequences in her life, perhaps even years later.

Renee never attended the Bible study again. We still pray for her, but none of us has seen her for months. I often wonder what's become of her.

George Barna's latest research shows that there is virtually no difference between the morality of Christians and non-Christians. Think about your life. Are you rationalizing any sin? Are you becoming deaf and defiant? Confess your sin right now and repent. Restore that fellowship with your Father.

Steps of Faith

Heavenly Father, when I think about the price You paid for the redemption of mankind, I am ashamed at my sometimes flippant attitude about even the "little" sins in my life. Shine Your light in my heart. Expose any hidden sin and set me back on the straight path.

Jennie's System

*Why spend money on what is not bread, and your
labor on what does not satisfy?*

ISAIAH 55:2

*J*ennie and I were roommates in college. As much as we joked about it back then, we both knew we had a serious problem. It wasn't unusual for one or both of us to run up $500 a month on our parents' charge cards just on "stuff." Whatever enticed us, we bought it. Shopping became a form of entertainment, an exciting mode of escape.

After we graduated, Jennie and I married and moved away with our new husbands. Craig took my credit cards and put me on a very strict allowance. I quit overspending cold turkey. Through his support and prayers, I was finally broken of the "addiction."

A couple of years ago, Jennie and I were both home at the same time and met at the mall for lunch. I noticed Jennie had a big department store shopping bag filled with boxes and packages. "Looks like you've been doing some shopping, girlfriend!" I teased. "What did you get?"

Jennie casually replied, "Oh, I bought this stuff a few days ago. I'm returning it." When she saw my puzzled look, she continued: "I can't seem to make a final decision in the store, but when I take it home, I don't cut off the tags. I just look at it now and then and ask myself, 'Do I really need this? Can we afford it?' Usually, after a few days, I return it. This way Danny doesn't drop dead when he gets the credit-card bill! It might not be the best system, but at least I'm taking steps to curb that impulse buying."

Do you suspect you may be an overspender or a shopaholic? It may boil down to a misunderstanding of who God really is and who you are in Christ. Scripture can be a mighty weapon in overcoming this problem. Meditate on Matthew 6:25-34; Luke 15:3-32; 24:6,7; John 14:13,14; Romans 5:8; 8:1.

Steps of Faith

Father God, thank You for loving me so much that You gave Your only Son, Jesus, so that if I believed in Him I would never die but spend eternity with You. When I meditate on the awesome reality of who You are and what I've become, the things of this world pale in comparison.

THURSDAY

Mrs. Milligan

In everything set them an example by doing what is good.
TITUS 2:7

I knew it wasn't right, but I needed a day off. Plus, my throat was a little sore and if I ventured out into the rainy, cold weather, I might end up with pneumonia! So I called in sick.

While snuggled under layers of blankets and slumbering blissfully, I was rudely awakened by the telephone. *Maybe it's the office; I'd better answer.* But it wasn't the office. It was Norma from the prayer chain, planning to leave a message about Louise Hinton, an elderly woman in the church who (actually) had pneumonia. When Norma asked why I was home, I reluctantly told her that I had called in sick. She told me not to worry, that Mrs. Milligan had made a double batch of chicken soup: one would go to the Hintons and the other would be sent to me. Before I could beg Norma not to send Mrs. Milligan over, she hung up.

Now I really did feel sick—sick with guilt and shame.

Three hours later Mrs. Milligan rang my doorbell. In her seventies and dripping wet from the rain, she carried in a pot of chicken soup. I wanted to crawl in a hole. She insisted I immediately go back to bed. Thirty minutes later she was serving me chicken soup on a tray. I felt ridiculous, but her joy was obvious. We chatted for a moment and then she said she'd let me eat in peace.

When I finished the soup, I took the tray to the kitchen. To my horror I found Mrs. Milligan on her hands and knees scrubbing my floor and wiping down the baseboards! Clean dishes sparkled on the drainboard.

No one deserved such torment! All I did was call in sick! I've never forgotten what the Lord and Mrs. Milligan taught me that day: a real servant puts another's needs first, and her own last.

Does your church have a "helps" ministry? Maybe you can start one. It's an effective means of assisting church members or other people in the community who are sick or in need. It's the church's way of being the hands and feet of Christ and demonstrating His love and care.

Steps of Faith

Oh Father, my Lord Jesus Christ was the greatest of all servants. I want to follow His example. Give me a servant's heart the next time I hear of someone who is sick or needs help in any other way.

Kindness at Home

Love is patient, love is kind.

1 CORINTHIANS 13:4

Sharon has always felt her special ministry was doing "good deeds" as described in 1 Timothy 5:10. Three mornings a week, she volunteers at a school for the hearing impaired. Once a week she provides child care for the women's prayer breakfast that is held at her church. She makes regular visits to the local nursing home. Hardly a week goes by that she does not take a casserole or home-baked goodie to a friend who is sick or is having guests.

The problem is not that Sharon does too much. She's excellent at time management; her family has never missed a meal or gone without clean clothes because of her activities outside their home. Sharon's husband simply wishes that she enjoyed doing things for him as much as she did for other people. He always feels as though her kindheartedness runs out just about the time he gets home from work.

Last night when he came home, Sharon's first words to her husband were, "Is *that* what you wore to work today? Why didn't you wear your other jacket?"

During dinner when he started to tell her about a meeting that had not gone well, she interrupted: "Look, my day's been really hard—I don't think I can listen to any more complaints today."

Later, after their children were in bed, he asked Sharon to watch a television program with him. But she wasn't interested: "Don't you have anything better to do with your time? Why don't you read a book instead of watching that silly box?"

Sharon's husband is beginning to resent the fact that she obviously cares more about being kind to other people than she does to him.

Why is it so much easier to practice kindness among strangers and acquaintances than it is in one's own home? Perhaps it is because we feel more appreciated by those who don't know us so well; or maybe we simply forget that our closest family members need kindness from us.

Steps of Faith

Dear Father, I want our home to be a refuge for my family—the one place where we can always expect to be treated with kindness. Remind me often that it is more important that I show kindness to my husband and children than it is for me to be known for my many good deeds.

Walk Thru the Bible Ministries

Walk Thru the Bible Ministries (WTB) began in the early 1970s when a young teacher named Bruce Wilkinson developed an innovative way of teaching surveys of the Bible. From these small beginnings emerged a multifaceted Bible-teaching ministry. By focusing on the central themes of Scripture and their practical application, WTB has wide acceptance in denominations and fellowships around the world. In addition, it has carefully developed alliances with over 100 Christian organizations. WTB has four major ministries:

International Ministries

WTB's International Ministry extends to over 70 countries, representing some 50 languages. With recent advances, WTB now has more than 3,000 trained seminar instructors worldwide. International branch offices are located in Australia, Great Britain, Singapore, New Zealand, South Africa, and Ukraine.

WTB Publishing

The Publishing Ministry began in 1978 with the launching of *The Daily Walk* magazine. WTB publications enable individuals and families to maintain a meaningful habit of daily devotional time in the Word of God. The publications include *Closer Walk, Family Walk, YouthWalk, LifeWalk,* and *Tapestry.*

WTB Seminars and Leadership Training

People of all ages develop a deeper understanding of the Bible through WTB's unique Old and New Testament surveys. Other seminars offered include: *The Seven Laws of the Learner, Teaching with Style,* and *The Biblical Portrait of Marriage.* The Leadership Training Ministry goes into secular business as well as churches and Christian organizations to communicate biblical principles of leadership. Each training module provides practical tools that make biblical truth relevant both in personal relationships and in the marketplace.

LifeChange Videos

The WTB creative team has developed a number of dynamic video courses for training leaders and for personal growth including: *The Biblical Portrait of Marriage, The Seven Laws of the Learner,* and *Personal Holiness in Times of Temptation.* Video makes it possible to bring WTB's lifechanging Bible teaching into churches and homes throughout the world.

No matter what the ministry, no matter where the ministry, WTB focuses on the Word of God and encourages people of all nations to grow in their knowledge of God and unreserved obedience and serve to Him. For more information about Walk Thru the Bible's publications, videos, or seminars in your area, contact Walk Thru the Bible Ministries, 4201 North Peachtree Road, Atlanta, GA 30341-1207 or call (770) 458-9300. Visit our web site at www.walkthru.org